EVALUATING SOCIAL WORK SERVICES AND PROGRAMS

ROBERT W. WEINBACH

University of South Carolina

Boston ▪ New York ▪ San Francisco
Mexico City ▪ Montreal ▪ Toronto ▪ London ▪ Madrid ▪ Munich ▪ Paris
Hong Kong ▪ Singapore ▪ Tokyo ▪ Cape Town ▪ Sydney

Senior Editor: *Patricia Quinlin*
Editorial Assistant: *Annemarie Kennedy*
Marketing Manager: *Kris Ellis-Levy*
Editorial Production Service: *Tom Conville Publishing Services, LLC*
Manufacturing Buyer: *JoAnne Sweeney*
Cover Administrator: *Kristina Mose-Libon*
Electronic Composition: *Omegatype Typography, Inc.*

For related titles and support materials, visit our online catalog at www.ablongman.com.

Between the time Website information is gathered and then published, some sites may have closed. Also, the transciption of URLs can result in typographical errors. The publisher would appreciate being notified of any problems with URLs so that they may be corrected in subsequent editions.

Library of Congress Cataloging-in-Publication Data

Weinbach, Robert W.
    Evaluating social work services and programs / Robert W. Weinbach.
        p.   cm.
    Includes bibliographical references and index.
    ISBN 0-205-41501-6
    1. Social service—Evaluation.   2. Evaluation research (Social action programs)   I. Title.
    HV40.W39 2005
    361.3'072—dc22
                                                                                2004044726

Printed in the United States of America

10 9 8 7 6 5 4 3 2 1   09 08 07 06 05 04

CONTENTS

CHAPTER THREE

**Traditional Methods for Monitoring and
Improving Social Work Practice   35**

CHAPTER FOUR

An Overview of Single-System Research   53

CHAPTER FIVE

Single-System Designs and Data Analysis   76

CHAPTER EIGHT

Evaluations to Improve Programs   149

CHAPTER NINE

Outcome Evaluations: An Overview   172

CHAPTER TEN

Preexplanatory Outcome Evaluations   196

CHAPTER ELEVEN

Explanatory Outcome Evaluations   222

Evaluation research is now a central part of both research and practice. It is no longer optional for today's social worker, and it will likely gain importance. However, it is often misunderstood or is viewed as so technical that it should be left to specialists. This book demonstrates that evaluation research is logical and understandable, and it is the province of all social workers.

INTENDED AUDIENCE

Evaluating Social Work Services and Programs was written for current or future social workers by a social worker. It is based on many years of teaching and work in the area. It has many examples and illustrations from the real world of social work practice.

The text can be used as the primary text in a one-semester graduate or senior-level, undergraduate course on evaluation. Or, it can be used as an additional text in a two-semester course on research methods and statistics. Practitioners "a few years out of school" who participate in evaluation activities that were barely mentioned in their academic programs may also find this text valuable.

GOALS AND ASSUMPTIONS

I have attempted to "demystify" evaluation research, to share with the reader how I believe it all fits together. At the same time, I have tried to avoid oversimplifying it, or to imply that it is not a complex topic. It is. However, I believe that an individual with a knowledge of social work practice and some basic understanding of research methods should be able to design and implement evaluations (with a little consultation, perhaps) that will be both informative and credible.

While some backround in research methods and statistics would be helpful for understanding the discussion, I have provided a review of concepts from areas that are most critical to understanding evaluation research. Their special meaning in the context of evaluation research is emphasized.

Overview

The book is not a "cookbook." For example, it does not contain "how to" directions for locating data collection instruments or describe how to conduct a focus group. I have held bibliographic citations to a minimum, not wanting to interrupt the logical flow of the discussion any more than absolutely necessary.

The book focuses on the basics of evaluation research, on what is common rather than what is unusual. Evaluation research is presented as an integrated activity. I have relied heavily on extended examples drawn from social work practice to illustrate important points, or to demonstrate how certain principles are applied. Ethical issues appear often because they are frequently encountered in evaluation research.

I have deliberately not included descriptions of this year's trend in evaluation research. My experience is that these fads come and go and are too specialized for what the book hopes to accomplish: that is, to provide the reader with a good understanding of what evaluation research is all about in its various manifestations. Thus the reader will not see such topics as utilization-focused evaluation, responsive evaluation, participatory evaluation, empowerment evaluation, or "360 degree." If instructors believe any of these is important (perhaps, because it is currently emphasized in their practice milieu) a supplementary reading or two can be used to illustrate their specialized focus and how it fits with the general themes described in this book.

CONTENTS AND ORGANIZATION

There are eleven chapters. Each might be a week's assigned reading with time left over for examinations or other applications of learning, such as assignments requiring that students design evaluations of various types. The chapters build on each other and are designed to be read in sequence. The amount of time and space dedicated to various topics reflects what I believe to be their relative importance in the world of evaluation:

- Chapter 1 contains key definitions and presents the focus of evaluation research within social work. Critical terms from research methodology and a few from statistics are defined as they are most commonly used in evaluation research.
- Chapter 2 examines the history of evaluation and the forces that contributed to its present importance.
- Chapter 3 reviews evaluation methods historically used to evaluate the effectiveness of social work services and programs, and introduces evaluation methods currently in use.
- Chapters 4 and 5 discuss single-system research and how and why it is conducted.
- Chapter 6 introduces the total enterprise of program evaluation, emphasizing commonalities of all program evaluations. Reasons for conducting program evaluations, as well as their components and the data sources used to evaluate them, are detailed.
- Chapter 7 discusses needs assessments as they are conducted for both proposed and existing programs.

- Chapter 8 examines evaluations that are conducted within on-going programs. Evaluability assessments, program monitoring, formative evaluations, and process evaluations are discussed with emphasis on their specific purposes.
- Chapter 9 discusses outcome evaluations in general, with emphasis on what they share in common and the ethical dilemmas that frequently surface.
- Chapters 10 and 11 introduce preexplanatory and explanatory designs for use as general frameworks for conducting outcome evaluations.

At the end of each chapter there are a list of key terms from the chapter, and study questions that determine the reader's understanding and ability to apply the major points in the chapter. In an academic setting, both can be used for class discussion or as homework assignments to help assess student learning.

ACKNOWLEDGMENTS

The greatest contributions to this book have come from students. While I taught courses on evaluation research for over a decade, they challenged my ideas and helped me refine them. Some have simply said, "It doesn't work that way in my agency," and explained why. Others have pointed out inconsistencies in the evaluation models I presented. Above all, students convinced me that evaluation research is both logical and comprehensible, and can even be enjoyable.

Two colleagues, Kathleen A. Bolland, University of Alabama, and Dean F. Duncan III, University of North Carolina at Chapel Hill, who reviewed an early draft of the manuscript, provided detailed, thorough suggestions for how it might be improved. With very few exceptions, I have taken their advice and, I believe, the book is much improved because of them. Patricia Quinlin and Annemarie Kennedy at Allyn & Bacon have again shown faith in my ability to complete the project and have provided assistance as needed. Acting Dean and long-time colleague, Leon Ginsberg, provided some tactical support, reflecting his commitment to productive scholarship, even among emeriti faculty. Finally, I am grateful to my wife, Lynne Taylor, who allowed me to sound out my ideas as they evolved and, in typical southern fashion, tactfully identified those that were less than profound.

CHAPTER ONE

WHAT *IS* EVALUATION RESEARCH?

Evaluation: The word has numerous connotations, many of them negative. To students, it suggests testing, grading, or some other process for determining whether they can continue in their studies or receive a degree. It is designed to determine whether they have the necessary knowledge or are otherwise "good enough."

To employees of an organization, evaluation most likely suggests that annual or semiannual ritual during which their supervisors apply certain criteria to their recent work. Employees are aware that the results can have a major impact on pay raises, promotions, or even continued employment.

To people working in a social program, evaluation may suggest having to demonstrate that a program is worthwhile. Its findings may ensure the program's continuation, or it may cost them their jobs.

There are many reasons why the word *evaluation* sometimes elicits anxiety or even fear. However, evaluation is a necessary and desirable activity. It provides valuable information. Why wouldn't students want to know if they are passing a course, or on the way to getting that needed passing grade? Why wouldn't employees want to know what their future in the organization is likely to hold? Why wouldn't the staff of a social program want to know if the program is worthwhile? In all cases, evaluation has the potential to offer what is needed for planning and decision making—but, only if it is done well.

A primary reason why evaluation has negative connotations to some people is that they don't believe they can depend on it to produce fair and accurate results. The specter of (and, sometimes, the experience with) subjective, unpredictable, and even arbitrary and capricious evaluators has left them fearful of evaluation. However, it doesn't have to be that way. In evaluating individual performance, or in evaluating larger systems such as programs or organizations, there are ways to make the results of an evaluation more fair, accurate, and, most importantly, useful. It entails the use of established research methods.

DEFINING EVALUATION RESEARCH

The NASW Code of Ethics recognizes the need to link evaluation and research.[1] Standard 5.02 is entitled "Evaluation and Research." In it, the ethical obligation of social workers to conduct evaluation research is described. Standard 5.02a states, "Social workers should monitor and evaluate policies, the implementation of programs, and practice interventions." Standard 5.02 states, "Social workers should promote and facilitate evaluation and research to contribute to the development of knowledge."

It is the introduction of the principles and methods of research that transforms evaluation from what is sometimes a useless, time-consuming, and resented enterprise into a valuable, efficient, and appreciated one. There is a big difference between the generic term known as *evaluation* and what is known as *evaluation research*. We will explore that difference in detail.

There are many definitions of evaluation research. They tend to vary based on the profession or activity to which they are applied, but all describe methods for assessing the value or merit of what people do. One very good one, a "standard" for many years, was proposed by Rossi and Freeman in 1982. They defined evaluation research as "the systematic application of social research procedures in assessing the conceptualization and design, implementation, and utility of social intervention programs."[2] In recent years, we have begun to think of evaluation research only a little more broadly as it applies to social work practice. Thus, we will begin with a simpler, slightly more inclusive, working definition that is specific to the current needs of our profession, that is, it describes the purpose of evaluation research in social work. We will then build from there.

> **Evaluation research** is the systematic use of *research* methods to make judgments about the *effectiveness* and the overall merit, worth, or value of some form of *social work practice*.

Three components of this definition require some elaboration: (1) evaluation research's place in the broad activity known as *research*; (2) what we mean by *effectiveness*, and; (3) what *social work practice* includes.

Research and Evaluation Research

All research is designed to produce knowledge. Research involves a rigorous, systematic method of inquiry that is believed to be superior to those other, less trustworthy sources of "knowledge" on which we sometimes rely. Because of its proven methods and built-in system of controls and checks and balances, it is less likely to lead us astray than, for example, authorities, traditional beliefs, common sense, or even logic. For example, research on the problem of homelessness over the past decade has given us reasonably accurate, up-to-date descriptions of who the homeless are, how they became homeless, and to a lesser degree, what methods of working with homeless people seem to work best. Other research on HIV-AIDS has kept us up to date on the changing demographics of people newly diagnosed with the disease and on changes in incidence and treatment. We can only speculate on how our understanding of homelessness or HIV-AIDS would be different if we had relied solely on the other sources. Research is not infallible; however, it has less potential for generating misinformation than all of the other sources.

What kind of knowledge does research seek? Much of the knowledge that social work research has generated in the past has been by **basic research.** It can be described broadly as "knowledge for the profession." It is knowledge that, it is hoped, will help social work practitioners understand some problem or phenomenon better, make better decisions, or otherwise do their jobs better. This knowledge, often described as our professional knowledge base, consists of what we, and people in related fields, have learned using scientific methods. Researchers have increased our understanding of human behavior and various forces that help shape it. They have helped us to better understand social problems and speculate on why the problems exist and how to address them. For example, research has produced reasonably accurate descriptions of spousal battery, its rate of incidence, what problems are most often associated with it, and the likely effects on its victims. As this descriptive knowledge has begun to accumulate, it has made it possible to more accurately predict what will occur if we do not intervene in some way. For example, we know that the risk of spousal abuse may increase if a batterer suffers a loss of employment or some other threat to self-esteem. Knowledge derived from research on a problem may eventually reach a stage of certainty that it can be used for more effective intervention. This "prescriptive" knowledge is less common than descriptive or predictive knowledge in our profession, but it does occur. Where it exists, it comes mainly through the use of evaluation research methods. Prescriptive knowledge, in our example, would tell us which intervention to use to prevent a repeat instance of spousal battery.

Generally, researchers seek knowledge that has broad applicability, that is, it can be used productively by many social workers for a variety of purposes. Knowledge of a more specific nature, that has more limited utility, is sometimes thought of as less valuable. However, it can be some of the most valuable knowledge that we can acquire. We cannot afford to neglect it. It is the product of evaluation research.

Basic research sometimes generates findings that exist unread in some obscure journal for years. They may gather dust on a shelf and never be used. However, the findings of evaluation research are immediately useful. Evaluation research is **applied research.** It is designed to provide knowledge that is of immediate use for decision making. It can tell us whether services and programs worked, appear to be working, or have the potential to work. What knowledge could be more valuable for social workers and their clients?

Effectiveness and Evaluation Research

Whether some form of social work practice works or seems to be working can be a very subjective decision. My idea of "working" may be different from yours, and neither of our definitions may agree with that of a third professional. The introduction of research methods is essential to evaluation research. As has been stated, "without using social science methods, little evaluation can be done."[3] It is used to remove subjectivity, as does the use of standardized definitions. A few are so central to the topic of evaluation that we will examine them "up front." When conducting evaluation research, we invariably refer to the effectiveness of an intervention. **Effectiveness,** in this context, refers to the degree to which an intervention is likely to achieve, or has already achieved, its stated objectives. Did it do what it was intended to do? For example, in evaluating our individual practice effectiveness, we may ask, "How much increase in assertiveness that Ms. Smith achieved can be attributed to participation in my group?" or, "Can I really demonstrate that my counseling has resulted in a decline of the derogatory remarks Ms. Jones made to her partner?" In evaluating a social program, effectiveness generally refers to the degree to which the program achieved its objectives. We may ask, "Did the job-training program really help participants to get and keep good jobs?" or, "Has the parent-education program produced a decline in the number of founded child-neglect cases?"

Of course, effectiveness, even if it can be demonstrated, is only one indicator of the overall merit, worth, or value of a service or program. And, effectiveness always comes at a cost. Some interventions may produce the same or comparable results as others, but they are more expensive in time, dollars, or other program resources. This introduces a second, related term: efficiency. **Efficiency** is a relative term, referring to the degree that we can produce satisfactory results (effectiveness) at the lowest possible cost. Some interventions are more efficient than others, and are therefore often, but not always, more desirable. Evaluation research necessarily looks at both the effectiveness and efficiency of various forms of social work practice. Sometimes, depending on the situation, one takes priority over the other in evaluative research. Generally, evaluation entails considering both, and then attempts to balance them to some degree.

Effectiveness and efficiency are the central focus of accountability. **Accountability** refers to the responsible use of something given or loaned to us by someone else. People contribute to human services in many ways. In the public sector, taxpayers provide most of the money to provide them. In the not-for-profit sector, funding may come from, for example, private donations, corporations, grants and contracts with government agencies (the taxpayers again), or private foundations. In private, for-profit organizations, clients themselves and third parties such as insurance companies help pay the bills. There are nonmonetary contributions to human service organizations too. Volunteers give their time and talents. Professional and nonprofessional staff members, even though paid, make a substantial investment in human services. In addition, of course, clients invest their time and energies in services and programs with the belief that the services will be beneficial to them. All contributing groups, known as **stakeholders,** have a right to know whether their resources have been used productively. We demonstrate accountability to them by showing that the resources expended on an intervention were used parsimoniously (with efficiency) and produced the desired, promised results (high effectiveness).

Social Work Practice and Evaluation Research

In the broadest sense, social work practice includes everything that social workers do in their role as professionals. That would include such diverse activities as supervision, consultation, management, fund raising, teaching, and advocacy. However, the primary focus of evaluation research is how social work practice benefits clients, and the vehicles used to attempt to help them: services and programs.

Services and programs are both forms of social work intervention that help to eliminate, or at least alleviate, some problem for an individual or other social system (such as a family, group, organization, community, or society). Services and programs are created and implemented because, logically, they should be effective. (If we didn't think they would be, why would we invest time and effort in them?) That is where evaluation research comes in. Always the skeptic, it asks and seeks answers to many questions about the value and worth of services and programs. Nothing is taken for granted only because it seems logical. Evaluation research relies on a variety of research methods (both quantitative and qualitative) to determine whether what is logical indeed has a basis in fact.

Service, Services, and Programs. We frequently use the terms service, services, and programs in written and verbal communication. But only to be certain that we share a common understanding of what each means, what they look like, and how they relate to each other, let's operationally define them now. When I use the terms in the chapters that follow, a **service** refers to a specific form of intervention designed to alleviate or eliminate a problem of a client or client system. It is what social workers and other professionals actually offer to a client or client system to try to alleviate a problem. A service may be treatment in the form of counseling or therapy, referral, case management, assessment, training, education, or any other form of intervention selected for its potential to help with the problem. A service may be offered by an individual practitioner or by more than one professional (as a team). Part of evaluation research entails methods to assess the effectiveness of a given service to a particular client, or client system, by a particular social worker or team of social workers.

Services (collectively) constitute one component (albeit a very important one) of social programs. In evaluation research, services are evaluated along with other program components as part of program evaluation. Box 1.1 on page 6 displays how services and programs differ and how they relate to each other.

A **program** is best understood as a subunit of an organization that has been constructed in a unique way to address some social problem. Sometimes an entire human-service organization (especially one that has a very narrow problem focus) is referred to as a program. However, an organization (often called a social agency in our profession) typically contains a number of ongoing programs. Programs are characteristic of all human-service organizations, that is, they are present in the public, not-for-profit, and for-profit sectors.

Programs come in two types: permanent and time-limited. A **permanent program** is an integral part of the agency or organization with permanent staff

■ ■ ■ ■ ■

BOX 1.1

SERVICES AND PROGRAMS

> **Services**   What helping professionals offer (along with goods) in order to alleviate or eliminate a problem of an individual client or client system.
>
> - Services may consist of various types of intervention including treatment, referral, case management, family assessment, and so on.
> - Services are offered by one or more professionals, and are only *one* component of a program.
>
> **Programs**   Subunits of organizations constructed in a unique manner to address a social problem.
>
> - Programs are more or less self-contained and have their own goals, objectives, policies, rules, procedures, services, strategies, staff, budget, space, resources, and so on.
> - Programs may be time-limited or a relatively permanent part of an organization.
> - Programs should be consistent with the organization's mission and vision statements.

---

and relatively secure funding (as secure as that of the organization itself). It is part of the organization's identity and exists to address some social problem, usually one that is not likely to go away (for example, poverty, family violence, unemployment, mental illness, or developmental disabilities). Some permanent programs are expected within certain organizations. For example, a state or county department of social services is expected to have, among others, child protection, financial assistance, and foster care and adoption programs. Many other permanent programs within organizations tend to be more innovative and unique. They began on a trial basis, often as a pilot project or pilot program, were evaluated, and found to be "worth keeping," as an effective way to address some social problem.

A **time-limited program** may or may not ever become a permanent program. It is, in a sense, "on trial." It may have financial support from the organization, or it may be supported primarily with funding from one or more outside sources secured through a grant or contract arrangement (sometimes called "soft money"). In the latter case, because the funding is time-limited (often renewable on a year-to-year basis or some other set amount of time), the term "life cycle" is often used in relation to these programs. A **program life cycle** of a time-limited program encompasses the entire life of the program, from its planning stages until the program is either terminated or is renewed for another cycle. Usually, if a program initially relies on outside funding, some way to make the program financially self-sufficient (and more permanent) must eventually be found, or the program will have to be terminated.

Programs vary widely in their degree of autonomy. Few generalizations apply to programs and their relationship to their organization and to those who provide funding for them. Some programs (such as some of those created by private, not-for-profit organizations) are quite autonomous. Others (such as those that are federally mandated within the public sector) function with much less autonomy.

A certain amount of autonomy is necessary for a program to function well. However, the degree of autonomy possessed by a program is often a source of tension within an organization. Programs that are more autonomous are likely to produce problems of "ownership." Program directors can become quite possessive of "their programs." They may be unwilling to, for example, be supervised by the organization's director, or to share "their budget" or "their staff's time" to address an organizational emergency. The degree to which a program is autonomous is often a matter of debate—few guidelines are available to resolve it. However, as discussed later in this book, the relationship of a program to its organization is very important, and must be examined in the process of program evaluation research.

A program is (to a greater or lesser degree) a self-contained unit of an organization. It may have its own specific mission, but its mission is usually consistent with the mission of its parent organization. But even this is not always the case. In pursuit of funding, some organizations have developed programs that seem to be only tangentially related to the organization's overall mission. While this may meet a financial necessity, it can also cause problems for the organization and its identity.

A program is likely to have its own goals, objectives, staff, budget, and services. It may have its own office space. It may even have its own rules, policies, and procedures that differ somewhat from those of the broader organization. For example, an organization-wide personnel policy about required work hours may be ignored within a program if it appears that it would hinder, rather than assist, the program in achieving its objectives.

The Interaction between Research and Practice. Both services and programs need to be evaluated. We need to know if limited resources are being used as effectively as possible and, if they are not, what changes need to be made. Fortunately, many of the same research methods and principles of statistical analysis that are used in traditional research activities can be applied successfully to evaluate a service or a program's effectiveness, efficiency, and overall value or worth. However, there is much about evaluation research that differentiates it from other forms of research. The most obvious difference is its purpose. As we have noted, it is not used primarily to build a knowledge base for our profession. While some of the knowledge that is generated may be a contribution to our body of knowledge, when this occurs, it is a bonus. More typically, the knowledge derived from evaluation research tends to be idiosyncratic: very specific to some unique service or program. Thus, it may not be "generalizable."

Who benefits from the knowledge derived from evaluation research? Individual practitioners and their clients tend to benefit most from evaluation of their own individual services. In fact, that is the primary purpose of one type of evaluation research—feedback to the practitioner on the effectiveness of his or her intervention with some client or client system. Evaluations of programs (including their services) are beneficial to several other different individuals and groups as well. These beneficiaries are discussed in Chapter 2.

The complex process of conducting good evaluation research can only be understood if we understand how research and practice interact. The cliché that "research informs practice, but practice also informs research" goes a long way toward explaining this relationship. It also helps to remember that research is a part of practice, not some outside activity that occasionally imposes itself on it. The "true knowing" that is the goal of evaluative research can only be accomplished when research and practice work together to seek the truth. The methods of evaluation research that I will describe in the chapters that follow are based on this assumption.

RESEARCH TERMINOLOGY FOR EVALUATION RESEARCH

You are likely to have completed (or are in the process of taking) one or more courses in research methods. You may also have studied how to conduct statistical analysis of research data. The research terminology that follows may seem like "old stuff," not worth studying again. However, evaluation research is not just application of research methods to the evaluation of services and programs. Therefore, the terms that follow and the concepts that underlie them have a unique connotation within evaluation research—please don't skip them!

Some research terminology and many forms of statistical analysis are useful in relationship to only one or two forms of evaluation research. Those terms will be discussed later where appropriate. However, the other terms that are relevant to many types of evaluation research are presented here. Each brief definition is enough to jog your memory and briefly describe how each relates specifically to evaluation research.

Methodological Terms

Let's begin with some terms you most likely encountered in a course on research design. They should be among those most familiar to you.

Design   a plan for conducting research. In evaluation research, data collection (one part of design) often occurs throughout the life cycle of a service or program rather than at a specific point in the research process. We will mention other important differences in our discussion of specific forms of evaluation research.

Cross-sectional design a research design in which all data are analyzed at about the same time, thus providing a "snapshot in time." In evaluation research, cross-sectional research is frequently used to evaluate the status of a service or program at a given time, such as when it is only getting underway, or nearing its conclusion.

Before-and-after-design (also referred to as a pretest-posttest design) a research design in which one or more key variables are measured once, and then again following some event. Before-and-after designs are commonly used in evaluation research to try to learn if a service or program may have made a difference in the severity of a problem and, if so, how much difference it may have made.

Longitudinal design a research design in which the same variables are measured repeatedly over an extended period to monitor changes as they occur. Longitudinal designs are often used in evaluation research to "track" changes in the severity of a problem among clients being served. A longitudinal design can identify when, and under what conditions, a service or program may have begun to make a difference, something that a cross-sectional design or before-and-after design cannot do.

Exploratory design a research design employed when we know very little about a research problem; often a relatively unstructured form of inquiry whose goal is to only know more about some phenomenon. In evaluation research, an exploratory research design would simply attempt to learn if any changes in a problem occurred after an intervention (a service or program) was offered. It could provide only an estimate of the relationship between a service or program and the problem. It would not allow us to learn if the intervention may have *produced* any change.

Descriptive design a research design which attempts to describe the distribution of variables within a research sample or population, or to identify associations or correlations between variables. Descriptive research designs are commonly used in evaluations of services and in certain types of program evaluations, for example, those during the early stages of a program. When they are used to evaluate program effectiveness, they can document the amount of change in a problem over the course of the program, but they still cannot allow us to conclude that the program produced the change.

Explanatory design a more rigorous research design that attempts to demonstrate a cause–effect relationship between or among variables; its purest form is the experiment. Explanatory designs are sometimes used to evaluate the effectiveness of individual services. They are also commonly used in program evaluations that seek to learn if a program has successfully produced changes in the severity of a problem. Through several methods (primarily random selection of cases and the random assignment to one or more control groups) threats to internal validity (see below) are better controlled than in exploratory or descriptive designs. While true experiments are ideal for determining the effectiveness of services and programs, both ethical and logistical constraints often preclude their use.

Qualitative methods   research methods whose goal is to understand human experiences from the perspective of those who experience them; methods characterized by use of inductive logic, subjectivity, lack of reliance on statistical analysis, flexibility, and (often) a heavy dependence on personal interviews or other less-structured methods of data collection. Qualitative methods are widely used in the evaluation of various aspects of programs, often as a balance or "check" on more quantitative evaluation methods. They are also used extensively for evaluating programs which do not lend themselves to more quantitative measurement of program value or worth, for example, in those programs seeking to maintain quality of life or which possess other objectives whose achievement can best be evaluated from the perspective of their clients.

Quantitative methods   research methods whose goal is to learn what *is* rather than what is *experienced* or is *perceived* to be; methods characterized by an emphasis on objectivity, freedom from bias, careful measurement, and deductive logic. Statistical analysis of data is often present. Quantitative methods are widely employed in evaluation research, especially in evaluating individual practice effectiveness and in evaluating the effectiveness of programs in relation to the achievement of their objectives.

Research ethics   principles that govern what can and cannot be allowed in the conduct of research; principles based on what a society views as right or wrong, justifiable or unjustifiable. While the usual research ethics standards apply to evaluation research (for example, protecting those who provide data), evaluation research produces many other ethical issues that are relatively specific to this type of research (for example, the presence of ulterior motives for conducting an evaluation).

Institutional Review Board (IRB)   a group convened primarily to protect the welfare and dignity of those participating in research. They review and approve research proposals, primarily to ensure that implementing them would not result in ethical violations (as specified in the code of ethics of professions such as sociology, psychology, or social work), for example, a lack of voluntary informed consent on the part of clients or their unnecessary pain and suffering. Depending on the nature of the research and other factors, IRB review of a proposal for evaluation research may be required.

Research question   the question that the research hopes to answer. If the answer can be found, it will help to alleviate the research problem (a gap in knowledge that limits practice effectiveness). While research questions vary widely in most other types of research, the basic research question in evaluation research is always some variation on, How valuable is this service or program? or, Is this service or program effective? There are also always a number of secondary questions that tend to vary more from evaluation to evaluation.

They often address the question of efficiency of a service or program or its value relative to other services or programs.

Research hypothesis   a tentative answer to a research question; a statement of a relationship between variables. It is sometimes referred to as the "alternative hypothesis" (as opposed to the null hypothesis). In evaluation research a research hypothesis may be a statement reflecting the belief that some intervention (service or program) produced (or has the potential to produce) some positive change in a problem. Or, it may be some other statement predicting what will be learned about the value or worth of a service or program. Research hypotheses are sometimes stated in evaluation research; other times they are not stated, but implicit.

Independent variable   the variable believed to affect the measurements of a second variable (the dependent variable). The terms *independent variable* and *dependent variable* are used to denote the relationship between two or more variables within a research hypothesis. In a research hypothesis within evaluative research, the dependent variable is often the intervention (a service or program).

Dependent variables   variables believed to be influenced by the independent variable or variables. Their variations and why they occur are of primary interest to the researcher (as opposed to the variation within independent variables). In a research hypothesis within evaluative research, the dependent variable is often the problem that the intervention (a service or program) is designed to address.

Confounding variables   a generic term used to describe any other variables that might somehow affect the appearance of the relationship between the independent and dependent variables; alternately referred to as an *extraneous variable*. In evaluation research, a potentially confounding variable is often any other variable that may affect the relationship between the problem (the dependent variable) and the intervention being evaluated (the independent variable). A confounding variable can make an intervention appear more or less effective than it really is.

Demographic variables   a generic term referring to the commonly measured descriptive characteristics of some group of people. In evaluation research, demographic characteristics of clients are generally measured and reported to provide the reader of a report with a clearer understanding of those being served. In reports of program evaluations, the demographic characteristics of others may also be reported. For example, the demographic characteristics of the community might be reported to suggest whether the program seems to be addressing its needs. Or, the demographic characteristics of staff members might be reported to suggest whether they reflect desirable diversity, or are otherwise qualified to deliver the program's services.

Nondirectional (two-tailed) hypothesis   a form of research hypothesis that states that the independent and dependent variables will be found to be related, but does not specify the direction of their relationship. In evaluation research, nondirectional research hypotheses are relatively rare. They sometimes occur when it cannot be predicted whether a service will reduce a problem or make it worse, or in those program evaluation designs where the researcher wishes to learn which of two or more promising interventions is more effective.

Directional (one-tailed) hypothesis a form of research hypothesis that states that the independent and dependent variables will be found to be related, and specifies the direction of their relationship. Directional hypotheses are the most common form of research hypotheses in evaluation research. Generally, we believe that an intervention will produce a positive change in some problem, or we would not implement it.

Null hypothesis the belief that the independent and dependent variables are really unrelated, *and* that any apparent relationship between or among them is a function of chance or sampling error. In evaluation research (as in other types of research), we test the null hypothesis through statistical analysis. If it suggests that it is safe to reject the null hypothesis, we have support for either a nondirectional research hypothesis or a directional research hypothesis. (However, the apparent relationship between variables may still have been caused by something else other than sampling error.) If there is insufficient statistical evidence to reject it, that would suggest that the intervention was ineffective or, if comparing two interventions, one intervention is no more effective than the other. Any apparent change in the problem or difference in its severity was only a "fluke," attributable to sampling error.

External validity an assessment of the degree to which research findings can be generalized beyond the research study itself. As suggested earlier, the findings of evaluation research studies often tend to have less external validity ("generalizability") than the findings of other, basic research. The primary purpose of evaluation research is to evaluate specific services and programs, not to contribute to our professional body of knowledge. Thus, the external validity of the findings of an evaluation study is usually relatively unimportant. If they have some external validity that is desirable, but not essential. However, the issue of the external validity of research findings can take on more importance in some evaluation research, for example, in studies designed to find answers to questions regarding the advisability of expanding or extending a service or program to other clients or locations.

Internal validity an assessment of how confident we are that something else did not produce an apparent relationship between the independent and dependent variables. The internal validity of research findings is very important in evaluation research, especially in studies that seek to determine whether a service or a program was effective. We assess the internal validity of our research findings by asking how likely it is that some other event or phenomenon (besides the intervention) might have produced positive changes in the problem. The most common threats to internal validity must be considered and are described in detail in Chapters 5 and 11. As we shall see, some are more plausible in certain forms of evaluation research than others. They are, briefly stated:

- *Direction of causation.* Did the intervention affect the problem or was it the other way around?
- *History.* Over the course of the intervention, what events occurred that might have produced changes in the problem?
- *Maturation or passage of time.* Did maturation or passage of time (and not the intervention) produce the changes in the problem?
- *Statistical regression to the mean.* Were what appear to be changes in the problem really not changes at all but a regression to a more typical level of the problem?
- *Testing.* Did measuring the problem before the intervention help to produce the changes in it?
- *Instrumentation.* Did the use of different measurements of the problem before and after intervention produce what appeared to be changes in it?
- *Selection bias.* Was the client or client group different in some important way that made the intervention appear to be effective in producing changes in the problem?
- *Overlap of "treatments."* How do I know that the intervention alone (and not some other help being received) produced change in the problem?
- *Experimental mortality.* Did "drop out" of clients or other lost measurements make the intervention appear more effective than it really was?

Secondary data   data collected and stored for some other purpose that may be analyzed as part of the research design. Evaluation research generally relies heavily on both new data collected specifically for the evaluation and on secondary data. Common examples of secondary data are a client's case record or a program's other records, budgets, job descriptions, or organizational chart.

Sampling bias   also referred to as *selection bias,* it is the unintentional or intentional systematic distortion of a sample. In evaluation research, sampling bias occurs when samples are collected in such a way that they are not representative in some important respect. For example, measurements of the "usual" level of the problem of an individual client or client system were atypical for some reason, or the sample of clients in a program was selected in some way that they were not representative of clients possessing the problem. Thus, any apparent success or lack of success of the intervention may be attributable to sampling bias—the intervention would not appear to be as successful if the sample had been more "typical," or it may have appeared to be more successful.

Sampling error   the natural tendency of samples (especially small ones) to differ from the population from which they were drawn. In evaluation research, if either a sample of measurements of a single client or client system problem or the number of clients in a program is small, sampling error could easily explain the apparent success of a service or program. When appropriate, we use statistical analysis to tell us the mathematical probability that sampling error alone could have produced it.

Simple random sample   a sample drawn so that every potential case had an equal probability of being selected. A random sample in an evaluation of a service might consist of the random selection of times or places when the dependent variable would be measured. In a program evaluation, a simple random sample of clients to participate in the program could be acquired by picking its clients at random from among all active clients who meet certain criteria.

Purposive sample   a sample that is compiled in a way that its cases will be the most useful, that is, informative. Purposive samples (also referred to as *judgmental samples*) often sacrifice representativeness for homogeneity and sometimes for diversity. In a program evaluation, the sample of clients in a program often is not selected using simple random sampling methods. They may be a purposive sample because, for example, they are only those clients whose problem is most severe or they were selected so that the sample would contain the widest possible variety of manifestations of the problem.

Convenience sample   a sample of cases that is selected primarily because of its availability. While it theoretically can be representative of the population from which it is drawn, it is highly unlikely. In evaluation research, convenience samples are often necessary for logistical reasons. For example, direct observations of a client's behavior may be possible only during treatment interviews and thus constitute only a convenience sample of measurements of the behavior. Or the clients in a program can only be those people referred to the organization who meet certain diagnostic criteria.

Reliability   the consistency of a measurement, its potential to produce similar results under a variety of conditions. In evaluation research, reliability is often an important consideration in selecting a scale or other instrument to measure the dependent variable. However, as in other types of research, the instrument should also be valid.

Validity   the degree to which the measurement of a variable measures what it is supposed to measure. In evaluation research, valid measurement of the dependent variable in a research hypothesis is especially critical. If not, any conclusions about the effectiveness of a service or program may be erroneous. The question is, Did our measurement really measure the variable we sought to change (the dependent variable), or did it measure something else? If, for example, a service or program is designed to increase assertiveness and our "assertiveness scale" actually measures hostility instead, we cannot say that the program was successful, no matter how much change appeared to occur.

Levels of measurement   labels applied to the measurement of a variable that relate to the degree of precision that the measurement reflects; nominal, ordinal, interval, or ratio-level measurement. The primary importance of levels of measurement in evaluation research is that they are major determinants in selecting what statistic or statistical test is appropriate for data analysis.

Statistical Terms

Here are just a few terms drawn from the field of statistics that have special importance and, in some instances, slightly different usages in evaluation research. They will not substitute for a study of the subject but, if you have at least some familiarity with it, they should serve as a good refresher.

Descriptive statistics various ways of summarizing and communicating the most important characteristics of data sets, including measures of central tendency, and measures of variability (dispersion). Tables and graphs may perform a similar function. In evaluation research, descriptive statistics are used simply to portray, often in abbreviated form, the distribution of variables that were measured, for example, the demographic characteristics of clients served by a program. In program evaluations conducted on programs in their early stages, descriptive statistical analysis may be the primary type of data analysis performed.

Inferential statistics the use of various formulas and mathematical tests to determine the probability that a relationship between variables within a research sample may have been produced by sampling error. Tests of inference are used in evaluation research to, for example, learn if there is statistical support for research hypotheses that predict a relationship between a service or program and changes in the severity of a problem or that predict which of two programs will be more successful.

Multivariate analysis the simultaneous examination of the relationship among three or more variables. While multivariate statistical analysis is used less frequently in evaluation research than bivariate analysis (which examines the relationship between the two most common independent and dependent variables: intervention and problem), it is being used more frequently now that computer analysis of data has become readily available. For example, it can be used in program evaluations to examine the relationship among multiple demographic variables of clients (age, ethnicity, education level, and so forth) and successful program outcomes. (To answer questions such as, With which clients was the program most likely to be effective?) Or, it can be used to examine the success of programs, which have multiple program objectives that may overlap to some degree. (To answer, for example, How successful was the child abuse prevention program in increasing knowledge of child development, increasing use of noncorporal methods of discipline, and increasing understanding of shaken baby syndrome?)

Statistical significance evidence, based on mathematics and the laws of probability, that a relationship between variables within a research sample is very unlikely to be the work of sampling error or chance. In evaluation research that examines the relationship between a service or program and a desirable change in a problem, a finding of statistical significance is not sufficient reason to conclude that the service or program is valuable or even that it is effective. A confounding variable, or one or more threats to internal validity, may have produced the relationship. Even if the intervention did produce it, the amount of change produced may not be enough to claim "success." If there are many measurements of the dependent variable or the number of clients in a program is very large, a statistically significant relationship between the independent and dependent variables is virtually assured. The determination as to whether a demonstrated relationship between an intervention and a desirable change in a problem is also sufficiently strong or meaningful requires the integration of knowledge drawn from both statistics and practice.

$p < .05$ the traditional cutoff point for rejecting the null hypothesis in statistical analysis; a conclusion obtained through statistical analysis that states that the relationship between two variables (given the size of the research sample) has less than a five percent likelihood of having been produced by sampling error. In evaluation research, a p-value of less than .05 is usually only one indicator that a service or program may have value or worth. Because true experimental designs are relatively rare, a finding of $p < .05$ following statistical testing of the relationship between an intervention and a positive change in a problem may be meaningless because so many other factors (for example, confounding variables, or threats to internal validity) could have produced the change. Even if it can be determined that they probably did not produce it, the actual impact of the intervention may not have been great enough to conclude that the service or program was valuable.

Statistical power   the capacity of the statistical analysis used to detect a true relationship between variables. Ideally, the analysis should be powerful enough to detect meaningful relationships between variables, but not so powerful that it detects trivial or meaningless ones. Several factors (including sample size) affect the power of a given statistical analysis. We may not be able to control the number of measurements of an individual problem that are available for analysis or the number of clients in a program (sample size). Thus, there is the potential that the analysis used may be too powerful or not powerful enough.

ADDITIONAL CLARIFICATION

This chapter began with a rather simple, straightforward definition of evaluation research. That definition was broken down and several of its components were elaborated. The review of selected terminology from research design and statistics further clarified what evaluation research is and how it is similar to, yet different from, other types of research. Now, in case the focus of evaluation research is still a little hazy, let me describe evaluation research a little more directly.

Evaluation research consists of the use of research methods to evaluate the value or worth of services and programs. This involves, in part, a focus on the effectiveness of (1) the interventions of individual social work practitioners, and (2) social programs as a whole (including the services that they offer). As discussed later in more detail, evaluation of individual effectiveness is designed primarily to benefit the practitioner himself or herself—to tell him or her whether what he or she is doing or has done to help a client or client system is working or has worked.

Program evaluation encompasses a much wider range of purposes than evaluation of individual practice effectiveness. Measuring program effectiveness is not always the primary purpose of program evaluations. Even when effectiveness is the major focus, it is usually not the only one. Many different aspects of program functioning are examined in order to learn the true value or worth of a program.

Program evaluations are conducted for and beneficial to many different parties and interest groups, not just those offering services. Program evaluations are conducted on programs that are relatively permanent and those that are time-limited. They occur at any stage in a program. For example, some program evaluations evaluate programs that are only getting under way—it might be fair to see if they are off to a good start, but certainly not to draw any conclusions about their effectiveness or overall worth. Still other forms of program evaluations examine the potential value of programs that haven't even been implemented yet, and may never be implemented.

CONCLUDING THOUGHTS

Chapter 1 provided a definition and general understanding of evaluation research and its relationship to research and social work practice. I highlighted some of the basic concepts of research that are critical to understanding it, while trying not to unnecessarily repeat what is usually covered in other research courses. I have also provided some working definitions of other key concepts to ensure that we have similar understandings of them in the discussions that follow. Much of what was introduced will be discussed in more detail later. Chapter 2 examines the origins of evaluation research and attempts to describe its status in our profession.

KEY TERMS

evaluation	efficiency	program
evaluation research	accountability	permanent program
basic research	stakeholders	time-limited program
applied research	service	program life cycle
effectiveness	services	

STUDY QUESTIONS

1. Why does the term *evaluation* often have negative connotations?

2. What makes evaluation research different from other types of evaluation?

3. What is effectiveness, and how does it differ from efficiency?

4. What is the relationship between a program and an agency or organization?

5. What is the relationship between a service and a program?

6. What does it mean when we say that a program is accountable?

7. How does the purpose of evaluation research differ from that of other forms of research?

8. How important is external validity in evaluation research? Explain.

9. What type of program design (exploratory, descriptive, or explanatory) is most likely to be used in evaluation research that seeks to learn if a program has been effective?

10. What is the most common research hypothesis in evaluation research? What are some other research hypotheses (stated or implicit) that evaluation research sometimes tests?

REFERENCES

1. National Association of Social Workers (1999). *Code of ethics.* Washington, DC: NASW Press.

2. Rossi, P., & Freeman, H. (1982). *Evaluation: A systematic approach.* Beverly Hills, CA: Sage, 20.

3. Scriven, M. (2004). "Michael Scriven on the Difference Between Evaluation and Social Science Research." *The Evaluation Exchange,* (IX, 4), Winter 2003/2004, 1–2.

CHAPTER TWO

THE HISTORY OF EVALUATION RESEARCH

Evaluation research is relatively new. However, conscientious professionals have always wanted to know if their interventions are effective. They relied on some indicator to tell them whether their services and programs made a difference. Unfortunately, more often than not, the indicators that they chose were only a slight improvement over a simple good or bad feeling about a service or program.

BEFORE EVALUATION RESEARCH

Ms. Butler has not missed an appointment in three years. She obviously is getting something out of her treatment.

The program can only accept about half of those who apply. We must be doing something right.

Both of the above statements (or a variation of them) have historically been used as indicators of success, and they may indicate client satisfaction with a service or program. But there are several reasons why client satisfaction is one of the poorest indicators of service or program success. First, some clients are "involuntary," that is, required to go by the court system or some other authority. They are unlikely to express satisfaction with services or a social program. Even if clients are "voluntary," they may continue to seek services or a program for any number of reasons, many of which are not what we might hope. It could be an unhealthy dependency (or co-dependency!), as in the first example. Or, it may be because it is "the thing to do" within a client's peer group. It may offer an excused absence from work or school. It may imply to others that the client really wants to work on a problem, when he or she really does not. Perhaps, it represents a chance for social interaction, or the building where a service or program is housed may be more pleasant or better climate-controlled than the client's home. We could probably come up with hundreds of "the wrong" reasons why clients might seek and be satisfied with a service or program, whether it was effective or ineffective.

> Since we began marriage counseling, the Taylors have decided to stay married until Gordon finishes high school.

> Since this program began, its clients have demonstrated consistent improvement in their social skills.

These two statements may be evidence of intervention success. However, they are subjective judgments that are vulnerable to the injection of personal values. One social worker may view preserving a difficult marriage as desirable and, thus, an indicator of counseling success. Another might view it as undesirable, given how it is affecting the social functioning of the family. Similarly, "social skills" may mean "acting as I act," or "acting as most people act" without regard to cultural differences that help determine what is in the clients' best interest.

> Group participation has really improved. Last week every member made at least two comments.

> We made over 900 job referrals this past year, nearly 20 percent more than last year.

The above two statements share a common problem—they suggest a focus on means rather than ends. They are examples of what is referred to as a **means-end displacement**—a phenomenon whereby people sometimes lose sight of a goal (an end) and focus instead on one or more means to achieving it.[1] Yes, verbal participation in a group is good. It is even necessary for most (but not all) people to benefit from group intervention. But it does not guarantee that the problems that clients are experiencing have diminished. Similarly, job referrals should not be an end in themselves. How many referrals actually result in appropriate, meaningful, and rewarding jobs? Referrals are means to solving the problem of unemployment; they are not ends in themselves. These statements only say that the means to solving a problem have occurred more often, and that is not saying much. Later chapters will examine other traditional indicators of service or program success in reviewing specific types of evaluation research.

Prior to the advent of today's evaluation methods, the criteria for evaluating the success of a service or program were quite "soft." They relied heavily on impressions, logic, and common sense. Of course, these subjective indicators were not the only ways in which services and programs were evaluated prior to evaluation research as we know it today. Much more systematic and comprehensive methods were also employed, such as those described in Chapter 3. They are still widely used, but primarily for monitoring the quality of services and programs rather than their effectiveness. Often, they seek to determine whether they are delivered "properly" (whatever that means!). As we shall see, some of these indicators may have utility for evaluating services or programs that are "in process," but they may lack validity as measures of intervention success. And, the need to demonstrate the success of our interventions was the impetus for evaluation research as we know it today.

FORCES FOR CHANGE

There was no single impetus for the increased emphasis on intervention effectiveness. It resulted from a combination of overlapping and mutually supportive developments during the twentieth century. Some can be linked to a specific date or event; others cannot. Working in concert, they produced a demand for evaluation research that eventually could not be ignored.

The New Deal

During the 1930s, many new federal social programs were established to address problems such as high unemployment and homelessness that were associated with the Great Depression. The programs were collectively referred to as the "New Deal" following a speech by President Franklin D. Roosevelt in which he used the term in outlining some of his plans. Some of the programs were undoubtedly successful; others were less successful. There were many calls for evaluation of these costly programs by their critics, most of whom were members of the opposing political party. As dissatisfaction grew, so did pressures for evaluation research.[2]

During World War II, some evaluation of various military and war-related programs took place, along with more frequent evaluation of social programs at home. During the 1950s, evaluation of both governmental and nongovernmental social programs continued to increase. Better methods of evaluation began to be developed by those social scientists who conducted them.[3]

The Consumer Movement

The term **consumer movement** was coined sometime back in the 1950s or 1960s; it is rarely used today. We rarely hear the term now because we simply assume that customers have the right to be treated fairly, ethically, and so forth. The movement has accomplished most of its goals. But the situation was different in the first half of the twentieth century. Consumers (and, for us, clients) pretty much had to accept what was offered. Their only recourses were to decline goods (or services) that they found unacceptable, and to tell their friends to avoid them.

Slowly, at first, people began to perceive the injustice of the current system and tried to change it. Their efforts were enhanced by some of the more dramatic disclosures about products offered to the consumer. Some products were found to be not only worthless—they were actually harmful, even life threatening. Consumers began to organize under the leadership of social activists and consumer "watchdogs" like Ralph Nader. They delighted in revealing research findings about design flaws in products such as the Chevrolet Corvair.[4] The consumer movement (alternately referred to as the consumer protection movement) ultimately gained additional legitimacy with the creation of the U.S. government agency known as the Consumer Protection Agency.

What, exactly, was the contribution of the consumer movement to the climate that created a demand for evaluation research? First, the movement helped to broaden the definition of a consumer. A *consumer* began to be defined as anyone who purchases or receives certain goods or services. Most significantly for us, that definition now included all of social work's clients. Clients who paid for their own services in the private sector always had some rights if they were dissatisfied with services or programs. They could withhold payment from, or even bring lawsuits against, the offending individual who offered a service or the organization that housed a program. But clients in the public sector had no similar recourse. The consumer movement helped our society to recognize that (1) clients receiving financial assistance and other services for which they do not directly pay are entitled to these services, and (2) they have a right to expect that the services will be delivered in a professional manner.

Over time, a third right began to be acknowledged—the right to receive services that are effective. In a sense, clients in the public sector were now seen as no different from any other consumer—the fact that their services were paid for by tax dollars was deemed irrelevant. We may look back at this now and wonder how it could have been any other way.

Even if they do not pay for them in dollars, clients invest time, effort, and other resources in a service or program. Shouldn't they be able to expect that the expenditure of these resources will be followed by the desired results? Yes, it is reasonable to expect that the service or program in which clients invest extensively is effective. A service or program should be able to demonstrate that it is effective. How?—through evaluation research.

Political Events

The 1960s marked both high and low points for social workers and other helping professionals. The growing number of people receiving public financial assistance provided opportunities, followed by threats. The latter especially helped to create a need for evaluation research.

Reason for Optimism.   There was consensus among American taxpayers that something must be done about the growth of welfare rolls. The Social Security Act of 1935 was intended to provide short-term financial aid to people who were unemployed because of the Great Depression. But, over the years, conditions had changed. What some Americans in the early 1960s perceived instead was a ponderous bureaucracy doling out taxpayer money to an ever-increasing number of people who saw public assistance as a way of life, a permanent source of assistance. This stereotype often included the belief that public assistance had become multigenerational, perpetuating a distinct social class of people content to be dependent on taxpayers to support them.

Of course, social workers who actually worked with recipients of public assistance did not buy into this stereotype. They saw instead large numbers of people trapped in a system that promoted dependency by offering them enough to survive, but not offering them enough of what they needed to escape it. Frustrated, overworked caseworkers complained that, among other factors, huge caseloads made it virtually impossible to use their helping skills successfully. All they could do was complete eligibility determinations and investigate continued eligibility for assistance. There was no time left to provide the counseling, which, they stated confidently, would provide a means for welfare recipients to become self-sufficient. Some small-scale studies seemed to lend credence to their contention. When intensive casework services were offered, they were successful in helping families to gain financial independence.[5]

When President John F. Kennedy took office in 1961, things began to look up for social workers. The "New Frontier" that he envisioned was designed to address many of the social problems of the day. In fact, it was so liberal in nature that few people held out much hope that most of its programs would pass the U.S. House and Senate. However, they did not anticipate two factors. First, Kennedy's personality and style in the White House quickly won over some of his critics. Secondly, his tragic assassination on November 22, 1963 resulted in a wave of sympathy and support for his proposed programs that might not otherwise have occurred. When Lyndon Johnson succeeded Kennedy, he was able to take advantage of the sentiment of the time to launch successfully both Kennedy's programs and reforms and his own. For example, his "War on Poverty" (the Economic Opportunity Act of 1964) introduced new programs such as Head Start.

The **Kennedy/Johnson years** were marked by the passage of many pieces of social legislation. However, the impetus for evaluation research came primarily from the **1962 Social Security Amendments** and the events that followed them. The 1962 Social Security Amendments made a number of important changes in the American public welfare system. Clients of the **Aid to Families with Dependent Children (AFDC)** program would continue to receive financial assistance, but they were to receive other services as well. The range of services included such social work staples as family counseling, budgeting assistance, and job-training referrals. The amendments mandated regular contact with caseworkers and set limits on caseloads, although the frequency of contact required and the size of caseloads (usually about 40 families) still did not allow for the intensive counseling that social workers sought to offer, or that had been offered in earlier pilot programs. They also made it possible for a family to receive AFDC benefits even if the father was present but unemployed, although this was an option that only about half of the states chose to adopt. Prior to the amendments, there was little incentive to work, because earnings were automatically deducted from monthly benefits. The net effect was that the "working poor" worked for nothing. But after its passage, they could keep the first $30 of their earnings without a reduction in benefits and a third of anything else they earned.

While the amendments did not go as far as social workers would have liked, the Kennedy/Johnson years were as close to the "golden years of social work" as we have seen. There was widespread support for the belief that social work services could end the cycle of poverty and reduce the welfare rolls. With some important limitations, we were told to do what we said we could do, if given the necessary resources. In short, social work's bluff was called.

What Happened?   Did we deliver? While many individual families undoubtedly benefited from enhanced casework services, the one indicator that the taxpaying public and its legislators were most concerned with—a decline in the AFDC rolls— did not happen. In 1962, there were approximately 3.5 million people receiving AFDC benefits; there were almost 10 million by 1970. The cost of the program quadrupled over the same period.

There are many reasons offered to explain why AFDC rolls grew rapidly following the 1962 Social Security Amendments. Contributing factors include simple population growth, rising unemployment, and inflation. The wording of the amendments and the changes that they precipitated may also have contributed to an increase in AFDC programs by making public assistance less stigmatized. They seemed to suggest causes for economic dependency outside the individual's control, and to assume that people do not want to be dependent on others—they may have no choice. In that way, they seemed to do less "blaming the victim." Perhaps, many people who were previously eligible for benefits but were too embarrassed to apply now viewed public assistance as socially acceptable, and applied for benefits.

During the 1960s, welfare recipients also began to organize. The Welfare Rights Organization sought to inform people of their eligibility for assistance (their right to it). It was widely believed that, because of clients' dislike of the current system, the organization's hidden agenda was to overload it so much that it would have to be reformed. The organization was undoubtedly successful in "spreading the word" and increasing welfare rolls.

In retrospect, we are not surprised that increased services did not produce the desired result. In addition to the reasons already noted, AFDC benefit levels remained low. As any student of human behavior knows, the most basic of human needs (food, clothing, and shelter) must be met before people are motivated by the next higher need level.[6] If AFDC benefits were inadequate to meet the basic needs, it was probably unrealistic to expect clients to be sufficiently motivated to seek to gratify higher-level needs for autonomy or self-esteem. Could we really expect welfare rolls to decline given all the forces working against them?

How can we explain the difference between the results of earlier pilot studies and those of AFDC programs in the 1960s? The conditions under which successful pilot studies had been carried out and the real world of AFDC in the 1960s differed markedly. As noted earlier, the intensity of contact with clients (mandated visits and caseloads) were very different. Perhaps equally important was the difference in professional training of those offering services. In the pilot studies, professionally educated social workers worked closely with clients to assist them in gaining financial independence. In AFDC programs, caseworkers often had little or no professional social work education and little on-the-job-training. In South Carolina, for example, many AFDC workers were people who had been previously employed as teachers in public schools but who could no longer qualify as teachers when educational requirements were upgraded.

The Backlash.   While an increase in the size of AFDC rolls in the 1960s appears inevitable in retrospect, it was widely viewed by the general public as social work's failure to deliver on a promise. Moreover, an important point for our discussion, the "failure" was widely blamed on social work's use of unproven methods of intervention, methods that "sounded good" but had not been documented as effective except in a few small studies lacking in design rigor.

An attitude of "never again" prevailed. Subsequent legislation (such as the 1967 Social Security Amendments) sought to simplify the process of applying and becoming eligible for financial assistance. But it also reflected a distrust of social work professionals. They were confined to "services" staff—a specific group of employees that offered social services (primarily counseling) to those families deemed to need them. An MSW degree might be required, or it might not, depending on the requirements of the state in which the program was housed. But the job of eligibility determination went to people who generally possessed little or no social work education. Families judged by their eligibility worker not to need social work services received none. This separation of "income maintenance" and "services" staff seemed to suggest the belief that counseling services were often a waste of time and money, and that much of the work previously performed by social workers could be done better and less expensively by "clerks" with little or no professional education.

Later, when the more conservative administration of Richard Nixon was wielding considerable influence over social programs, the public was regularly reminded of the "failure" of earlier programs during the 1960s. Top advisers such as John Ehrlichman promoted the idea that social work and related fields should be held accountable using the same methods for evaluating effectiveness that were used in business and industry. Programs should be funded only if it could be demonstrated that they really work and that they are efficient. If they fail to work or prove to be too expensive, they should receive no more federal money. Many social workers objected, arguing that methods for measuring business success were inapplicable when evaluating human services and programs. After all, it is hard enough to know for sure what a success is in the human services, and harder still to demonstrate that a service or program (rather than something else) produced it.

Despite objections from social workers and others in the helping professions, the "age of accountability" had arrived and it would not go away. Because business methods for demonstrating accountability were so often inappropriate, a logical alternative was to develop our own models for evaluation research. And, that is exactly what began to happen. One of the better-known, early models was called Differential Program Evaluation.[7] While not downplaying the importance of effective programs, it emphasized fairness. For example, it proposed different evaluation questions and strategies for a social program based on its stage of development.[8]

Social Work Critics

External critics of social work programs were major contributors to demands for accountability. They were given additional ammunition for their criticism by the reports of federally funded evaluations of programs such as the Seattle-Denver Income Maintenance Experiment (SIME-DIME). It concluded that conventional welfare seemed to erode the work ethic of its clients, and was associated with an increase in other problems among its recipients.[9] But demands for accountability were not limited to those who might naturally be critical of the helping professions. Some social workers had begun to question the lack of empirical evidence showing that our services and programs were effective, even before others exposed it. They continued their challenges into the 1980s and beyond. Many of them were academicians, men and women who understood and conducted research themselves and who wondered why we advocated the use of research for developing general knowledge for use by practitioners but rarely relied on its methods to see if our services and programs really worked. They perceived an anti-intellectual bias among those in the "real world" of practice—or was it a fear that some of the methods of intervention that were practiced would not stand up well in light of objective evaluation?

One of the more controversial challenges to social work practice from within was undertaken by Joel Fischer[10] during the early 1970s. Using an established research procedure (meta-analysis), he reviewed the reports of over 80 research studies that purported to evaluate the effectiveness of social casework as a method of intervention. He did not include the great majority of studies in his data analysis because they did not employ a control group, a group of potential clients not offered services that could be compared with those who received them. He concluded that, without a control group, it would be impossible to learn whether any improvement in client functioning could be attributed to the casework intervention, or whether it would have occurred without it.

Only eleven studies met Fischer's design criteria, that is, they were regarded as sufficiently rigorous. Of those, none demonstrated that people who received social casework services reflected a statistically significant higher rate of improvement than their counterparts in control groups did. Even worse, many clients who received services actually appeared to be functionally less well after receiving services.

Fischer's findings were, to say the least, controversial. He had listed many of his own methodological limitations, for example, he acknowledged that many of the clients were involuntarily receiving services and, thus, they may have been very resistive to receiving assistance. His critics eagerly sought out other potential flaws in his research methods. A lively and, sometimes, almost mean-spirited debate occurred within our professional literature as some writers sought to discredit Fischer, while others defended him. His critics found him to be a difficult target—he seemed to have no vested interest in his findings. He was both an academician and a social work practitioner who taught and wrote extensively in both areas of social work research and practice.

The reaction to Fischer's research findings was not surprising. After all, who wouldn't respond negatively if someone came along and declared that some method of intervention that you believe to be effective, and that you had built a career around, didn't really help people, and maybe made some of them worse!

Eventually the controversy died down, and in the end, it probably does not matter whether his critics were correct in their attempts to discredit his research, or were merely being defensive. What did matter was that following Fischer's work, it became increasingly acceptable among social workers to question whether practice (services and programs) were really effective. An article published nearly thirty years later identified Fischer as one of fifty leading research scholars in social work.[11]

During the late 1970s, both the Council on Social Work Education (CSWE) and the National Association of Social Workers (NASW) created and convened task forces to attempt to bridge the apparent gap between research and practice. Their members concluded that evaluation research might just be the answer. It seemed to be a way that research could serve practitioners and ensure that research findings would be more relevant to practice than they had been.

Among other objectives, the task forces sought ways in which social work could move closer to other professions such as medicine or psychology, both of which regularly used research to evaluate various aspects of their practice. In one of the publications that emerged, Scott Briar proposed what he called the clinical scientist model[12] as a way for social workers to be more accountable in their practice. The model places heavy emphasis on evaluation of practice effectiveness and reliance on those intervention methods that have been proven to be effective.

Eventually, there was general consensus within the profession that some of the emphasis on accountability that had been forced on us by the federal government and by the general public might be justified, and maybe was not such a bad idea after all. Maybe it was a good idea to conduct evaluations of practice to ensure that our limited resources were not being spent on services and programs that have limited or no value.

Efficiency Concerns

By the end of the 1970s, concern about the effectiveness of social work services and programs was well-established, both within and outside the profession. However, a variety of forces during the last two decades of the twentieth century contributed to an increased emphasis on efficiency. In the public sector, the cost of public assistance programs continued to rise. Legislators and members of the general public began to question whether, to a large extent, this was occurring because caseworkers were making too many errors in eligibility determinations. Perhaps, they were incorrectly concluding that some people were eligible for financial assistance when they were not eligible, or failing to disqualify other people for assistance when they became ineligible. Some highly publicized audits of case records seemed to confirm that this might be exactly what was happening.

The solution that was proposed was to apply the same quality-control methods used by manufacturers to assure that errors are kept to a minimum. In a manufacturing plant, this entails randomly pulling products off the end of a production line and submitting them to rigorous quality testing. Workers might be rewarded or penalized, depending on the number of flaws that were found. In the public sector, a popular variation of quality control entailed the introduction of a new focus—error rate. Federal auditors could now randomly select case records and carefully scrutinize them to determine whether eligibility standards had been applied correctly. Then the percentage of errors, the error rate, could be computed. If the error rate was above a certain standard, federal reimbursement for a state's program would have to be returned. The fear of loss of federal reimbursement should result in more conscientious eligibility determination and, thus, reduced welfare rolls, it was assumed. It did create somewhat of an obsession with error rate among administrators and public welfare employees, and thus may have reduced costs somewhat. However, did it actually help to promote financial independence? Probably not. Inevitably, in some agencies, staff members began to be evaluated (at least in part) based on their error rate. A good caseworker was one who could demonstrate a low error rate; a caseworker with a higher error rate might receive a reprimand or some other sanction, even though he or she might be offering good services to clients and errors may not have been his or her fault. (For example, clients may not have reported changes in their economic situation as required). So, we only had another example of a means-end displacement—a focus on one possible means to an end (eligibility determination) rather than on the end itself (which should have been client economic self-sufficiency).

During the 1990s, cost consciousness contributed to another phenomenon, privatization of services and programs. It was widely believed in many circles that the large bureaucracy characteristic of state and federal agencies was highly inefficient. Why couldn't private entrepreneurs do the same jobs for less money? Increasingly, private for-profit organizations were allowed to try. State agencies began to contract out to the private for-profit sector for services in areas such as corrections or foster care. Competition, not previously a factor, began to drive social agencies to cut costs. They did this by identifying those services and programs that promised to be effective, but were less expensive. Evaluation research promised to provide answers to such questions as, Can we treat people just as effectively (and for less cost) by treating them in a group, rather than in individual counseling? or, Can we get the same, or nearly the same, results from a program that is shorter or less expensive than the present one?

The rapidly rising cost of health care in the 1990s was yet another impetus for an emphasis on evaluation research. As health care costs skyrocketed, the message from health insurance companies to social workers (and other health professionals) was, "Cut your costs, or we will cut them for you!" A concern with "unnecessary" medical procedures, tests, medications, and even surgery led logically to a concern with "over-treating" our patients and clients. Several methods for monitoring and cost containment were implemented in the medical fields; they remain with us today. Professional standards review organizations (PSROs) routinely review cases to determine (among other concerns) if certain procedures, tests, or continued hospitalization appear necessary. Health Maintenance Organizations (HMOs) and other health insurance organizations seek to contain costs by developing and applying diagnostic related groups (DRGs), based on the usual medical procedure performed to treat a specific diagnosis. DRGs are developed based on, for example, the average time that a client or patient has been hospitalized following quadruple heart by-pass surgery and what he or she requires in the way of treatment. Then, suppose a patient requires the surgery. The DRG specifies what will be "covered" (treatment, tests, follow-up care). It also authorizes a specified number of days of hospitalization. If the patient goes home earlier, the hospital is financially rewarded. If he or she stays longer and no adequate justification can be provided that results in preauthorization for the extended stay, the hospital will not be reimbursed for the additional costs of hospitalization. DRGs also specify when treatment can be done as an outpatient or when inpatient treatment is required. Over recent years, more medical procedures are being added to the list of those required to be performed on an outpatient basis.

Overall, demands for greater accountability have increased incrementally during the twentieth and into the twenty-first centuries. They have caused social workers to ask more questions and, increasingly, to justify their actions. For example, can we demonstrate that the knowledge and skills of an MSW social worker are really needed to complete a discharge planning summary? If not, the job of discharge planner may go to someone else (perhaps a BSW social worker) who can do it at less cost. Can we demonstrate that more than three days are required to conduct a thorough psychiatric evaluation? If not, we will have to do it in three days or not receive third-party reimbursement beyond the third day. Can we demonstrate that an eight-week job-training program really produces better results than a six-week one? If not, the eight-week program may lose its funding.

Evaluation research has become ever more critical as we have had to assume "the burden of proof," that is, to demonstrate both the effectiveness *and* the efficiency of what we do. It is undoubtedly a threat to services and programs that may be worthwhile but, because of the nature of the problem that they address, have a difficult time operationalizing what is a "success" and identifying when one has been achieved. However, social workers who offer services and programs that can demonstrate both effectiveness and efficiency have learned that evaluation research can provide a sense of security, especially in tight economic times. They are unlikely to suffer cuts in staff or funding.

The forces that have just been described (along with many others) have combined over the past half century to produce the current market for evaluation research. We are now at a point where, for a variety of overlapping and mutually supportive reasons, social work professionals recognize the need for it and have come to value it as an integral part of professional practice.

EVALUATION RESEARCH TODAY

There are many specialized forms of evaluation that focus on one particular aspect of a service or program. We will examine them in Chapter 3. However, the "mainstream" of social work evaluation research consists of single-system research (for evaluating one's individual practice effectiveness) and program evaluation (for evaluating all aspects of programs including, but not limited to, the services they offer).

Single-System Research: Definition and Purpose

One distinguishing characteristic of single-system research is its primary purpose. **Single-system research** is designed and conducted by social work practitioners to tell them if an intervention that they have introduced in order to alleviate some problem was effective, or, if it is currently being used, if it seems to be producing the desired results. It is not designed to advance knowledge of the profession or to determine whether a method of intervention is effective (generally). It answers the question, Does *this* specific intervention that *I* am using with *this* client or client system seem to be effective in reducing *this* particular problem of *this* client or client system? Thus, the findings of single-system research are assumed to lack external validity. Some designs have greater potential for internal validity than others do but, generally, when an intervention appears to be effective, it is often difficult to conclude that nothing else (besides the intervention) may have produced the apparent "success." Even in situations where social workers exercise considerable control over clients and client systems (such as in-patient psychiatric facilities); there are still many factors (for example, threats to internal validity) that could have produced it.

Many senior social work practitioners may have never heard of single-system research. While it has been around for a long time, it was not seriously discussed or taught in schools of social work until the 1970s, and did not appear regularly in social work curricula until the 1980s. Today, when it is covered in any detail, it sometimes appears in research courses and, other times, in social work practice courses. Sometimes it is discussed in both. Students are encouraged to use it to evaluate their practice, but they may encounter problems with field instructors who are not familiar with it and regard it with some suspicion.

In practice, pressure to conduct single-system research is very uneven. Some practitioners are convinced of the value of evidence-based practice and conduct it routinely; others may have conducted it, or studied about it as students, but are still unconvinced of its value. They may use it only occasionally, or not at all. Some supervisors and administrators support its use; others question whether it isn't a waste of valuable staff time. In the twenty-first century, a realistic picture of single-system research has begun to emerge. It is not "the best thing since sliced bread," but it is far from worthless. Most social work practitioners now regard it as a valuable asset in some situations and they are finding it helpful and informative on more occasions. Single-system research, and its strengths and limitations, will be discussed in more detail in Chapter 4.

Program Evaluation: Definition and Purpose

Program evaluation is a generic term. It encompasses a wide range of activities and methods, so we will define it rather broadly. **Program evaluation** is the application of both quantitative and qualitative research methods to assess the merit, worth, or value of a program. It seeks to test the theoretical models of social programs. It is used to examine programs that are at any stage of development—from the planning stage to completed programs—and to assist in decision making about their futures.

Like other types of research, program evaluations can be described as primarily exploratory, descriptive, or explanatory. Or, "hybrid" designs can employ elements of two, or all three, types of research. Designs for program evaluations can also be cross-sectional (before and after), or longitudinal. They can be primarily quantitative or qualitative, but most frequently are a mixture of the two. Program evaluations can be initiated from outside an organization or from within it. Frequently, there is pressure to evaluate a program from some outside source, for example, a funding organization that is providing financial support for it. Evaluation may be one-time or periodic (such as annually or every six months). It may entail self-evaluation, the use of outside evaluators, or some combination of the two.

Program evaluation is essential to good management. A good manager wants to make decisions about programs within an organization based on as much reliable information as possible. Consequently, managers may, on their own initiative, design and implement various ways for evaluating existing programs, either by themselves or with assistance from their staff members.

Some programs are constructed based on a theoretical model of intervention that has been developed and refined over many years. They may have the advantage of knowing that a previous program evaluation of the model has already demonstrated its effectiveness somewhere else or with another client group. Questions remain, however. For example, Will the model work here and with our clients? or, How valuable will the program be within our community? In other instances, a program may be based less on a formal model and more on an idea that may have never been tried. However, there is still a theoretical model reflecting certain beliefs about the origins of some problem and what intervention will successfully address it. The theoretical model is the underlying reason why it is believed that the program should work. The question is, will it?

Most programs sound good, but there are numerous examples of programs that have failed despite logic telling us that the program would be effective. Sometimes we have simply misunderstood the problem or made some erroneous assumptions about its causes. For example, a program to reduce unwanted teen pregnancy that is based on the assumption that the problem stems solely from a lack of knowledge of contraception methods will fail. Sometimes, programs fail because the people planning and implementing the programs did not really understand the subculture of those whom the program sought to help. For example, certain subcultures or age groups respond differently to a program than their planners thought they "should" respond. "Scared Straight" serves as a good illustration. Wasn't it logical to assume that teenagers starting to get into trouble would benefit from a visit to a prison and a talk with incarcerated hardened criminals? However, an evaluation of the program[13] produced no evidence that it helped them to avoid subsequent criminal activity and, in fact, may have had exactly the opposite effect! Similarly, has the DARE program resulted in a reduction in drug abuse among young people? No.[14] Or, has a program designed to get high school students to sign a pledge that they will not drink and drive on prom night produced a decrease in prom night drinking or in fatal traffic accidents? Probably not. Only a well-designed program evaluation will be able to provide definitive answers.

Unlike single-system research, there may be beneficiaries of program evaluations besides social work practitioners themselves. It has already been suggested that managers use the results of program evaluations for decision making. Other beneficiaries might include: (1) those offering services who want to know whether their work is making a difference; (2) funding organizations who want to know that they are getting the most "bang for the buck"; (3) policy makers who use the results to shape public policy; and (4) the general public which wants to be assured that tax dollars and charitable donations are being used wisely. Of course, the prime beneficiary of program evaluations are the clients they serve. In later chapters, we will examine the specific ways that program evaluations benefit all of these groups.

One way in which single-system research and program evaluations are similar is a lack of emphasis on the external validity of their findings. Like clients, programs are often unique. Even if a program is repeated or is duplicated elsewhere, the conditions under which it is offered a second time invariably differ from those of the first program. Sometimes we can learn from the successes and failures of another program and increase the likelihood that our program will succeed. However, as noted earlier, evaluation research is not designed to make a major contribution to our profession's body of knowledge. Thus, when most program evaluations are conducted, a major beneficiary is not the profession, only a limited number of professionals who have some investment in a given program or a similar one. If, as it occasionally happens, something is learned in the course of a program evaluation (such as insight into the true nature of a problem) that has wider utility, that is generally regarded as a "nice bonus."

CONCLUDING THOUGHTS

This chapter introduced the origins of evaluation research and attempted to arrive at its definition. No one can identify all of the events and forces that brought us to the current status of evaluation research, or quantify how much each contributed. What I have described is one person's (admittedly subjective) impressions of what have been important reasons why we moved from point A to point B. When I first entered social work in the 1960s (point A), there was little talk about evaluating services and programs. Certainly, some responsible social workers were doing it, but it was hardly a central focus of attention. In the early twenty-first century (point B), evaluation research is "center stage," viewed by many as the most important type of research conducted within our profession. The combination of events described may be viewed as important contributors to this dramatic change, but they certainly are not the only ones.

Single-system research and program evaluation constitute most of what falls under the rubric of evaluation research today. Both are forms of applied research, that is, research designed to provide specific answers to specific questions rather than to contribute to our professional body of knowledge. The definitions and descriptions provided are not universal ones; they are ones, which, it is hoped, will provide a good general understanding of the goals, beneficiaries, and richness of evaluation research. The chapters that follow will "flesh them out."

KEY TERMS

means-end displacement	1962 Social Security Amendments	single-system research
consumer movement	Aid to Families of Dependent	program evaluation
Kennedy/Johnson years	Children (AFDC)	

STUDY QUESTIONS

1. Describe some ways that social workers in the past have sought to demonstrate that their services and programs were effective. Why are these means not valid indicators of effectiveness?

2. How did the consumer movement help clarify the rights of clients who receive our services?

3. What were some of the frustrations that social workers providing public economic assistance experienced prior to President Kennedy's election?

4. Why are the Kennedy/Johnson years sometimes referred to as the "golden years" of social work?

5. What are some of the reasons why social workers were unable to reduce AFDC rolls in the 1960s?

6. How did Joel Fischer's research on the effectiveness of social casework contribute to our current emphasis on evaluation research?

7. What is quality control, and how was it used in social programs to examine efficiency?

8. What developments during the 1990s contributed to a demand for evaluation research?

9. Describe another program (other than those mentioned in this chapter) that sounded good, but proved to be ineffective.

10. Why is program evaluation sometimes described as a management decision-making tool?

REFERENCES

1. See, e.g., Sils, D. (1970). Preserving organizational goals. In O. Grusky, & G. Miller (Eds.) *The sociology of organizations* (p. 227). New York: The Free Press; or Merton, R. (1957). *Social theory and social structure*. New York: The Free Press, 199–200.

2. Rossi, P., & Freeman, H. (1982). *Evaluation: A systematic approach*. Beverly Hills, CA: Sage, 21–24.

3. See, e.g., Weiss, C. (1972). *Evaluating action programs: Readings in social action and education*. Boston: Allyn & Bacon.

4. Nader, R. (1965). *Unsafe at any speed: The designed-in dangers of the American automobile*. New York: Grossman.

5. Brown, G. (1968). *The multi-problem dilemma: A social work research demonstration with multi-problem families*. Metuchen, NJ: Scarecrow Press.

6. Maslow, A. H. (1943). A theory of human motivation. *Psychological Review, 50*(4), 370–396.

7. See Tripodi, T., Fellin, P., & Epstein, I. (1971). *Social program evaluation*. Itasca, IL: F. E. Peacock; or Tripodi, T., Fellin, P., & Epstein, I. (1978). *Differential social program evaluation*. Itasca, IL: F. E. Peacock.

8. Ibid., 105–142.

9. See, e.g., SRI International (1983). *Final report of the Seattle-Denver Income Maintenance Experiment, Vol. 1: Design and results*. Washington, DC: SRI International.

10. Fischer, J. (1973). Is casework effective? A review. *Social Work, 18*(1), 5–20.

11. Rothman, J., Kirk, S., & Knapp, H. (2003). Reputation and publication productivity among social work researchers. *Social Work Research, 27*(2), 105–115.

12. Briar, S. Incorporating research into education for clinical practice: Toward a clinical science in social work. *Sourcebook on research utilization*. New York: Council on Social Work Education, 132–133.

13. Finckenauer, J. (1979). *Evaluation of juvenile awareness projects: Reports 1 and 2*. Newark, NJ: Rutgers School of Criminal Justice.

14. Lynam, D., et al. (1999). Project DARE. No effects at 10-year follow-up. *Journal of Consulting and Clinical Psychology, 67*, 590–593.

CHAPTER THREE

TRADITIONAL METHODS FOR MONITORING AND IMPROVING SOCIAL WORK PRACTICE

Today's evaluation research did not just appear one day following ever-increasing pressures for accountability. It is an outgrowth of, and a response to, the strengths and weaknesses of more traditional methods for monitoring and improving individual practice and the work of social programs. They are still in use today, sometimes as components of current evaluation research designs and sometimes as "stand alone" methods for monitoring what goes on within human service organizations and for identifying ways to improve it.

METHODS TO IMPROVE THE QUALITY OF INDIVIDUAL SERVICES

In the ideal world, all human service workers are dedicated, competent, and skilled. They use only highly effective methods of intervention and perform all other necessary tasks in ways that guarantee that their clients will be helped to solve their problems. Of course, in the real world, this is not always the case. Over the years, various methods (besides single-system research) evolved to attempt to ensure that clients receive the effective services that they deserve.

Job Requirements

Historically, job requirements have been used to ensure that staff members possess at least the potential to deliver effective services. Well-educated, knowledgeable, and experienced helping professionals should be more able to provide effective interventions for their clients than those who are less qualified. It only makes sense. It would seem that one way to increase the likelihood of successful intervention is to only employ people who have certain educational achievements, experience, and who have been judged by others to be effective practitioners, that is, by requiring staff to have undergone a process of **credentialing.**

Professional Degrees.   A degree indicates that a person has been exposed to certain knowledge, values, and skills and he or she has demonstrated some degree of professional competence. He or she has undergone a process of socialization. But did it "take"? Unfortunately, it is possible to complete the required work, get a professional degree (and even earn good grades), but still have major shortcomings in one or more areas.

Work Experience.   Many years of work experience can be valuable, but they still may not ensure that a staff member will deliver effective services. The experience may have been bad experience; for example, experience in the use of ineffective methods of intervention or in the use of ethically questionable methods. If so, the experience may not be an asset at all. It can represent an obstacle to intervention effectiveness.

Professional References.   While not totally worthless, professional references (written or verbal) are often misleading. If the individual applying for a job is currently a valuable employee, the person providing a reference may offer a less than glowing description of him or her to attempt to avoid losing the individual. If the employee is not very competent, the person providing a reference may offer a very positive description of his or her work (omitting certain characteristics) with the hope that the individual will become someone else's problem. Even if the individual is a former employee, it is unlikely that a reference will be very accurate. Because of concern over potential lawsuits, few administrators and supervisors are willing to risk putting in writing a description of a former subordinate's flaws. They are somewhat more likely to present an accurate description "off the record" in a confidential conversation, but even that practice carries certain legal risks. In short, references are of very limited value. Like academic degrees and work experience, they *may* suggest that an individual helping professional is an effective practitioner—but they certainly do not guarantee it.

Licensure.   Social workers currently must possess a state license to hold most social work jobs and to describe themselves as social workers. However, as we know, meeting licensure requirements such as passing a written licensure exam or undergoing a certain number of hours of supervision by a senior colleague only indicates that a social worker probably has a certain amount of relevant knowledge. It provides no assurance that the knowledge will be applied effectively (or even ethically) in work with various client systems. Because licenses are requirements for employment, the threat of their loss probably helps prevent ethical violations among social workers. But merely possessing a license and meeting continuing education requirements does not ensure practice effectiveness. While under our code of ethics, there are prescribed steps for dealing with a colleague's obvious incompetence (including reporting it to licensing and regulatory bodies),[1] censure or loss of a state license for incompetence occurs very rarely. Lesser shortcomings, such as not using the best interventions or using good interventions but not very well, are virtually impossible to prove and thus tend to go unpunished. In fact, licensure boards are merely required to investigate (but are very unlikely to act on) complaints about social workers who just are not very good at what they do.

Additional Credentialing.   Some social work jobs require additional credentialing related to their specific area of practice. Examples would include a graduate certificate in gerontology or addictions counseling. The completion of the required coursework (like completion of a degree) merely ensures that a social worker has mastered a certain body of specialized knowledge. It does not ensure that a social worker's interventions will be effective. Perhaps more important, it does not provide the objective feedback that helps professionals to learn what works for them and what does not—feedback that can help them to improve their effectiveness. Day after day, a practitioner may believe that he or she is offering effective interventions when, in fact, they have produced limited success or no success at all.

Client Feedback

Historically, another indicator of the effectiveness of our interventions has been client feedback. Clients have always provided feedback in one form or another. Unfortunately, what they have provided has often been of questionable validity.

Actions.   Some clients have not followed through on referrals. Voluntary clients who were seen for services a first time may have registered their assessment of their services when they returned for more help (or they did not). The problem was, and continues to be: we can never be sure what is meant by these actions. Why was a referral not completed? Was the "word on the street" that the services were useless and ineffective, or did the client simply lack transportation or have a scheduling conflict relating to a new job? Why did the client not return after a first interview? Was the first interview enough for the client to determine that intervention was a waste of time, or was the interview so effective that help was no longer needed? Or did something else, unrelated to the services received, prevent the client from returning?

Complaints and Compliments.   Client complaints and frustration with services have also been used as indicators of service quality, but they have questionable validity. Clients may not like the services offered for various reasons, but the services may be exactly what they require. Or they may simply be unhappy with some other aspect of their lives and choose to vent their frustrations on a relatively safe target: helping professionals. Similarly, unsolicited client praise, thank you notes, and so forth, while more pleasant to receive, are equally dubious indicators that intervention has been effective. They may be nothing more than transparent attempts to ingratiate to the helping professionals, or to manipulate them in some way.

Satisfaction Surveys.   When the consumer movement (see Chapter 2) occurred, it created a permanent change in how services (and programs) are evaluated.

Evaluation is no longer the sole preserve of those offering services or those paying for them. The consumer movement legitimized the right of consumers (our clients) to have a "say so" in the services that they received. As time went on, some client input into evaluation of services became desirable and even mandatory, especially for those services that were paid by health insurance or other third-party payments. Efforts were made to try to acquire it in a way that seemed to promote objectivity. Thus, the client-satisfaction survey was born.

Client-satisfaction surveys, often in the form of a questionnaire containing professional-looking Likert-type scales, can appear impressive. Random-sampling methods can seem to increase their credibility. But there are many reasons why client-satisfaction surveys fall short as reliable and valid indicators of the effectiveness of services. For one thing, there is little impetus for clients to answer candidly, and several reasons not to. Do our clients sometimes deliberately fail to provide honest answers? Certainly. Even with a carefully worded, mailed data collection instrument, there is nothing to prevent clients or former clients from giving the safe, socially desirable, or politically correct answer. Or, they may provide a positive evaluation of services received in order to express gratitude for a professional's efforts, despite receiving little or no help. Or, for any number of reasons, they may express great dissatisfaction with services that were effective.

There are other problems as well. One relates to return (or completion) bias. Those clients most likely to return the survey are those most satisfied with services and, perhaps, a smaller number who were least satisfied with them—an uneven, biased response rate that underrepresents the group in the middle.

The "I appreciate your asking" phenomenon is especially troublesome: Some respondents not at either extreme choose to respond simply because they appreciated being asked about their opinion of their services. These respondants may report "very satisfied" despite feeling less than satisfied with services received.

Overall, client-satisfaction surveys (whether used for evaluating services or programs) usually have a positive bias. They can make the social worker feel good, but they are not a good barometer of service effectiveness. The presence of a past or present helping relationship with clients and client groups almost invariably influences the findings of a client-satisfaction survey. Even personal characteristics of the social worker (perhaps, a physical similarity to a favorite uncle or to one who verbally abused the client) may also tend to influence client satisfaction with services received.

Of course, the major problem with using client-satisfaction surveys as indicators of intervention effectiveness, or of the quality of a service, is that satisfaction with services and successful intervention are not the same. For example, a client could be satisfied with an intervention because it cost nothing, got her out of the house, provided the opportunity to complain about her family members, or for any number of other reasons, even though the intervention was ineffective in addressing the client's problem. Or, conversely, dissatisfaction may be registered because the social worker offered some effective but unappreciated intervention (for example, confrontation when the social worker "cut her off" whenever she attempted to blame her problems on others). Even if questions and scales attempt to measure client progress rather than satisfaction, they are vulnerable to client perceptions that may be inaccurate for many of the same reasons. It may sound a little harsh, but clients sometimes do not know what they need and what is in their best interests, especially in situations where they are engaging in denial or in projecting the responsibility for their problems onto others. And, for various reasons, they may be unable to recognize effective intervention when they see it, or they may perceive it when it does not exist.

Client-satisfaction surveys remain a part of today's evaluation research, both as part of evaluation of individual practice and as a component of most program evaluations. However, we now recognize both their many limitations and understand where and when they can provide useful (if not very valid) data. We will return to the topic of client-satisfaction surveys in later chapters.

Case Supervision

Theoretically, the regularly scheduled supervisory conferences characteristic of social work practice should contribute to individual practice effectiveness. **Case supervision** should be used to help social workers recognize and eliminate ineffective practice methods and to continue to use those methods that have been identified as effective. Undoubtedly, some very helpful evaluation of services has taken place in case supervision in the past. In supervisory conferences, social workers have been encouraged to evaluate their work with clients objectively. Along with the supervisor (a more experienced professional with acknowledged expertise in service delivery), successes have been identified and less successful interventions were analyzed in order to learn what went wrong and what needed to be done differently. However, it has not always worked that way. Honest, open discussion of one's work can only occur in an unthreatening environment, when there are no negative consequences for discussing shortcomings. And, this often is not the case.

Individual supervisory conferences perform dual functions, and that is the problem. Supervisors serve as mentors and consultants, but they also provide administrative supervision. In the latter role, one of their duties is to perform annual or semiannual performance evaluations of their subordinates. And, where do they acquire most of their knowledge about a subordinate's competence as a practitioner?—in supervisory conferences. This is not conducive to an honest, open discussion and critique of one's work. If you knew that describing your consistent inability to find an intervention that worked with some client or client system or your inability to provide adequate structure in a treatment group that you are leading could make you appear to be incompetent and might thus jeopardize salary increases or promotions, would you do it? You probably would not, even if it deprived you of useful feedback and constructive suggestions. There would be a natural tendency to describe your successes, but to keep your frustrations in working with other clients to yourself.

Recently, supervision and the role of the supervisor have changed to the point that it is an even less useful source of valid feedback. With rising health care costs, settings such as hospitals and psychiatric facilities have eliminated many supervisory positions and reassigned social workers to be supervised by people from other disciplines (such as nurses). If a social worker has a supervisor at all, it may be someone who is seen face-to-face only rarely and is unfamiliar with social work's methods of intervention. To increase efficiency, alternative models of supervision (for example, group supervision, peer supervision, or even remote supervision via phone or e-mail) are increasingly replacing the traditional supervisor-worker relationship. Each has certain advantages (for evaluating one's services), but has inherent disadvantages too.

Group supervision employs a group meeting in which a supervisor provides supervision to all of his or her workers at the same time. Social workers take turns discussing cases, usually those that are frustrating in some way; for example, the intervention doesn't seem to be working. Ideally, this venue should provide for a wealth of feedback, as there is the opportunity to get many different perspectives (rather than only one) on the problem. However, it often does not work that way. The supervisor's presence can result in a kind of sibling rivalry in which social workers become more interested in presenting themselves and their work in the best possible light rather than to talk honestly about the problems they are having with unsuccessful interventions. Again, valid feedback is a casualty.

In **peer supervision,** there is no supervisor present so, theoretically at least, everyone is equal. That eliminates to some degree the problem of people trying to appear very competent to increase the likelihood of desirable personnel actions or to look more competent than one's peers. (Of course, people being what they are, some will probably try to assume the role of expert!) However, the lack of an experienced supervisor—one who should have superior knowledge and who also represents the program or organization and what it defines as successful services—can be a liability. Without a knowledgeable authority figure, no one may have the answer to a problem and feedback may be limited.

Remote supervision has the advantage of more easily available access to supervision. However, phone calls or e-mails generally tend to be brief and to-the-point. The quantity and quality of supervisor feedback may be limited.

Case supervision has historically been a favorite method for evaluating services provided by individual social work practitioners. However, for all of the reasons that have been discussed (and others), feedback provided by it has tended to be limited and lacking in validity.

Performance Evaluations

The fact that supervisors provide supervision and also evaluate social workers limits the value of supervision as a vehicle for feedback about individual practice effectiveness. But don't the evaluations provide some feedback about individual practice effectiveness, especially if they are based on more than what is reported during supervisory conferences? To a limited degree, yes. But generally, they are not reports of careful, objective research on worker effectiveness conducted by the supervisor. They tend to be based on a combination of overall perceptions (which can be highly subjective and influenced by personal characteristics) and criteria that may relate only indirectly to practice effectiveness (such as arriving on time for work, or having all necessary paperwork up to date). Forms and instruments that are used for performance evaluations may be inappropriate for the specialized nature of an individual's job. They rarely undergo validation using appropriate statistical analyses and are often little more than a reflection of the personal preferences (work style) of their creator. Evaluations also may be based in part on occasional firsthand observations, data provided by the individual being evaluated, and the impressions of other employees. Sometimes a very unscientific analysis of case records may also be used. Unless they are done conscientiously using tested, standardized methods, performance evaluations provide limited feedback to the social worker about his or her practice effectiveness. Their primary utility is for providing feedback about how secure one's job is and (for the person conducting them) for justifying subsequent personnel actions.

Goal Attainment Scaling

Over the years, social workers and other helping professionals came to acknowledge that all of the potential sources for monitoring and improving individual practice effectiveness that we have examined were inadequate. They either (1) failed to focus on what should be the primary indicator of practice effectiveness: success in alleviation of a client or client system problem; or (2) lacked objectivity because of one or more "human" factors. In response to these failings, some social workers turned to another method of evaluating the success of an intervention method, **goal attainment scaling (GAS).** GAS usually relies on consumers (clients) to provide data on changes in their problem following services (rather than their satisfaction with services), and that is good. However, it has other shortcomings.

GAS was first used back in the 1960s among therapists working with psychiatric patients. However, it is equally applicable for use with any client system, including organizations and communities. When using GAS, a social worker identifies (with input from the client or client system) a small number (usually three to five) of specific problems that an intervention seeks to address. Problem behaviors (or, if appropriate, the lack of desirable behaviors) of the client or client system are often selected because they are easier to measure than, for example, attitudes or emotions. Of course, the problems should be ones of importance to the client or client system, ones that are interfering with functioning in some important way. They should also be problems for which it is reasonable to expect that the intervention will produce some positive changes, usually because it has worked to at least a limited degree in the past.

Reasonable goals for the intervention are specified for each problem. This is expanded to a range of five levels of potential goal attainment for each problem. They are assigned a number between –2 and +2. A zero is assigned to the expected outcome if intervention is successful, often the level of success experienced when the intervention was used in the past. "Plus" scores are assigned to goal attainment that is greater than expected, and negative scores to goal attainment levels that are less than expected. For example, a social worker working with the family of a teen-ager might (among other goals) attempt to decrease the number of angry parent-child confrontations per week. Suppose that currently they have an average of about seven such confrontations per week. The following GAS scale might be used to mea-sure the practice effectiveness of counseling after four interviews:

Most unfavorable outcome (–2)   10 arguments
Less than expected outcome (–1)   7 arguments
Expected outcome (0)   5 arguments
More than expected outcome (+1)   3 arguments
Most favorable outcome (+2)   1 argument

The decision as to how much reduction in angry confrontations (arguments) would represent the expected outcome (0) and the numbers for the other four lev-els would be based on a number of factors. They may include an assessment of what was realistic given the current severity of the problem, the clients involved, the time available for the intervention, and what past experience has taught the social worker about the likely effect of the intervention. While this entails the intro-duction of some "facts," it still allows considerable room for subjectivity.

The results of goal attainment in addressing each of a client's targeted prob-lems can be combined by averaging the respective scores to suggest, overall, how effective a social worker has been in working with a client or client system. Or, if some problems are considered to be more "major" than others, the scores can be weighted to reflect the relative importance of their problems. Other calculations can be used to convert results to a scale with scores that can range between 1 and 100.

GAS works best with well-motivated clients who want to change, and who will cooperate in setting realistic goals and honestly reporting the degree to which they change. It also works well with larger client systems like communities where valid measurements of problems are available, such as delinquency rates, percent of voter registration, or illegal gang activity. It is useful only with social workers who want honest feedback about the effectiveness of their interventions, not those who only want to appear competent. It is easy to "stack" the results of GAS to get whatever results are desired if one is not really seeking feedback. If, deliberately or because of a lack of thorough planning, the various levels of success are scaled too high or too low, the results of GAS will be of little value as feedback. For example, if both the social worker and an adolescent with a problem of not doing her home-work set an expected goal of two homework hours per week (–2 equals zero hours; –1 = 1 hour; +1 = 3 hours, +2 = 4 hours), a 0 level or even a +2 level might be easily accomplished, at least in the short term. The social worker would appear success-ful. But would this really indicate successful intervention? Probably not—the goal levels were set too low, and could too easily be achieved. It could also be argued that time spent doing homework (along with whatever distractions might be pre-sent) may not be a valid indicator of success. Class grades or percent of satisfactory homework completed might provide better measurements of intervention success.

GAS has been an improvement over the previous methods for helping social workers to learn if their interventions are effective. It is better because (1) it uses measures of intervention success that can be easily measured, and (2) success is defined as desirable changes in the client or client system rather than some characteristic or behavior of the social worker. However, it is still quite vulnerable to manipulation, deception, and subjectivity. It is still in use, though probably not as widely as it once was. It is a less desirable method than single-system research for evaluating individual practice effectiveness.

GAS is occasionally used to evaluate the effectiveness of a service (a program component) within a program evaluation. However, a series of single-system research studies usually has more credibility for evaluating a given service and is preferable, unless it cannot be used for some ethical or logistical reasons.

METHODS TO IMPROVE THE QUALITY OF PROGRAMS

Most of us are familiar with the traditional or classical methods for monitoring and evaluating the quality of programs. They tend to be characterized by a rather narrow focus. They are still used regularly within programs, often because of the awareness of a specific problem or the fear that one might develop. Like GAS, they also sometimes are used to evaluate some part of a program, that is, as one component of the current, more comprehensive methods of program evaluation that we will examine in later chapters. We will briefly describe some of the better-known ones, because conducting or participating in a program evaluation requires a basic familiarity with them.

Financial Accountability

The funding for social programs can come from one or, more typically, from a variety of sources. These sources include grants and contracts from government agencies or charitable foundations, allocations from "umbrella" organizations (such as United Way) to which individuals and corporations contribute, direct contributions from individuals and service organizations such as Rotary International, fees collected from clients for services, and occasionally, income from investments or real property donated to the organization. Historically, one way that programs have been evaluated has been to determine whether a program has been a good "steward" of its funds. Several methods have been used to examine whether the program's funding was used in a way consistent with the wishes of those who provided it.

Budget Review. A budget is a plan for spending a program's funds. But it is much more. A budget helps to shape the activities of a program, that is, what it can and cannot do. Whatever their source, the total funds available to a program are broken down and distributed in the form of a budget, helping to control the activities of a program.

Not surprisingly, budgets have often been a prime focus of evaluations of programs and have undergone careful scrutiny. A budget can take a number of different forms. The organization in which a program is housed is likely to have a **program budget,** that is, a budget that breaks down, by program, where the organization's money goes. Factored into the cost of each program (but not usually specified in a program budget) is its share of expenses for shared costs such as rent, utilities, public relations, office supplies, and so on. Each individual program, in turn, is likely to have its own **line-item budget,** a budget that specifies the exact amount of money allocated for various expenses incurred by the program. Typically, a line-item budget is broken down into broad categories (with dollar amounts) and then each of these is subdivided into several more specific categories (sometimes with dollar amounts) reflecting the types of expenses included. For example, for the broader category "employee benefits," specific categories might include "health and dental insurance," "401(k) contributions," "group life insurance," and "other." Other broad categories, similarly broken down, might include salaries, payroll taxes, supplies, postage, equipment purchase, rental and maintenance, the program's share of occupancy costs, telephone and fax, printing, and so forth.

Historically, program evaluation methods that focused on budgets themselves have looked first at whether, overall, a budget was reasonable, neither extravagant nor so austere that it could not possibly provide the support needed for program success. Then, individual categories within the budget and their appropriateness were examined. Many questions might be asked. For example, was the budget too "personnel intensive" (without adequate support in other areas) or with too much expense concentrated in certain forms of administration and not enough in direct services? Did it fail to include an allocation for some important component, such as publicity or legal expenses? What category would provide for reimbursement for necessary travel expenses for staff and clients?

Other budget reviews have focused on how well an existing budget was managed. However, there has not been very good consensus about just what good budget management is, much beyond "staying within budget." It has been much easier to identify budget mismanagement, for example, unnecessary spending or spending too much for some goods or services.

Accounting.   **Accounting** is a very specialized skill, one that social workers rarely possess. It entails keeping accurate, up-to-date financial records of funding received and expenditures. Often agencies (and larger programs) hire a "finance manager" or someone with a similar title who has a background in accounting. The expectation is that this individual will "log in" any deposits, checks written, and so forth. If the finance manager is doing the job well, he or she is always aware of the financial situation of an organization or program. A good accountant can check the books and inform a manager of just how much money is available for a given need at any time. He or she will also alert the manager if overspending in some area is beginning to emerge. Then adjustments can be made such as seeking additional funding or imposing a moratorium on spending for a while. In this way, accountants help to prevent mismanagement of budgets, which can reflect negatively on both a program and its manager.

Good accounting helps ensure that expenditures are made in such a way that no portion of a program's budget will be exhausted too soon, leaving some important activity without resources. However, a budget is merely a projection of financial needs. No one who designs a program or who provides funding for it is clairvoyant; miscalculations are inevitable, based in part on changing conditions and costs. One or more categories of a line-item budget may be underbudgeted; others may be overbudgeted. A good accountant often is the first person to recognize this and to make recommendations as to how to remedy the situation.

One issue relating to budget management has always been the degree of rigidity versus flexibility that is contained in a budget. It can be a major source of misunderstanding and disagreement. Some people take the position that a budget is virtually written in stone. They believe that a surplus in a category must remain in a category and be spent for only the items in that category. Others view a budget as a general guideline, and that shifting from one area to another based on over-projection of costs in one area and demonstrated need in another is perfectly acceptable and necessary. Probably, some degree of flexibility built into a budget is ideal. Some shifting of funds (officially or unofficially) is both inevitable and desirable. It avoids a wasteful "spend it or lose it" mentality. At the other extreme, if a budget is so loose that shifting of funds can be accomplished with impunity, the budget loses its effectiveness as a planning device. As a plan, a budget is supposed to shape future events, not be led by them.

The amount of line shifting that can be made is sometimes not left to management discretion—it is spelled out in the grant or contract that provides financial support for a program. Then the responsibility of an accountant is to know where there is flexibility (and how much) and where none exists, and to share this knowledge with the manager who must make important budget decisions.

Auditing.   While accounting is generally an "in-house" function, **auditing** is usually conducted by someone who is not connected with a program, or at least who is not in its employ. Like accountants, auditors have very specialized skills. The auditor may be an employee of a major auditing firm, a representative of a program's major funding source, or anyone else with expertise in financial auditing who is assigned to make sure there are no financial irregularities. Whatever their affiliation, auditors share in common a sensitivity to problems that may be identified within the records and accounts of a program (for example, on employee time sheets or travel records), through interviewing staff, or in other data to which they are given access. Program audits are often feared, because audits may uncover financial irregularities. Of course, this can result in constructive suggestions. They can also document that financial management is "kosher" and give a program a "clean bill of health." However, they are best known for uncovering intentional or unintentional misuse of funds, sometimes called "audit exceptions."

What kind of financial irregularities can auditors uncover? They range from careless errors to deliberate fraud. The more severe audit exceptions can result in employees losing their jobs or even facing criminal prosecution. Irregularities can assume an almost infinite number of forms, since they often evolve from the "creativity" of those who perpetrate them. Examples might include:

- Poor accounting practices such as a failure to record transactions or otherwise maintain accurate, up-to-date records.
- Overbilling or double billing third parties for services, or billing for services not actually received.
- Using charitable contributions designated specifically for one purpose for something else.
- Personal expenses falsely billed to a program as legitimate program expenses.
- Use of program employees to conduct managers' personal business or provide personal services.
- "Padded" expenses for professional travel or claims for travel that never occurred.
- Duplicate counts of clients being served.
- Unauthorized shifting of funds from one line item to another.
- Purchase of supplies or equipment that is charged to a program, but used elsewhere in the organization.
- Use of program funds for dining or entertainment of staff.

A clean audit, like good financial accounting, is often characteristic of a well-managed, good program. However, some programs that demonstrate excellent financial accountability are still not good programs, that is, they may not be effective or valuable. Others may be a little slack in some financial areas, but still manage to make an important difference in the lives of their clients.

Identifying Inefficiency

Good programs generally are efficient, that is, they use their resources so as to minimize waste. In many programs, personnel costs (especially salaries) are the most expensive component—more money is allocated to them than for anything else. Thus, efficient use of staff time has often been a focus (although usually not the major one) for evaluating programs.

Of course, there are many ways to determine whether staff members are using their time wisely. One method, developed in the manufacturing industry many years ago, has been adapted for use within human service agencies. It is known as the **time and motion study** and was defined as "an analysis of the efficiency with which an industrial operation is performed."[2] Time and motion studies examine and document how staff members spend their time. They are used to (1) identify waste and inefficiency; and (2) suggest changes for making a program more efficient. While they can be used any time, they have been used most often when it was believed that wasted time and effort were becoming problems within a program.

The stereotype of a time and motion study (which has a basis in reality in early twentieth-century industry) includes some outside efficiency expert (with pad and pencil in hand) carefully recording how staff members occupy every minute of their workday. It includes an image of the efficiency expert stopping employees to ask them what they are doing and why they are doing it. Not surprisingly, time and motion studies are not very popular among professionals. Social workers in the public sector often have encountered some variation of them, although they may not be identified as such. For a set number of days or weeks, they have been required to keep a careful log of their daily activities—what they did, why, how long it took them, with whom they did it, and so forth.

Professional staff members often view time and motion studies as demeaning and insulting. The studies seem to imply that someone believes they are "slacking off" too much. Critics often point out how they result in "inefficient efficiency." They cynically observe that participating in a time and motion study can occupy so much time that workers have little time left to do their jobs. Others question the validity of any findings, especially if they rely exclusively on self-reporting. They contend that people will simply lie as necessary to present themselves in the best light. They question, How many people would be likely to report that they spent ten minutes daydreaming, planning their weekend, or attempting to date a co-worker? Would they acknowledge that they made a personal phone call? Not likely.

Even if staff members are totally honest, the interpretation of findings from time and motion studies is another area of debate. Is taking a ten minute break to clear one's head prior to seeing the next client a waste of time? Should social workers be required to be productive at all times while on the job? How can we possibly be asked to do stressful, productive tasks eight hours a day without a break? What about burnout? And, how can we operationally define "productive"? Does making a social call to a colleague in another organization to inquire about her recovery from surgery constitute wasted time? Or, is it a productive effort at relationship building and networking that will pay benefits for the program sometime in the future?

Time and motion studies certainly have their problems, not the least of which is the bad reputation that they have developed. They offer a very narrow perspective on a program's functioning—whether time is managed efficiently. However, they are not without value. If used conscientiously and constructively, they can identify problems and precipitate changes that can enhance the quality of programs. For example, a time and motion study might reveal that staff members waste considerable time standing in line at a copy machine or going up two floors to get approval for some action from a supervisor. Perhaps, either problem could be addressed if some changes were made in the physical location of machines and people. Time and motion studies are a kind of specialized form of systems analysis. Thus, they can produce a more efficient system (program), but offer little or no insight into whether a program is truly effective.

Maintaining Standards

There is another way in which, historically, we have sought to determine whether organizations and their programs are good. It entails the application of standards, developed by people at a local, state, or national level. The standards are sometimes applied to an entire organization; other times they are applied to a program (usually a relatively permanent one) within it. If standards are met, the organization or program is allowed to continue with the endorsement of those who developed the standards. If not, its credibility is seriously weakened and it may be required to cease operating. The two methods for assuring that an organization or program meets established standards are licensing and accreditation.

Licensing.   Certain types of programs are mandated by law to be licensed. For example, states require **licensing** to operate a day care facility. While no license is needed to have an older relative live with you, having several older people move in (and being paid for their care) constitutes running an extended care facility (nursing home), and extended care facilities must be licensed. Similarly, foster homes must be licensed. If no license is obtained, the facility will be shut down under state law. Generally, some organization of state government has ultimate authority for licensure of facilities and programs (for example, health departments or the department of social services) where specific expertise is assumed to exist. These organizations then conduct inspections, respond to complaints, and issue, deny, or revoke licenses.

The standards for acquiring and keeping a license vary both by type of facility or program and by jurisdiction. Many of them relate to protection of clients (from abuse, neglect, crowding, other unhealthy living conditions, and so forth). Others relate to what is believed to be the minimum level at which goals can be accomplished, for example, staff-client ratio, personnel standards, amount of expenditure (per client) for meals, or availability of specialized personnel.

It is important to recognize what a license signifies and, perhaps more important, what it does not ensure. A license means that a facility or program has met a number of minimum standards. The standards have been set (sometimes based on research and sometimes based on subjective judgment), by groups of people who have an interest in and, hopefully, expertise in some field of human services. In developing standards over the years, group members have often used an inductive process. It entails identifying what are, by group consensus, outstanding facilities and programs and then noting what each of them has in common. Secondly, as problems and abuses have been brought to light, additional standards have been added to attempt to guard against their reoccurrence.

There is absolutely nothing wrong with the process that has just been described. It is logical and, lacking complete cause-effect knowledge of exactly how a facility or program should look and operate, it is the best that can be done. However, we should not deceive ourselves, believing that a licensed facility or program is necessarily a good one producing desirable results. The presence of a license only means that a facility or program has demonstrated to the licensing organization that it has in place the resources (human and otherwise) to produce them. And, that is all. It cannot guarantee, for example, that qualified staff will always have good attitudes about their work, or that they will enjoy working with their clients or patients and want to do all they can for them. They may simply treat their work as "a job" and their patients and clients as "a necessary evil."

Whether the idealistic goals of a licensed program actually are achieved with a given client (or with any clients for that matter), is not generally addressed by licensure standards. However, to be fair, there is a trend beginning in licensure to go beyond those easily measured indicators such as staff-client ratios or square footage of client rooms. There is more of an attempt to look at the goals that are more difficult to operationalize, such as whether healthy changes may be occurring for clients or whether they have a good quality of life. Hopefully, this trend will continue.

Accreditation.   **Accreditation** bears many similarities to licensure. Both are used to attempt to ensure the potential for success in a relatively permanent program. Both employ standards and make judgments that can grant society's legitimization to a program. However, while licensure is required by law for some types of programs and services, accreditation is, to a greater or lesser degree, voluntary. In fact, organizations like colleges and universities have little choice but to seek accreditation. A master's or bachelor's program in social work, for example, would not attract many students if the program were not accredited by the Council on Social Work Education (CSWE). A degree from a CSWE-accredited program is a minimum requirement for employment in most areas of social work practice. It also is required to take a state licensure examination. Thus, a program must become and remain accredited if it is to remain competitive with other similar programs in recruiting students.

For some organizations and programs, national accreditation is not yet available. The field of work either has not begun the time-consuming job of developing accreditation standards and procedures and being legitimized as an accrediting body, or they have simply decided that accreditation is unnecessary or undesirable. However, in certain fields of practice (for example, family services or the not-for-profit child-protection sector), there is the opportunity to seek accreditation from a national organization. Some agencies seek it; others do not. For those who do, there are certain advantages and disadvantages. National accreditation carries with it a certain amount of prestige and may connote to potential clients and to the general public that an organization has achieved certain standards of professionalism. There are other benefits as well. National consultants may be made available at little or no cost to work with staff of accredited agencies and programs. National meetings and conferences provide excellent opportunities for networking with, and learning from, the successes and failures of professionals performing similar functions. Also, much of the work of individual managers has already been done and its products are available to members, saving time as well as potential legal problems. For example, the national office may already have some very good written materials on sexual harassment policies, screening and supervising of volunteers, or conducting employee performance evaluations.

So, why doesn't every organization or program that has the opportunity seek to become accredited? The two most commonly cited reasons are cost and loss of autonomy. The cost of becoming accredited (self-study costs, report publication, employment of consultants, travel and lodging expenses for site visitors, and so forth) can be very expensive, especially for smaller organizations and programs. Accreditation also may force agencies to align themselves with a national model, adopting the same mission, goals, and vision statements. What if the unique needs of a community suggest that something else is needed? Some managers simply conclude that autonomy, the freedom to develop programs and services based on their best professional judgment of what is best for their community, is worth more than the benefits that national accreditation can offer.

There is still one other way in which accreditation and licensure are similar. They both bear many similarities to what is sometimes called **structure (or structural) evaluations.** Structure evaluations have been in use for many years. They focus on outward indicators (some would say superficial ones) of program quality. These might include the attractiveness of the facilities in which a program is housed, the number of advanced professional degrees held by its staff, staff diversity, or the presence of the latest technology. They focus on whether everything is in place "as it should be." Structure evaluations also seek to determine whether services are being delivered in the best manner possible. But, as their critics have contended, they don't tell us what we most need to know—does a program really work and what is its overall value?

Structure evaluations (like several other evaluation methods that have been described) focus on the means to an end, rather than on the end itself, that is, the reduction of some social problem. However, the presence of the means does not ensure program success. For example, it is almost always desirable to have staff with appropriate credentials, appropriate ethnic and cultural diversity, many years of experience, and who are adequately compensated for their services through generous pay scales and fringe benefits. We could probably even demonstrate statistically that programs in which staff members have these desirable characteristics are more likely to be successful than those that lack them. But that does not necessarily mean that a given program that possesses them will be successful. Accreditation and licensure only increase the likelihood that programs will be effective—they neither guarantee it (what can?) nor, more important for our purposes, provide evidence that a program seems to be working or has already proven effective.

TRADITIONAL METHODS IN PERSPECTIVE

The traditional methods for attempting to monitor and improve our practice that have been described in this chapter remain in use today. We still attempt to screen out incompetent practitioners by setting rigid job requirements and verifying credentials of applicants. We then use client feedback, case supervision, and performance evaluations to help practitioners know when they have done their jobs well, and when they have been less successful.

The current method for evaluating individual practice effectiveness, single-system research, is an improvement over goal attainment scaling. Like GAS, it focuses on measurement of client progress toward alleviating a problem as the primary indicator of individual practice effectiveness. But it is less vulnerable to subjectivity and manipulation, and even applies statistical analysis to determine the likelihood that any apparent improvement in a client's problem may have been the work of sampling error or chance.

In evaluating programs, we still rely in part on the methods (budget review, accounting, and auditing) described in this chapter for assessing financial accountability of programs. We use various forms of structure evaluations to determine if a more permanent program meets licensing or accreditation standards. However, today these and other methods that will be discussed later (such as cost/benefit analysis and cost/effectiveness evaluation) are not generally regarded as program evaluation models in their own right. They are sometimes used to evaluate the individual practice effectiveness of certain social workers who are only indirectly involved in the provision of services to clients, for example, those whose primary function is managing, fund raising, or marketing a program. Or, they may appear as indicators of overall program quality (as in the case of accreditation and licensure), or as only one of several components of broader scale program evaluations.

Instead, today's program evaluations rely heavily on the application of proven research methods for making recommendations about the value and future of social programs. In examining a program, program effectiveness and efficiency (or at least the potential for them) now occupy "center stage." As we shall see in Chapter 6, this entails a focus on certain key components of a program.

CONCLUDING THOUGHTS

As long as there have been human services and programs, people have been evaluating them, at least informally. Only the focus of evaluation has changed over the years. This chapter described some of the more common methods that have been in use for many years and that are still with us today.

During the latter part of the twentieth century, attributable in large part to the forces described in Chapter 2, efforts were made to make the activity of evaluation more objective and thus make the results of evaluation more credible. This meant a change in focus, with less emphasis on the process of intervention, and more on its products. In the chapters that follow, we will look at how services and programs are evaluated today, using the tried and tested tools of the researcher.

KEY TERMS

credentialing	remote supervision	time and motion study
licensure	goal attainment scaling (GAS)	licensing
client-satisfaction survey	program budget	accreditation
case supervision	line-item budget	structure (structural)
group supervision	accounting	evaluation
peer supervision	auditing	

STUDY QUESTIONS

1. How do job requirements attempt to ensure that clients will receive effective services? Why are they no guarantee that a practitioner will be effective in his or her work with clients?

2. Why are the findings of client-satisfaction surveys usually very favorable?

3. Why do the various forms of case supervision often not provide valuable feedback about individual social worker effectiveness?

4. Why is an annual or semiannual performance evaluation not a very valid indicator of individual practice effectiveness?

5. What are the strengths and weaknesses of goal attainment scaling as a method for monitoring practice effectiveness?

6. How does a program budget differ from a line-item budget?

7. Explain the differences between accounting and auditing as methods of program evaluation.

8. What is the primary focus of time and motion studies?

9. Why does licensing of programs fail to ensure that programs are effective?

10. For programs in which accreditation is truly voluntary, what are the advantages and disadvantages of being accredited?

REFERENCES

1. National Association of Social Workers (1999). *Code of ethics.* Washington, DC: NASW Press, 18.
2. *American heritage dictionary of the English language* (4th ed.). (2000). J. Pickett, et al. (Eds.). Boston: Houghton Mifflin.

CHAPTER FOUR

AN OVERVIEW OF SINGLE-SYSTEM RESEARCH

Most all of my clients seem to like coming to see me.

My group attendance has never been so high.

Rosina and Felipe hardly ever argue during my treatment sessions anymore.

Outside funding has increased by 12 percent in only one year.

After I organized the protest, the regressive tax proposal was defeated.

It is not difficult to see why the above observations may not be valid indicators of the effectiveness of an individual social worker's practice. Fortunately, we no longer have to depend on them and others like them to be able to judge whether our interventions are successful. In this chapter and the next, we will see how research methods can be applied to inject more objectivity into the process of evaluating practice effectiveness.

As noted earlier, single system research (also referred to as $n = 1$, single-case time series, single-subject research, and idiographic research) is the current method of choice for evaluating a practitioner's individual services. As in all other evaluation research, social workers conducting single-system research collect, record, and analyze data, and then they interpret it for use in their practice decision making. There are other similarities to more traditional research methods as well. There are many different research designs. Some are described as exploratory, some as descriptive, and some as explanatory. All single-system designs can be described as longitudinal research, or, more specifically, as a **longitudinal time series,** because they entail the repeated measurement of the same variable over time.

One difference between single-system research and most other forms of evaluation research is especially noteworthy. In the other forms, research specialists from outside an organization are often used to conduct the research. They are not associated with the service or program that they evaluate. They are clearly in the role of "researcher" or "evaluator." Even when the research is conducted internally by employees of an organization, the employees tend to "switch hats"—they leave the role of practitioner behind for a while and assume the role of evaluator. In contrast, in single-system research social workers never really leave the role of practitioner. They only conduct their research as part of their practice in order to help them become more effective practitioners.

THE "BASICS" OF SINGLE-SYSTEM RESEARCH

Single-system research is not designed to evaluate all aspects of a social worker's practice. It attempts to answer the question, Was my specific intervention effective with this client or client system?

Terminology

There are some terms that have specific meanings in single-system research. They are central to conducting and understanding it.

Single System.   The "single system" can be any client system. Although it can be (and most frequently is) an individual client, it also can be a couple, a family, a group, an organization, or a community—all systems where social workers seek to intervene to address problems. Box 4.1 provides examples of some problems that are commonly the focus of social work interventions. Notice that some of the problems relate to the functioning of the entire system, while others relate to some portion of the system such as an individual or group within a larger system. All of these problems possess the potential for evaluation of practice effectiveness using single-system research.

Target Problem.   The specific problem (behavior, attitude, emotion, and so forth) that the social worker is seeking to influence is called a **target problem** ("target behavior" is often used in older literature). It is the dependent variable for research purposes and is measured repeatedly throughout all phases of the research.

BOX 4.1

EXAMPLES OF PROBLEMS WITHIN DIFFERENT SOCIAL SYSTEMS

- Behaviors of a client during or outside of individual treatment.
- Individual or couple behaviors within a dyadic relationship.
- Individual or group behaviors within a group.
- Behaviors of one or more individuals within families or family behaviors.
- Individual, group, or organization-wide behaviors within an organization.
- Individual, group, or community behaviors within a community.

The target problem must be easily and accurately measured. It can be (and often is) only one symptom of a greater problem or even some behavior that may be only tangentially related to the greater problem, but is still creating difficulty for the client. For example, a social worker working with a client who has been diagnosed as paranoid schizophrenic may conduct single-system research using a specific form of intervention to attempt to increase the number of times that the client goes out in public or is in compliance with her medication regimen.

Intervention.   Even the term intervention has a precise meaning in single-system research. It is *not* simply "whatever assistance I offer the client or client system" as it might be in other contexts. It refers to something very specific, often something additional (an "add-on") or something substituted for all or part of what might usually be offered. The intervention is the independent variable in single-system research.

The intervention in single-system research cannot be something like "weekly supportive counseling" or "group therapy." They are far too vague. However, an appropriate single-system research intervention might be "providing the client with recordings of her supportive counseling sessions" or "having group members assigned to seats by random selection." The research could then be used to determine whether the specific intervention attempted by the social worker was associated with, or (better yet) can be shown to have produced some desirable effect on some problem of the client or (in the latter example) on group behavior.

Phases.   Single-system designs consist of one or more time periods (phases) during which the intervention is offered. Most designs also consist of one or more other phases during which it is not offered. Labels are used to differentiate these phases from each other. A period of time (of predetermined length) in which the intervention is present is referred to as the **B phase** or "treatment phase." Sometimes the term *B phase* is used in a generic sense to denote any phase in which an intervention is offered. (I will be using it this way in this chapter and in Chapter 5). However, in those research designs that contain two or more different interventions offered at different times, the different interventions are given different labels—B, C, D, and so forth—to denote the sequence in which they are offered.

An **A phase** is a block of time during which the specific intervention being evaluated is not offered. However, this does not mean that the client or client system is simply ignored or denied help. During an A phase, other forms of assistance to the client (often the usual assistance that would be offered) may be initiated or they may continue as before. If the intervention being evaluated is only something offered in addition to the usual assistance that would be offered (an "add-on"), an A phase and a B phase would be identical (in what is offered to the client) with one exception. In the A phase the intervention is absent; in the B phase it is present. Of course, if the B phase entails substituting the intervention for what would usually be offered to the client during an A phase, the A and B phase will be considerably (if not totally) different.

A phases are supposed to serve a function similar to that of control groups in experimental research designs. They provide a reference point, a source of comparison that indicates the severity of the target problem when the intervention either (1) has not been introduced or (2) is withdrawn following its presence. Thus, differences between A phases and subsequent B phases *may* be the effects of the intervention. If A phases are used as "control groups," then B phases are the counterpart of experimental groups in true experiments. Of course, the lack of both a true control group and the use of random assignment to experimental and control groups that is characteristic of true experiments leaves open the likelihood that threats to internal validity may explain why an intervention may appear to be successful in addressing a target problem.

Theoretically, an A phase following a B phase can be accomplished by either withdrawal of the intervention or a **reversal:** a deliberate attempt to reverse the changes in the target problem that occurred within the prior B phase. However, reversal is very rarely (if ever) used in second and subsequent A phases in social work single-system research. Generally, to do so would be highly unethical. How could a social worker ethically attempt to increase the practice of unsafe sex, substance abuse, or some other behavior that may be life-threatening for a client following the introduction of an intervention that appeared to be successful? Or, how could a social worker ethically attempt to increase homophobic beliefs in an organization or apathy among community members during a subsequent A phase only to attempt to learn if it really was the intervention that produced a desirable change? We could not do it.

When a research design calls for an A phase following a B phase, social workers usually use withdrawal of the intervention. If the B phase entailed offering something additional, it would simply not be offered anymore. If the B phase entailed substituting the intervention for the usual assistance offered, the subsequent A phase might entail returning to the usual method of intervention.

Baseline.   An A phase is sometimes referred to as a **baseline.** However, the term is really only an accurate description for an A phase that occurs prior to the *first* time that the intervention is introduced (the first B phase). A true baseline is supposed to be an accurate representation of the usual severity and way that the target problem manifests itself for the client or client system, what is "typical." If a good baseline has been compiled, it is possible to determine just how much change in the problem occurred following the introduction of the intervention.

What is a good baseline and how long does it take to acquire one? This question is not easily answered. It really is a judgment call. Any baseline is only a time-limited (not a random) sample of the target problem. Thus, the measurements of the target problem that are taken during it will not be perfectly representative of the pattern of the target problem. But when is a baseline "representative enough"? Generally, a baseline is considered sufficiently representative if it is believed to have captured the "general pattern" of the target problem prior to the introduction of the intervention—how often it occurs, how severe it is, whether it is decreasing, increasing, or remaining pretty much at the same level, and so forth.

Sometimes, depending on the target problem, a good baseline can be obtained in a short period of time; sometimes it takes much longer. For example, a social worker who plans to use an intervention with an adolescent to try to get him to avoid using the words "like" or "basically" in his speech (good luck!) might be able to compile an adequate baseline in a thirty-minute interview. However, another social worker working with another adolescent client who is attempting to reduce the number of incidents of her shoplifting may need several weeks or even months to compile an adequate baseline.

Sometimes it is not necessary to measure the target problem for a period of time in order to create a baseline prior to introducing the intervention. A baseline can be created retroactively. This is most likely to be the case when records have been kept or careful observations and measurement of the target problem already have been made and are available (for example, school records, financial records, and so forth). Then the usual pattern of the behavior can be accurately identified and a baseline constructed from these secondary data. This is a timesaver and allows the social worker to offer the intervention immediately, thus eliminating any ethical issues related to withholding a promising intervention in order to create a baseline. Another advantage of using secondary data is that they are "not vulnerable to such biases as the client's desire to please the worker or the worker's desire to see progress."[1] There is no way that the social worker could have influenced the baseline measurement. Of course, that does not preclude someone else (whoever compiled the data) from influencing them.

In the past, medical records have been a good source of baseline data for single-system research. However, passage and implementation of the 1996 Health Insurance Portability and Accountability Act (HIPAA) has made their use more difficult and, in some instances, impossible. The act contains standards for maintaining the privacy of individually identifiable health information. While undoubtedly a good thing for clients, the act severely limits the availability of medical recordes data for research purposes.

There are many reasons why a social worker might not decide to use available records data to form a retroactive baseline. Data may have been collected haphazardly or in a subjective manner. They may contain deliberate distortion: for example, they may understate or simply not report a child's absence from school because excessive absences might require loss of funding or a referral to juvenile authorities. The quality of records data is also dependent on the way in which the target problem was conceptualized and operationalized by whomever performed this function. For example, if the dependent variable is "number of disruptive behaviors," the teacher who recorded them may not share the same operational definition of the variable as the social worker conducting the research. Thus the baseline measurements may be reliable, but they would not be considered sufficiently valid.

Treatment Carryover. The removal of the intervention does not necessarily mean that its effects will go away immediately, or at all. If it does not, this phenomenon is known as **treatment carryover.** Thus A phases that immediately follow B phases may not be valid indicators of the pattern of the target problem without the intervention, and are not considered true baselines.

While the presence of treatment carryover may make it a little more difficult to evaluate the findings of single-system research, it is generally not an undesirable phenomenon from a treatment perspective. In fact, generally it is exactly what we hope to see happen. We want our clients to sustain, and even build on, improvements made because of our interventions. With the rare exception of interventions that seek to promote dependency as a substitute for some other, less desirable form of dependency (for example, antabuse for cocaine), treatment carryover is often an indication that an intervention has been successful.

Assumptions and Hypotheses

The basic assumption of single-system research is that if an intervention is effective, a client or client system should show a desirable change (in the target problem) when the intervention is offered. Beyond that, additional indications that an intervention has been effective depend on (1) our knowledge of the target problem and of the client or client system, and (2) the goal of the intervention. For example:

- *The target problem is something that is likely to "revert" when the intervention is withdrawn or the goal of treatment is to positively affect it only during the intervention.* An indication of intervention success would be if the target problem goes back to its usual pattern (a baseline) or at least gets somewhat worse when the intervention is withdrawn. The stronger the pattern of agreement between the presence or absence of the intervention and this pattern of the target problem, the greater the evidence that the presence of the intervention makes a difference. If improvement in the target problem occurs during repeated introductions of the intervention and the target problem gets worse every time the intervention is removed, the evidence that the intervention makes a difference is especially strong. Such consistent patterns would constitute an unlikely coincidence, one that would defy the laws of probability.
- *Improvement in the target problem is unlikely to revert when the intervention is withdrawn or a goal of the intervention is that it does not.* An indication of intervention success would be continued improvement in the target problem or, at least, continuation at the same level as at the end of the intervention (B phase). In other words, treatment carryover would be an additional indicator of intervention success.

Because social workers are most likely to use single-system research to evaluate an intervention that they believe (or at least hope) will create a desirable change in the target problem, most single-system research has an implied directional (or one-tailed) research hypothesis. It can be stated (in general terms) as:

The introduction of the intervention will be accompanied by a desired change in the problem.

If the research design can be considered to be "explanatory," the general research hypothesis could be stated as:

The introduction of the intervention will cause a desired change in the problem.

Less frequently, a social worker might wish to learn if a proposed intervention will have any effect whatsoever on a target problem and, if so, will it make it better or worse? Then the research hypothesis would be nondirectional (or two-tailed):

The intervention will be accompanied by a change in the problem.

As in all research, the research hypothesis is not tested directly. Instead, we test its null form. The null hypothesis can be stated as:

The introduction of the intervention will have no effect on the target problem.

Rules, Principles, and Conventions

As in any research, there are rules that govern how single-system research should be conducted. There are also a number of principles and conventions that can be very helpful for designing and conducting it. They are based primarily on experience. While they are not rules per se and sometimes can be ignored, adherence to them can increase the likelihood that the research will produce meaningful findings.

Examine Only Direct Effects.   The intervention should be something that the social worker does to attempt to *directly* influence the problem. It should not be something the social worker instructs the client to do to influence it, or that the social worker otherwise simply sets in motion. For example, a social worker counseling an adolescent could conduct single-system research to see if five minutes spent each week discussing careers with her will increase her school attendance or the amount of time she spends doing homework.

However, single-system research would not be appropriate for evaluating whether an intervention reminding a student to ask for help will result in her father increasing the amount of time he spends helping with her homework. In the latter example, the social worker would not be evaluating the effectiveness of his intervention; he would be evaluating the effectiveness of the student's interaction with her father. Any success of the client in this regard would not be directly attributable to what the social worker said or did, and thus would not be a good indicator of his practice effectiveness.

To illustrate this important point (one that is often confused) again, consider this example. Suppose that a social worker is counseling a client (Charles) who is recovering from prostate cancer surgery. Charles is attending a support group of cancer survivors only occasionally and the social worker believes that he would benefit from regular attendance. Single-system research could be used to see if an intervention (perhaps, a brief discussion of what transpired in the most recent group meeting each time they meet) might positively influence Charles's group attendance.

However, suppose the social worker is also counseling another man (William) who is also recovering from prostate cancer surgery. Single-system research would not be appropriate to learn if her referral of William to the support group was effective in producing a decline in his clinical depression. First, her intervention occurred once, at a single point in time (when she made the referral), and that is not the way single-system research works—the intervention must reoccur over a time period. Second, the support group was not her intervention. It was someone else's (the support group leader's), and thus the amount of decline in William's clinical depression would be an indicator of the support group leader's practice effectiveness, not hers.

Do Not Evaluate Theories.   Clearly, single-system research is *not* appropriate for evaluating the effectiveness of some interventions that social workers use (for example, referrals, one-time advocacy, decisions about clients, or other helping methods that do not occur repeatedly over a period of time). It is also not designed to test the effectiveness of a treatment theory or type of service per se, for example, it cannot be used to determine whether aversive therapy is effective in treating pedophilia—that is the work of basic research. Or, if the service is a component of a program, it could be tested as part of the program evaluation that examines the overall effectiveness of the program.

Single-system research is used most frequently to try "something different" with a client or client system, to see if it might be effective. Traditional, accepted, and proven methods of intervention for a given problem are not generally tested using single-system research. There would be little to be learned from the research. Exceptions might be if the social worker has never used some specific intervention before, in which case the research would suggest whether *he or she* was able to use it effectively ("I wonder if *I* can use it successfully?"); or if the intervention has been used only with clients that differ from the clients currently being served ("I wonder if it would also work with *this* client or client system?").

There Should Be a Pattern in the Target Problem.   Most often, single-system research is designed for situations in which there is a clear pattern reflected in the target problem and the goal of the intervention is to disrupt that pattern in some desirable way. If the problem appears to be occurring somewhat randomly, it may be impossible to use single-system research as a method of evaluation of practice effectiveness. Box 4.2 provides some examples of patterns of behaviors that suggest that single-system research may be feasible.

In some situations, maintenance of the status quo (rather than a change in the target problem) may be an objective of the intervention. For example, the objective of the intervention in working with a hospice patient might be to maintain the client's current level of functioning, or to delay certain changes as long as possible.

■ ■ ■ ■ ■

BOX 4.2

EXAMPLES OF PATTERNS OF PROBLEMS THAT EXIST

- **Declining:** e.g., family recreational activities. Goal: stabilize or increase.
- **Increasing:** e.g., verbal abuse of a partner. Goal: decrease.
- **Widely varying but in a consistent way:** e.g., child study patterns with studying occurring primarily the night before a test. Goal: stabilize.
- **Stable:** e.g., community funding of services. Goal: increase.

These might not be appropriate target problems for single-system research. However, there might be others, for example, the number of times a client eats meals with his or her family, or the number of times that the client makes phone calls to friends or relatives.

The Target Problem Should Be Easily Measurable.   If the target problem cannot be easily, regularly measured, single-system research may not be appropriate. In the past, most single-system research has focused on changes in client behavior, because behavior is more easily measured than other problems. However, that is changing as better methods for measuring other problems have been developed. When something more complex such as an attitude or a change in a family relationship is the target for change, self-administered indexes and scales are often used to measure it.

Don't Define the Target Problem Too Narrowly.   The way that the target problem is measured and how it is defined should be specific enough to identify meaningful changes. It should not be so specific that it will suggest that the intervention has been successful when it really failed. This can happen because of a phenomenon called **symptom substitution.** For example, suppose we define a child's target problem as "spitting at his sister." We might count fewer incidents of the spitting during a B phase than during a baseline A phase and conclude that our intervention is effective. But the child may have simply substituted hitting for spitting, or is now spitting at his brother instead! That would not be success. It might have been better to define the target problem as "aggressive acts toward a sibling," thus including all aggressive acts and all siblings.

Of course, there is also a potential problem if a target problem is defined too broadly. Then, it can encompass many different phenomena that may vary widely in severity, including some that are not especially problematic in some situations. For example, the broad definition "aggressive acts toward others" may include certain actions that include defending oneself or are quite normal and even desirable on a soccer or football field for an adolescent, but not in the home or in social situations.

Define the Target Problem in Positive Terms.   A problem of a client or client system may be too much of something or too little of it. For example, the goal of intervention with one client may be to reduce some form of substance abuse; with another client it may be to increase time spent interacting with a family member. Whichever situation exists, it is desirable to define the goal of intervention in positive terms whenever possible. This is consistent with social work practice values (the "strengths perspective"). For example, it would be preferable to define our goal as "increasing the number of times Lois makes unsolicited comments during group treatment" rather than "decreasing the number of times Lois refuses to participate in group discussions."

Use One Intervention with One Target Problem.   Some single-system research designs (including some presented in Chapter 5) contain more than one target problem or more than one intervention. However, the designs adhere to a rule of single-system research—at any time there can be no more than one intervention and one target problem. The same intervention is never offered to try to influence two different target problems simultaneously. Also, two or more interventions are never offered simultaneously to try to influence a target problem. This rule is designed to help keep the design as "clean" as possible, that is, to not introduce other variables or confounding factors that will make the findings more difficult to interpret. If it were not the case, it would be difficult, if not impossible, to sort out what the findings suggest, to determine "what did what to what."

Use Logical Time Parameters.   The overall duration of single-system research studies varies widely. A study should last long enough to be able to draw conclusions about the effectiveness of an intervention, but not go on for an excessive amount of time. Setting the time framework for a study entails logic and a knowledge of social work practice. The length of a study is influenced by such factors as how long a social worker anticipates working with a client or client system, the frequency that a target problem occurs, the number of phases in the research design, and what the social worker believes is a reasonable time for the intervention to "take effect" with a unique client or client system.

Target problems that occur frequently are generally measured using small time intervals between them, such as days, hours, or even minutes. For example, speech mannerisms or certain involuntary behaviors such as foot jiggling or twisting one's hair may occur so frequently that, theoretically, a study consisting of several alternating A and B phases might be completed in only a few hours. For target problems that occur less frequently or that are not easily susceptible to change, larger units of time (a period of weeks, months, or even years) may be required. For example, evaluating the effectiveness of regular, five-minute phone calls (the intervention) to increase a former client's compliance with his medication may require many months, if the client has a long-standing history of noncompliance.

The length of a single-system research study does not have to coincide with the course of social work treatment. In fact, it often doesn't. The research can begin after clients have begun receiving (the usual) services, and it can end while services are still being offered.

MEASUREMENT TASKS AND ISSUES

As in all research, good measurement of the dependent variable (the target problem) is very important. In planning to measure it, several issues need to be addressed.

Use of Operational Definitions

Measurement of the target problem requires that the social worker know and specify exactly what is meant by it. This is done by first conceptualizing what it means and then finding or constructing an operational definition of it. Suppose the target problem is the temper tantrums of a three-year-old. It would be necessary to state exactly what constitutes a temper tantrum (preferably in the form of behaviors such as foot stomping, screaming, lying on the floor, and so forth). An operational definition of most any target problem can usually be found and borrowed from our professional literature. It need not be the best one ever created—only good enough for us (or whoever is conducting the measurement of the target problem) to determine with accuracy whether it occurred.

What to Measure

Once having operationally defined the target problem, there are frequently many different ways in which it can be measured. Let's use the same example of a target problem, temper tantrums. Some of the most common ways that may generate interval or ratio-level measurement include:

1. *Frequency.* For example, we might ask a parent to keep a record of how many times the child throws a temper tantrum each week.
2. *Duration.* For example, we might ask the parent to record how long each tantrum lasts.
3. *Interval.* For example, we might ask the parent to record the length of time between each tantrum.
4. *Magnitude.* For example, we might ask the parent to record the magnitude of each tantrum using a Likert-type scale or similar measurement instrument.

A major determinant in deciding how a target problem should be measured is the goal of the intervention. A determining factor might be what the parent currently finds most intolerable—the frequency, duration, interval between, or magnitude of the tantrums. Another factor to consider would be what the social worker and the parent realistically believe can be accomplished if the intervention is successful, knowing the child and his or her maturity level and personality.

Of course, the social worker may conclude that little can be done about the child's tantrums, or that they are not excessive and are only symptomatic of a developmental stage and thus not an appropriate target problem for single-system research. However, the social worker concludes that the mother could use some help in "handling" them better, perhaps, by becoming less verbally abusive of her child when tantrums occur. Then the parent's behavior may be the target problem (and the focus of intervention) and the possible ways of measuring it would be different:

1. *Frequency.* For example, we might ask her to record how many times she handled the tantrum without berating the child afterward.
2. *Duration.* For example, we might ask her to record the length of time that she berated the child following a tantrum.
3. *Interval.* For example, we might ask her to record the time between incidents in which she berated the child following a tantrum.
4. *Magnitude.* For example, we might ask the other parent or partner who witnessed the tantrums to record the magnitude of the abuse following them using a Likert-type scale or similar measurement instrument.

Of course, frequency, duration, intensity and magnitude are not the only ways in which target problems are measured in single-system research. Depending primarily on the goal of the intervention, there is an almost infinite number of other options. For example, if the target problem is a behavior, measurement might entail the awareness of others, place or time where the behavior occurs, or the level of acceptance or nonacceptance of it by the client. If the target problem is not a behavior, still other ways can be used. For example, if it is an attitude that the social worker seeks to change, it would be possible to measure its intensity, toward whom it is directed, or the way it manifests itself.

Who Should Measure

In conducting single-system research, valid measurements of the target problem sometimes can be found in the form of records: case records, arrest records, attendance records, employment records, or some other secondary data source. However, because of increased legal and privacy restrictions such as HIPAA, it has become virtually impossible to gain access to them. Almost invariably the social worker must now measure the target problem, or ask others to provide measurements of it.

Deciding who should conduct the measurement of the target problem often involves a compromise between what is ideal and what is feasible. Valid measurements are most likely to occur when either first-hand observations can be made by the social worker, or they can be carefully made and verified by others who have no personal involvement with the target problem of the client or client system. However, neither of these alternatives may be possible given the nature of the problem, where and when it occurs, and so forth. Other people theoretically can provide valid measurement, but when they do, its quality may be questionable. This is frequently the case when measurement must rely on a client's self-report or the recollections of friends, relatives, co-workers, or others who must "live with" the target problem. Whenever there is no alternative but to use sources like these, every effort should be made to enhance their credibility by, for example, using multiple observers and standardized data collection instruments.

Acceptability of Measurement

Certain ethical issues also affect measurement of the dependent variable in single-system research. The researcher is, first and foremost, a social work practitioner. The welfare of his or her clients must remain the top priority. Thus measurement should be as nonobtrusive as possible. (Videotaping or other recording of clients' speech or actions, for example, rarely meets this criterion.) Measurement should not interfere with either the intervention being evaluated or any other assistance that the client or client system is receiving. Both the measurements themselves and their methods of collection should be acceptable to clients, not imposed on them simply because a power differential allows it to happen. Measurements should not occur that, for example, violate a client's right to privacy, cause discord with significant others, or are embarrassing to a client in some way.

RECORDING AND GRAPHING DATA

As previously noted, the target problem continues to be measured over the course of the research. This may entail the use of a standardized data collection instrument, for example, an attitude scale administered each week prior to a client being seen for counseling. Or, it may entail a "counting" of some behavior during times when the social worker interacts with the client or client system, for example, how many times a facial tic occurs during each weekly counseling session. Ideally, measurement involves using more than one observer or some other method to ensure that the measurements of the behavior are reliable and valid. However, in reality, the reliability and validity of measurements are not always assured. For example, client self-reports of behaviors (such as substance abuse during the previous week) are often what must be used. Measurements are recorded as they are made, and are used to produce graphs (frequently scattergrams) that can then be analyzed and interpreted.

The absence or presence of the intervention (A or B phase, respectively) constitutes the two value categories of the independent variable; measurement of it is thus regarded as nominal level. The dependent variable (the target problem) can be considered to be at any level of measurement (almost always either nominal, interval, or ratio), dependent on how it is measured. Scattergrams are used if its measurement can be regarded as interval or ratio level (such as "incidents of verbal abuse" or "number of supportive statements made to a child").

On the graph, time intervals are labeled by phase, for example, "A" (for an A phase), "B" (for a B phase), and so forth. Possible measurements of the target problem are plotted along the vertical axis; the passage of time (along with the measurements that occurred within it) is displayed along the horizontal axis. Thus, each dot on the scattergram portrays both a measurement of the target problem and the time when the measurement took place. Figure 4.1 is an example of a graph that displays the graphing of a ratio-level variable. Notice that there appears to be an increase in the frequency of the dependent variable (supportive comments) during the fifteen weeks when the intervention (some intervention that the social worker used with the parent) was present.

If the target problem is a dichotomous variable (for example, "school attendance" or "meals in which all family members are present"—a yes or no situation), a graph may not be necessary—only keeping a count of the measurements in the respective A and B phases may suffice. If a graph would make it easier to visualize the findings, an even simpler graph is used. A single horizontal line separates the two variable categories of the target problem and a dot or an "X" is inserted either above or below the line to indicate a measurement at a given time. Figure 4.2 is an example of this type of graph.

The primary purpose of a graph is to facilitate data analysis and interpretation. As such, it should contain anything else that assists in this process. It is com-

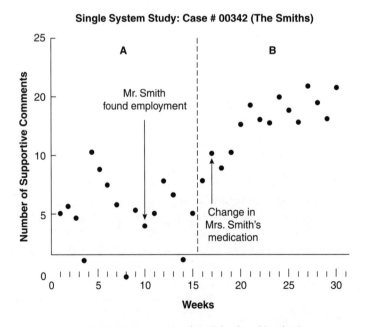

FIGURE 4.1   A Scattergram Used to Display Single-System
Research Data (Ratio-Level Dependent Variable)

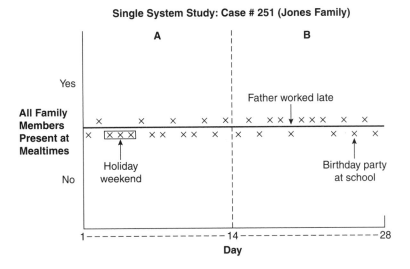

FIGURE 4.2   **A Graph to Display Single-System Research Data (Nominal-Level Dichotomous Variable)**

mon practice to label any threats to the internal validity of the findings, that is, any important events that occurred over the course of the research besides the intervention that might have produced change in the target problem or might have precluded it from happening.[2] For example, changes in health, financial or employment status, changes in family situation, or changes in sources of available help all may have influenced the target problem. If it is reasonable to think that this might have occurred, they should be included with a line or arrow indicating exactly when they occurred (as in Figures 4.1 and 4.2).

THE SEQUENCE OF EVENTS

It should be clear by now that single-system research is a systematic approach to evaluating individual practice effectiveness. There is nothing haphazard about it. It should not be surprising that, as in other types of research, a general sequence of steps is followed in conducting single-system research. Box 4.3 displays them. Notice that seven of the steps in Box 4.3 are conducted before any data are collected. This emphasizes the importance of planning in single-system research. Steps 2 and 3 are especially critical to the quality of the research and its findings. It is important both to specify exactly what the intervention consists of and what exactly the target problem is and how it will be measured. If this is not done thoughtfully, little of value will be learned. Steps 9 and 10 have not been discussed yet. They are the subject of Chapter 5.

■ ■ ■ ■ ■

BOX 4.3

HOW TO CONDUCT SINGLE-SYSTEM RESEARCH

1. Identify and specify the overall problem of the client or client system.
2. Specify the target problem that will be addressed (usually a symptom or one aspect of the problem) and the pattern of its occurrence.
3. Specify the method of intervention that you are considering.
4. Review the professional literature to either identify theoretical support for the proposed intervention or to determine how it should be modified. Modify it if indicated.
5. Specify how the target problem will be measured.
6. Determine which research design would be most appropriate based on ethical constraints, time limitations, your knowledge of the client, your knowledge of the target problem, and treatment goals.
7. State the research hypothesis, indicating what pattern of the target problem would constitute support for it.
8. Conduct the research, carefully recording all measurements.
9. Analyze the data, both visually and by using the correct test of statistical significance, if appropriate.
10. Interpret the findings in light of the research design used, analysis of the data, and your awareness of other factors that may have influenced the results.
11. If the intervention appears to have been effective, consider replicating it with another similar client or client system.

Earlier versions of this box, created by the author, appeared in Yegidis, B., & Weinbach, R. (2002). *Research methods for social workers* (4th ed.). Boston: Allyn & Bacon, 291; and Compton, B., & Galaway, B. (1999). *Social work processes* (4th ed.). Pacific Grove, CA: Brooks/Cole, 472.

LINGERING ETHICAL QUESTIONS

There are a number of ethical concerns that continue to surface regarding the use of single-system research. A few are real, but when examined carefully, most of them are really nonissues that arise from misunderstandings about how single-system research is conducted and what priorities constrain it. For example, contrary to some common misconceptions, A phases need not be (and usually are not) time periods during which no services are offered. The intervention that is being evaluated is withheld, but other needed assistance is not. Similarly, there is nothing unethical about a design that ends in an A phase. The final A phase does not mean that the client is left with no help, only because the research design requires it. Other forms of assistance to a client or client system can begin before, continue during, and continue after the time frame of the research. An intervention that was evaluated also can be reintroduced after completion of the research.

The following are some of the most frequently mentioned ethical issues in research. They relate primarily to the protection of research participants, clients or client groups in single-system research studies.

Need to Conduct the Research

One potential ethical issue, unnecessary research, is rarely an issue in single-system research. It would be illogical for a social worker to conduct a single-system study, only for the sake of doing it. Even though single-system research can be done quickly and inexpensively, why would anyone devote any time to it unless he or she wanted to evaluate the effectiveness of some intervention with a client or client system?

The only occasion where the question of unnecessary research might be an issue would be if conducting single-system research were made a requirement by a social worker's supervisor or by a student's professor. Conceivably, the social worker could conduct research already knowing the answer to the research question, Is this intervention effective? and not caring about the findings. But he or she would not know for sure if the intervention will be effective with *this* client or client system. Besides, the problem of conducting research "only to get experience in doing it" is not unique to single-system research and is no more likely to occur than in other types of research. Problems can best be avoided if the person requiring the research is careful to remind the social worker of his or her ethical responsibilities as a professional.

Anonymity and Confidentiality

Because data from single-system research is kept either in the social worker's own files or in the secured records of clients, the confidentiality of what is revealed in the course of single-system research is generally not an issue. In medical and psychiatric settings, current HIPAA requirements relating to privacy of health information must be addressed. In those relatively rare instances in which the results of a study are published in a professional journal or otherwise disseminated to others, the social worker must carefully "de-identify" the client to the extent that privacy and confidentiality are not violated. As in other forms of research, this is usually accomplished by describing the client or client system in only general terms, omitting any demographic characteristics or behaviors that might betray the client's identity. If there is any question of possible noncompliance with a legal standard, it is advisable to seek legal advice.

No Unnecessary Pain and Suffering

The issue of "no unnecessary pain and suffering" is pretty much a nonissue. Client well-being is our top priority. We would never attempt an intervention unless we believed that it might help a client with a problem. No ethical social worker would ever insist that a need for research-based knowledge should take precedence over the welfare of our clients.

The same principle would apply in making decisions about whether to terminate a research study. Suppose that a single-system design calls for a change, for example, the removal of an apparently successful intervention or the introduction of one that, based on recently acquired knowledge about the client, may harm him or her in some way. Perhaps, removal is likely to create extreme anxiety or other physical symptoms. Would the research continue as planned? Certainly not! The research may simply have to be terminated or the design altered. But either decision may result in a loss of valuable feedback about the effectiveness of the intervention! Then, so be it! What if the design calls for no change to occur? However, what is occurring in the current phase appears to be harming the client or at least causing a delay in providing what the client needs. The response is the same—the research may have to be terminated or the design altered in some way. As in all forms of research conducted by social workers, practice values and ethical concerns must always take precedence over the research. In single-system designs, ending the research prematurely is far less costly (there is less invested in it) than in other more traditional types of research.

Voluntary Informed Consent

There is one ethical issue related to single-system research that is a little more complicated and is less easily dismissed than the others. To a great extent, it revolves around different perceptions of the respective roles of the social worker and the client and the possible existence of a dual-role relationship. It is the issue of "voluntary informed consent" and how it should be addressed.

The "informed consent" part of the ethical requirement often can be addressed rather easily by (1) describing (at least in general terms) what data will be required from the client and how it will be used; and (2) asking the client to sign a consent form granting permission for the social worker to use the data for research purposes. (Of course, this would not be easily accomplished if the "client" is a larger system such as a community.)

The "voluntary" part of the phrase *voluntary informed consent* can be a little trickier. Suppose the client is an individual. Because clients may not wish to displease the social worker, they may sometimes agree to provide data or permit measurement for single-system research that they would otherwise prefer not to allow. Or, clients may feel compelled to provide data because of the power differential that exists or because of some other factor inherent in the social worker–client relationship. Is participation really "voluntary" when these situations exist? If not, the consent form may be meaningless. Of course they will agree to sign it.

Within our profession and even within social work education there is a lack of consensus about how to address the issue of voluntary informed consent in single-system research. Specifically, there is disagreement over whether the client or members of the client system should be required to sign a standard consent form before research can be conducted, as research participants are required to do in other types of research. (The form provides at least some protection for both the researcher and the participant, including the statement that the participant can drop out of the research at any time without penalty.) Those people and organizations who advocate or require the signing of a consent form take the position that single-system research is still research, and thus its research participants require protection. The question of whether the form is probably meaningless is generally not addressed—perhaps it is really protection of the organization rather than the client that is being sought.

Those who do not agree that signing a consent form is necessary justify their position by pointing out that, although single-system research uses research methods, it does so only as part of good practice. They see nothing unethical about using a method to systematically monitor and evaluate one's practice in order to ensure that the best possible interventions are offered. In fact, they suggest, it would be irresponsible for a professional not to do so. Besides, in a sense, clients have already granted permission for treatment and, thus, for the evaluation that is a part of their treatment, when they applied for services.

This latter position seems (at least to me) to be the more logical because, as I have suggested, the social worker conducting single-system research remains a practitioner; his or her primary role does not change simply because of the use of research methods in his or her practice. Thus there is no dual role relationship, only a single one—that of social worker and client. However, because positions and requirements differ on this issue, a social worker conducting single-system research would be wise to investigate if a standard consent form must be signed and if review of single-system proposals by institutional review boards (IRBs) are required. In some settings (for example, teaching hospitals), a client receiving services generally has already agreed to participate in research and no additional requirements may exist. Other settings may require consent forms and IRB review for their legal protection as well as for protection of clients.

CURRENT STATUS OF SINGLE-SYSTEM RESEARCH

Single-system research has now been advocated and reported in the social work literature for more than thirty years. When it was rediscovered and advocated as a logical bridge between research and practice by NASW and CSWE task forces of practitioners and researchers in the 1970s (described in Chapter 2), it initially caught on fairly slowly. Later, as more and more practitioners learned how to use it, it became more popular. Yet its critics still existed, and they continue to exist today.

Support for single-system research in the workplace is growing. There was a time when some social workers had to "sneak it" past their supervisors who did not understand it, were suspicious of it, and who often viewed it as wasting time. However, most supervisors now have at least a beginning appreciation for it and, even if they do not use it themselves, tend not to interfere with others who use it.

Over the years, three developments have created changes in the way that single-system research is conducted. First, social work researchers such as Walter Hudson have created and refined scales for the measurement of such hard-to-measure variables as marital adjustment and family relations,[3] variables that are often the very problems that social workers seek to address. These instruments have been found to produce reliable and valid measurements when used over and over again with the same clients: a requirement for single-system research. Secondly, other researchers have developed more new, specialized single-system research designs for use in answering different research questions.[4] There now is a suitable design for nearly every situation. Third, researchers have also developed software to make the recording, graphing, and statistical analysis of data both fast and efficient. Now most of the major statistical software packages, and even some designed to support individual textbooks,[5] can quickly and easily accomplish these tasks. The "old days" of keeping pencil and paper records of ongoing research on graph paper may soon disappear.

Advantages

Single-system research is especially well-suited to providing early feedback about new or experimental methods of intervention or those that we are just wondering about. After a preliminary evaluation using a single-system design, they can then be either discarded or, if the findings seem to suggest that they may be effective, they can be evaluated more thoroughly using more traditional research methods.

In many ways, single-system research is a bargain. Feedback on the effectiveness of a social worker's intervention is received at little or no cost to the client or the practitioner. Single-system research costs very little in time and other resources, something that generally cannot be said of program evaluations, which often are very expensive to conduct. Learning to conduct single-system research is also quick and easy. After only a single workshop on the topic or a few hours reading about it, social workers are generally ready to use it in their practice.

Once they conduct a few studies, most practitioners learn to like doing single-system research. Positive findings offer evidence of, and thus reassurance about, a practitioner's effectiveness. And, if an intervention does not appear to be working, it is possible to make adjustments while there is still time to do so. Unlike basic research, in which application of findings may occur years down the road or may never occur, application in single-system research can always occur in a timely fashion.

It can also be argued that the process of conducting single-system research itself creates better practitioners by keeping them "focused." It requires a social worker to specify the objectives of intervention and be regularly reminded of them. He or she must also specify what method of intervention will be used and what the theoretical rationale is for it. These are desirable actions (good practice) that can easily carry over to work with other clients where single-system research is not appropriate.

Limitations

Generally, the shortcomings of single-system research relate to its lack of design rigor. Critics often ask, What can it really tell us about the effectiveness of an intervention?

A major limitation of single-system research is its questionable ability to control for threats to internal validity. It has been suggested that single-system research can provide evidence of a correlation between the presence or absence of an intervention and changes in the target problem. It can also "provide evidence of the control of variables other than the intervention that might be responsible for change."[6] But does it really control for them? Because it lacks a true control group, it is impossible to conclude that the intervention (and not some other event or phenomenon) produced any changes in the target problem that may have occurred. Thus any such conclusions must always be regarded as tentative. However, this is a common problem in all research, especially when the research involves human behavior. Besides, a basic characteristic of all knowledge acquired using scientific methods is that it is regarded as "provisional," that is, subject to later modification if proven incorrect.

Generally, the findings of single-system research also are considered to have little or no external validity. However, sometimes a study can be replicated, perhaps many times. **Replication** can appear to produce more generalized knowledge, knowledge about the effectiveness of an intervention per se in working with a given client problem. How is replication accomplished in single-system research? It might entail a social worker conducting a series of identical studies with the same dependent and independent variables, the same design, and clients or client systems that are very similar (at least in relation to the problem addressed). If the findings of all of the studies are similar, they might be assumed to have external validity. Nevertheless, the external validity of findings based on replication of single-system studies remains suspect. As human service professionals we know about the uniqueness of all people and their environments. Every person is a unique sample of one. Every social worker (and his or her skills, personality, and so forth) is different; so is every client or client system.

CONCLUDING THOUGHTS

If we were to objectively evaluate the place of single-system research in the overall enterprise of evaluation research we would probably conclude that it plays a relatively small, yet important, role. It certainly is no substitute for comprehensive program evaluations or even for components of them that evaluate a particular service that is offered by many professionals working in concert. And, it is not meant to be. However, it does evaluate some part of practice, the effectiveness of individual social workers in their work with individual clients and client groups.

Perhaps most important, single-system research helps to create a mindset among practitioners, one that emphasizes the importance of objectively determining what works and what does not work. The presence of that mindset can facilitate all other forms of evaluation that occur within human service organizations.

Social workers need to know, Was it the intervention or something else that produced changes in the target problem? Some of the more complicated designs (those that contain multiple A and B phases) can be used to produce at least a tentative answer to this question. However, implementing complicated designs with many measurements of the dependent variable over longer periods of time is not always feasible. Even if it is, a complicated design may sacrifice one of the greatest features of single-system research, its simplicity.

The findings of single-system research studies are intended for use by the individual practitioner. They are not intended to be used by supervisors for evaluating the professional competence of social workers (as data for performance evaluations). They also are not designed to evaluate the effectiveness of types of services in general, or to evaluate the effectiveness of services that are a component of a social program. However, they have sometimes been used in this way. This is a mistake. As later chapters discuss, there are much better methods for evaluating the effectiveness of services within social programs—methods that do a better job of addressing the question of threats to internal validity.

KEY TERMS

longitudinal time series	A phase	symptom substitution
intervention	reversal	replication
target problem	baseline	
B phase	treatment carryover	

STUDY QUESTIONS

1. What is the purpose of all single-system research?

2. What is the difference between a true baseline and an A phase that follows a B phase?

3. If a B phase is the counterpart of an experimental group in a true experiment, what is the function of an A phase?

4. Why do most hypotheses tend to be directional or "one-tailed"?

5. Why would it be better to use the target problem "days in which homework was completed" rather than "days homework was incomplete" in conducting single-system research with an adolescent client?

6. What is a good way to avoid the problem of symptom substitution?

7. If the target problem is child abuse, how would we measure its duration? How else could it be measured?

8. What type of graph is created if the measurement of the target problem generates data that are considered to be interval or ratio-level?

9. What is a *real* ethical issue in conducting single-system research (rather than a non-issue based on a misunderstanding of it)? Explain.

10. What are the greatest strengths and limitations of single-system research?

REFERENCES

1. Berlin, S., & Marsh, J. (1993). *Informing practice decisions.* New York: Macmillan, 109.
2. Ibid., 116.
3. Hudson, W. (1982). *The clinical measurement package: A field manual.* Homewood, IL: The Dorsey Press.
4. See, e.g., Bloom, M., Fischer, J., & Orme, J. 2003. *Evaluating practice: Guidelines for the accountable professional* (4th ed.). Boston: Allyn & Bacon.
5. See, e.g., *Singwin,* a software package developed by Charles Auerbach, David Schnall, and Heidi Heft Laporte for the book, *Evaluating practice,* ibid.
6. Tripodi, T. (1994). *A primer on single subject design for clinical social workers.* Washington, DC: NASW Press, 81.

•

■ ■ ■ ■ ■

CHAPTER FIVE

SINGLE-SYSTEM DESIGNS AND DATA ANALYSIS

Chapter 4 presented a broad overview of single-system research. By now you should have a good general understanding of how it works and what it is all about. Conducting single-system research is relatively simple; it relies heavily on logic and social work practice knowledge. However, there are two very important tasks, selecting a research design and analyzing the data, that also rely heavily on the knowledge and skills usually acquired by studying methods for conducting research.

The discussion that follows was written based on the assumption that you either have studied, or are studying, research methods and statistics. If it has been a while, or if you have very little background in the subjects, it may be necessary to refer to books on research methods and statistics to better understand and use this discussion for planning and implementing a single-system research study.

RESEARCH DESIGNS

In any research, a research design is a plan for conducting a research study. The general characteristics of single-system designs can be described using some of the same terms used to describe research designs in more traditional research. As noted in Chapter 4, all single-system designs are longitudinal, thus designs that are before and after (or pretest-posttest) or cross-sectional cannot be considered single-system research. The clumsier term "single case time-series" that is sometimes used to describe them makes this point. Single-system studies also are considered to be primarily quantitative (with emphasis on accurate measurement, deductive logic, objectivity, and so on).

As in other types of research, the general nature of the research design in single-system research determines what can be learned from it. **Exploratory designs** provide beginning insights into the effectiveness of an intervention in addressing a target problem. Not surprisingly, exploratory designs are the most simple ones. They lack an A phase and only seek to answer the question, Does change in the target problem occur when the intervention is introduced?

Descriptive designs help us better understand the effects of an intervention. They contain a single baseline A phase and seek to answer the question, How *much* change occurs when an intervention is introduced? If either an exploratory design or a descriptive one is used, the social worker must rely heavily on practice knowledge and knowledge of the client in drawing any conclusions about whether an intervention really worked. Definitive answers about the effectiveness of an intervention cannot be obtained.

Some designs are described as explanatory. (Some writers even use the term "experimental,"[1] but that seems to me to be an overstatement because they lack a true control group and the random selection and random assignment normally required.) **Explanatory designs** attempt to answer the question, Does the intervention *cause* changes in the dependent variable? They contain a series of alternating A and B phases. This is done primarily to attempt to control for threats to internal validity, at least to the degree possible. For example, if it can be shown that a decrease in the target problem occurs *every* time the intervention is introduced and it increases *every* time that it is withdrawn, it would be highly unlikely that history, maturation, regression to the mean, and so forth may have produced these changes. Even if an explanatory design is used, practice knowledge and knowledge of the client or client system still play important roles in drawing conclusions about an intervention's effectiveness. Statistical analysis can also help to make any such conclusions more definitive.

Design Selection

In selecting a design for a single-system study, a social worker considers some of the same issues that are considered in other research—and some different ones too. As in all research, different single-system designs are used for different purposes. For example, some designs compare the effectiveness of two or more different interventions. Others are more suited to examining whether a single intervention seems to work more effectively for addressing one target problem than another. Others are designed to learn what intensity or quantity of an intervention is most effective. Still others seek to determine what sequence of interventions is most effective for addressing a given problem.

In addition to issues about which design will best provide the answer to some question, in single-system research two other factors are considered in the selection of a research design. First, a social worker must consider the ethical implications of various designs. Specifically, the social worker must consider how the client may be affected by the use of a baseline prior to the introduction of a promising intervention, or the withdrawal of an intervention offered during a later B phase. The welfare of the client or client system must be a first priority. One design may promise more definitive answers to a research question than another. But if it puts the client in some jeopardy it must be rejected in favor of a design that is less desirable from a research perspective. Secondly, a social worker conducting single-system research needs to estimate the likely impact of the intervention on the target problem if it is effective, as anticipated. This entails the application of knowledge drawn from our professional literature and the social worker's knowledge of the specific client or client system. Among the questions to be considered may be:

- How long should it take for the intervention to be effective?
- Would change in the target problem be likely to occur after only one use of the intervention, or would it require reinforcement?
- If it is effective, would I expect that the problem will revert back to its old level if the intervention is withdrawn, or will treatment carryover likely occur?
- Would treatment carryover be consistent with treatment goals?

Design Labels

In single-system research, most designs are referred to using letters. The labels reflect the sequence in which A phases and B phases are scheduled to occur and the number of each. For example, an ABAB design would have two A phases and two B phases. The first A phase would be a true baseline during which the "usual pattern" of the target problem would be monitored and measured, unless the baseline could be established from secondary data such as accurate records of the history of the target problem. The second A phase would be characterized by withdrawal of the intervention. The first B phase would be when the intervention is first introduced; the second would be when it is reintroduced following withdrawal (the second A phase). In contrast, a BAB design would begin and end in a B (intervention) phase with a withdrawal of intervention (A phase) in between. It would have no baseline prior to the first intervention (B phase).

In more complicated designs (such as those that use a baseline for two or more interventions or those that contain phases with different intensities or quantities of the intervention), subscripts and superscripts are added to the A and B phases. For example, the respective baseline phases for the baselines of four different interventions would be labeled A_1, A_2, A_3, and A_4. The phases that contain four different intensities or quantities of an intervention would be labeled B^1, B^2, B^3, and B^4.

Different Designs for Different Purposes

There are an almost limitless number of designs that can be used for single-system research. I will describe some of the simpler, and more commonly used, ones with special reference to when they are most appropriate.

B. The B design consists of the introduction of the intervention and then the monitoring of any changes that occur in the target problem during some predetermined time period. It is what good social work practitioners usually do, but in a more structured way. What makes it different is: (1) the careful, repeated measurement (quantification, if possible) of the target problem; (2) the duration of the research (unlike services to the client) is limited and specified in advance; and (3) the measurements are recorded and interpreted throughout the research.

BC, BCD, BCDE, and so forth.   Different interventions are introduced in a predetermined sequence to try to determine whether one or all produce change in the target problem. These designs (like B) are considered only exploratory because they lack a baseline. They are sometimes used when there is concern that the use of an A phase either before or following a B phase might be detrimental to the client in some way. However, this concern is generally unfounded, because an A phase does not require that no assistance is offered, only that the specific intervention(s) being evaluated are withheld.

The designs offer some beginning understanding of the relative effectiveness of several different interventions. However, because they lack A phases, they do not do a good job of answering the questions, To what degree was the effectiveness of an intervention affected by previous ones? or, How much change did the interventions produce overall?

AB.   AB designs are quite common and are considered descriptive. AB consists of a beginning A (baseline) phase of predetermined duration during which the intervention whose effectiveness is being evaluated is not offered. The baseline phase is then followed by a B phase during which the intervention is provided.

AB is appropriate when permanent learning or nonreversible behavior or attitudes are a likely consequence (and a goal) of the intervention. If the target problem entails certain types of learning (for example, acquired daily living skills) and it occurs, withdrawal of the intervention would be unlikely to produce "unlearning." Thus the introduction of another A phase (an ABA design) is not necessary—it would produce only expected findings. In addition, we know that some behaviors (for example, assertiveness, social skills, health practices) and attitudes (for example, racism, agism, homophobia) once they change for the good, are unlikely to revert back if the intervention that produced them is withdrawn. Often, this is because the new behavior or attitude is self-reinforcing—it produces rewards in the form of improved social relationships or otherwise meets the client's needs better than the old one.

An AB design is quite limited. It cannot answer the questions, How do I know that it was the intervention (and not something else) that caused changes in the target problem? or, What would happen to the target problem if I were to discontinue the intervention? Unfortunately, these are two questions that are often central to the evaluation of our practice effectiveness.

ABC or ABCD.   Social workers sometimes identify two or more different interventions that may seem promising for addressing a single-client problem, and would like to know which work bests. With these designs (ABC, ABCD, and so on) each intervention is introduced for a predetermined period of time. These designs attempt to describe changes that occur in the target problem when several different interventions are introduced, one at a time. Thus, they are used to begin to examine the relationship between several independent variables (interventions) and a single dependent variable (a target problem).

Ethical concerns related to use of ABC or ABCD designs are not as great as with some other designs, especially those that require the withdrawal of an intervention that may appear to be successful in order to go into a subsequent A phase (such as ABA). However, these designs may still require withdrawing an apparently successful intervention in order to substitute another (albeit a promising one) that may not work as well. However, if the target problem seems to get worse when the new intervention is introduced, the social worker can (and should) reintroduce the earlier, apparently more effective one. Ethically, there may be little choice. The ABC research is thus terminated, and the research effectively becomes (after the fact) an AB design.

When using descriptive designs (such as AB, ABC, or ABCD) that have only a single A phase (baseline), the social worker does not control for other factors (besides the intervention) that might produce change in the target problem. For example, a desirable change in a child's behavior may have been the effect of the intervention, but it is impossible to know for sure. It may also have been the result of a one-time change in her diet or her medication, her grandmother's moving into the home, intimidation by a sibling or peer, maturation, or many other factors working either alone or in concert to produce the change.

ABA. Described as "explanatory," an ABA design makes some effort to control for threats to internal validity by including a second A phase after the intervention is introduced during a B phase. Suppose the target problem reflects improvement during the B phase and then gets worse again during the second A phase. On the surface, this would seem to suggest that it was the intervention (and not something else) that produced the improvement during the B phase.

The ABA design can provide convincing results. It can determine if improvement in the target problem occurs only when the intervention is present. The problem is (as suggested earlier), most social work intervention is not designed to promote dependency on the part of clients. We hope to empower our clients to continue to improve, even when we no longer offer assistance to them. So, what if instead, the improvement persists into the second A phase or even accelerates? How should this be interpreted? Is it desirable treatment carryover and thus support for the effectiveness of the intervention in working with the client or client system? Maybe. But the continued improvement in the target problem when the intervention was withdrawn may simply mean that something else (not the intervention) produced the changes in it during the B phase.

What if little or no improvement is found to occur during the B phase? How is this interpreted? The intervention may simply have been ineffective. Or, perhaps the intervention really would have been effective, but it did not continue long enough to produce any change in the target problem. Or, some event or phenomenon may have somehow nullified the effect of the intervention and prevented it from being effective.

Interpretation of the results of an ABA design can be difficult. Despite being regarded as explanatory, not too much that is conclusive can be learned from it.

True, it can answer the question, What happens to the target problem when the intervention is withdrawn? (which an AB design cannot do). But that is about all. It does not provide definitive answers for social workers who hope to learn that their intervention promotes positive changes in a target problem that are sustained when the intervention is no longer present—a common social work practice goal.

ABA is also not a favorite among social workers for another reason—it both begins and ends with an A phase. Unless secondary data can be used to create the first A phase (baseline), it requires a waiting period before offering a promising form of intervention. Later, it requires the withdrawal of the intervention, even if it appears to be effective. This does not parallel the usual course of treatment in many social work practice settings where services that are believed to be effective are offered as soon as possible and continue until the client no longer needs them. (Termination of services is a time when they may be especially needed.) However, as noted earlier, during A phases only the specific intervention (the independent variable) that is being evaluated (often just an additional form of intervention) is denied to the client. The usual services are offered. Besides, as observed earlier, the duration of the research does not have to coincide with the duration of other services to the client. So ethical concerns about ABA designs may be largely unfounded. Their major shortcoming is their limited capacity to answer important questions about practice effectiveness.

ABAB.   The presence of an additional B phase in an ABAB design helps to provide some evidence for (or against) a cause–effect relationship between the intervention and changes in the target problem. Thus ABAB does a better job of controlling for threats to internal validity than the ABA. Suppose the target problem shows dramatic improvement during the first B phase. If the same pattern in the target problem persists in the second half of the research (the second A and B phases) as in the first, it is likely that the intervention and not something else produced any desirable changes in the target problem. However, if the pattern does not continue the same during the second A and second B phases as it did in the first, then most likely the apparent success of the intervention in the first two phases was produced by something else.

The ABAB design also can even more readily identify dependency on the presence of the intervention. Like ABA, it is appropriate in situations where a social worker wants to know if desirable changes in the target problem are dependent on the presence of the intervention.

Since the ABAB ends in an intervention (B) phase, it is often liked better than ABA by many social workers. Justifiably or not, this only seems more in keeping with social work values.

BAB.   BAB designs both begin and end in an intervention (B) phase, with an A phase in-between. Thus, they are especially well suited to those situations where the social worker believes that to wait and first conduct a baseline measurement prior to offering the intervention would be unethical, and it is believed that following a period of intervention (perhaps crisis services) the intervention can then safely be withdrawn.

When using a BAB design, ethical concerns center on the timing of the decision to withdraw intervention. When is it safe to move from the first B phase into the A phase? Decisions regarding research designs (including the length of all phases) should, whenever possible, be made prior to the onset of the research. Just like most other research, it it is not a good idea to make changes once data collection is underway. However, without extensive foreknowledge of a client or client system and with little knowledge of the pattern of the target problem (because no baseline is present), it is difficult to determine when would be a safe time to withdraw the intervention. For this reason, BAB designs are often terminated (or sometimes modified) before they are completed. This is the only ethical response if it becomes evident, for example, that the problem is more severe than previously believed, or that removal of the intervention at the prescribed time might be premature. Of course, a client or client system may have been receiving services from the social worker for some period of time before the actual BAB design was implemented. Then, it may be possible to know the situation well enough (even if measurements of the target problem were not made and recorded) to plan a time to enter the A phase that does not have potential to harm the client.

ABC, ACB, BAC, BCA, CAB, CBA.   Sometimes, we believe that several interventions have a compounding effect on a problem. We'd like to know the best order in which to introduce them to produce the maximum effect. It was noted earlier that ABC, ABCD, and so forth do not help to answer the question, Which *sequence* of interventions (designed to address a single problem) is best? A design such as ABC, ACB, BAC, BCA, CAB, CBA can answer that question. By using it, we could, for example, learn which sequence of interventions works best for a given client in reducing incidents of some form of substance abuse. We would change the sequence of interventions again and again to identify the sequence following which the greatest decline took place. The research would begin in an A phase, then introduce interventions B and C in sequence. Then the next sequence would be interventions A, C, and B, and so forth. Obviously, the use of ABC, ACB, BAC, BCA, CAB, CBA designs would not be possible with many types of target problems; it would not be suitable where a problem or behavior either disappears quickly or does not persist at some level over an extended time. However, problem recidivism is not uncommon in the human service fields. It is found in problems such as verbal abuse, truancy, delinquency, bullying, and low self-esteem.

ABAC or ABACAD.   Designs that add an A phase between each pair of interventions provide us with an indication of whether treatment carryover occurred. If it appears (from studying the data) that it did not, then a comparison of the effectiveness of various interventions is facilitated. Of course, if carryover into subsequent A phases is obvious, we may not be able to make a determination as to which intervention was the most effective for addressing the target problem.

$AB^1B^2B^3$.   If we wish to learn what intensity, quantity, or dosage of an intervention is most effective, we might use the $AB^1B^2B^3$ design or some variation of it.

Each of the B phases represents a different amount of the intervention. For example, it might be the amount of time spent in play therapy with a child during a treatment hour designed to reduce some behavioral problem or (to use a more "macro" practice example) the length of speeches in meetings designed to increase community participation. Generally, the amount of the intervention increases in each subsequent B phase. This makes it possible to learn when the intervention becomes "too much of a good thing" (the point when there is an undesirable change in the target problem). Or, it can locate the "point of diminishing returns" (when adding more of the intervention ceases to produce additional improvement in the target problem—improvement levels off).

Multiple Baseline. I have mentioned some common designs for examining the effectiveness of an intervention (the independent variable) for affecting change in a target problem (the dependent variable). Others discussed are appropriate for examining the relationship between several promising interventions (independent variables) and a single target problem (dependent variable). However, sometimes we have a promising intervention (still the independent variable) and want to learn in which of two or more situations (that often bear some relationship to each other) it might prove most effective. If this is the case, a multiple-baseline single-system design may be appropriate.

Multiple-baseline designs are commonly used in social work to determine the answer to one of three questions: (1) With which client or client system *problem* does an intervention work best? (2) In which *setting* does an intervention work best? or (3) "With which *type of client or client system* does an intervention work best?" Of course, multiple-baseline designs can be used to answer other questions too, those that entail a single intervention and multiple situations in which the intervention may be more or less effective in promoting positive changes in the dependent variable.

There are many variations of multiple-baseline designs, some quite complicated. In one of the simpler ones (illustated below), an A phase precedes the introduction of the intervention to all client problems, settings, clients, and so forth. During that phase, baseline measurements are compiled for each. Then the intervention is introduced to attempt to influence first one of them, and then (sequentially) the others. While the intervention is offered to attempt to change the first (the first B phase), baseline measurement of the others continues, thus creating an extended A phase for each of them. Then, intervention shifts to the second client problem, setting, client, and so forth while a second A phase occurs for the first dependent variable (the intervention is no longer applied to it). The third dependent variable continues in an extended baseline phase. Then, the intervention shifts to the third, while the first two are in an A phase. A final A phase may be added (or extended) after the final B phase, so that withdrawal phases can be compared for all dependent variables: client problems, settings, clients, and so forth.

Graphing the findings of a multiple-baseline design can be quite a time-consuming process when performed by hand, especially if there are three or more situations in which the intervention is introduced. These graphs are more difficult to create and interpret than the graphs of the other designs that we have examined. An example will help to illustrate this point.

Wendy leads three "socialization" groups in an in-patient psychiatric treatment facility. One group consists of adolescent boys, another of adolescent girls, and the third group consists of young adults (male and female), aged 20 to 35. Participation is voluntary, but strongly encouraged. There are potentially 20 group members in each group (20 beds for each client category), but attendance has been as low as 20 percent (4) and no higher than 55 percent (11) in any of the groups over the past year. Wendy discussed the problem of group attendance with a friend, Michael, who worked as a social worker in a high school setting and ran a voluntary group for students referred to him. He remarked that his group attendance seemed to improve after he began announcing the "agenda" for the next meeting at the conclusion of each meeting and then posting it outside his door. Since two of her groups consisted of patients about high school age, and the members of the third group were not much older, Wendy wondered whether some variation of what Michael had done might be effective with one or more of her groups, and if so, with which group it would work best. Because both her clients and her work setting were different from Michael's, and her groups met daily rather than weekly, she was uncertain whether it would work with all three or any of her groups. However, she decided to try it, using a multiple-baseline design. The graph for Wendy's research is shown in Figure 5.1.

As Figure 5.1 shows, Wendy used her intervention (announcement of the agenda for the next meeting and posting of it prior to the meeting) for two weeks (ten weekday meetings) with each of her three groups. She began with a two-week baseline with the adolescent girls (A_1), (although if she had trusted her records data, she could have used them to construct a two-week baseline for all three groups). Then, at the end of the first two weeks (day 10), she introduced her intervention to the girls' group and continued it for two weeks, during which time she continued with an extended baseline for the young adults group (A_2) and for the adolescent boys' group (A_3).

At the end of the fourth week (day 20), Wendy introduced her intervention to the young adults' group and continued it over the next two weeks. During this time, the adolescent girls' group no longer received the intervention and the adolescent boys' group continued in its extended baseline phase (A_3).

At the end of the sixth week (day 30), Wendy introduced the intervention to the adolescent boys' group and continued it for the next two weeks. As she introduced it, she withdrew it from the young adults' group. At this time (day 30) the young adults' group reentered an A phase and the adolescent girls' group continued in its second A phase for two more weeks.

Frequently, the results of multiple-baseline studies require considerable study and thought in order for the social worker to be able to draw conclusions from them. Figure 5.1 presents a relatively "clean" picture of how the independent variable (the intervention) may have affected the dependent variable (group attendance) differently with three different groups. Since the groups did not interact with each other, there was no possibility that the first introduction of the intervention

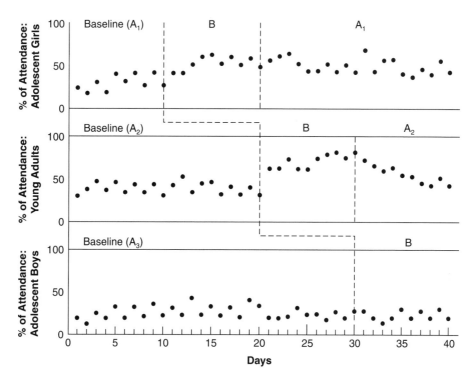

FIGURE 5.1 **Graph of Multiple-Baseline Design: Group Attendance in Three Socialization Groups**

could have produced an effect on group attendance in the other two groups. This avoided what some authors regard as a major problem in some multiple-baseline designs, "the possibility that changes associated with introduction of the first intervention with the first baseline may show up in the other baselines as well."[2] The problem is most likely to occur when the social worker wishes to learn with which related problem of a single client or client system an intervention is most effective. For example, when an intervention designed to increase social interaction is introduced to increase a client's time spent shopping, changes in shopping may also have the effect of increasing (or decreasing) other social activities, such as visiting friends and relatives, or making phone calls. The different behaviors that the intervention is designed to affect (referred to as "problem variables") are likely to be highly correlated with each other.[3]

In Figure 5.1, it is quite apparent that the intervention was most effective with the young adults; their attendance jumped quickly when it was introduced, and continued at a high level until the intervention was withdrawn (at day 30). Assuming Wendy could be reasonably certain that nothing else might have produced the increase in young adult group attendance, she had a tentative answer to her research question—the intervention seemed to work better with young adults than with adolescents. Statistical analysis (discussed below) could now be used to see if the amount of increase in the young adults' group attendance was statistically significant.

In the adolescent girls' group, the intervention was accompanied by a slight increase in attendance in weeks 11–20, but attendance continued pretty much the same after it was withdrawn. If the pool of adolescent girls had remained the same throughout the study, this might have indicated the presence of treatment carryover, a good thing. However, Wendy knew that this was a short-term treatment facility (girls came and left the facility fairly quickly), so treatment carryover could not explain the relatively stable attendance during the B and subsequent A_1 phases. Perhaps, she had only "drawn" a rather atypical time of low group attendance for her baseline (the first two weeks) and the next six weeks were a more representative sample of group attendance. If so, the intervention was probably ineffective with the adolescent girls' group.

Wendy would probably be safe in assuming that the intervention was ineffective in the adolescent boys' group. There was no noticeable increase in group attendance when the intervention was introduced (day 30), although attendance had been the lowest of all three groups during the baseline phases. However, it is possible that only a two-week intervention was not enough to increase attendance in the boys' group. Perhaps, if the intervention had lasted longer it might have produced better results.

It should be noted that Wendy may appear to have violated one principle of single-system research. Her intervention seemed to have two parts to it—the announcement and the posted notice of the agenda. That sounds like a **compound intervention,** and such interventions are generally to be avoided in single-system research ("Use one intervention with one target problem"). When they occur, it can make matters confusing. If desirable change in the target problem occurs, was it the one action that produced it, or was it the other action? Or, if no change occurred, perhaps the two parts of the intervention "canceled each other out." However, Wendy's intervention was not a true compound intervention. She really had only one intervention—publicizing the agenda of each upcoming group meeting. The two activities were only two parts of her intervention, one designed to reinforce the other. It would matter little whether it was one, or the other, or both that produced any desired changes in the target problem. Both cost little or nothing. If proven effective, Wendy could easily continue to offer both as a single intervention.

The example also illustrates another point about single-system research—the target problem need not be the major problem experienced by the client or client system. In Wendy's groups, the problem which all of the clients shared in common was shyness or a lack of social skills. A manifestation of the problem that the groups shared was a lack of verbal participation in groups. However, the target problem of her research was group attendance. Of course, group attendance is both the client problem and the group problem. Clients could not verbally participate or work on their social skills in the groups if they did not show up!

ANALYSIS OF SINGLE-SYSTEM RESEARCH DATA

As in any research, once the data have all been collected, they need to be analyzed to determine how they should be interpreted. The steps in analyzing single-system data that consists of at least one A phase and one subsequent B phase are pretty straightforward:

1. Complete a graph of the data.
2. "Eyeball" the graph to see if there even appears to be any support for the intervention's effectiveness (the research hypothesis). If they would be of assistance, use descriptive statistics to compare A and B phases.
3. If there still appears to be support for the research hypothesis, use the appropriate test of inference to determine the mathematical probability that sampling error might have made the intervention appear to be effective.
4. If statistical support for the research hypothesis was achieved, consider what threats to internal validity might have produced the changes in the target problem.

The most common statistical analyses of single-system data entail the comparison of measurements of the target problem within a true baseline phase (A) with those within the first B phase, that is, when the intervention is introduced. (It cannot be used with data from exploratory designs such as BC or BCD, which contain no A phase.) For example, suppose a social worker created a baseline by recording how many times a client made disparaging remarks to her partner during ten weeks of couple counseling sessions (baseline). Then measurements of the same variable were made during the next ten weeks (B phase) when some additional intervention (the independent variable) was present. The two sets of measurements (samples) could be compared using one or more statistical tests of inference.

In conducting statistical analysis, we recognize the fact that (1) the samples were neither randomly selected nor were they comprised using random assignment, and (2) even if they had been, the samples would still tend naturally to differ from the population from which they were drawn and from each other. Any two samples of measurements (such as those in the baseline and those in the subsequent B phase) are likely to differ somewhat, even if no intervention takes place. This is attributed to the phenomenon known as *sampling error*. So any apparent improvement in the target problem during an A phase may not be improvement at all. Either or both samples of measurements (A or B) may have only been not very representative of the true severity of the target problem. For example, suppose the target problem is self-esteem, a variable that fluctuates over time among people based on many factors. Because of sampling error (chance) we might have drawn a sample of measurements of self-esteem in the baseline phase that were among a client's lowest of the year, and the measurements in the B phase might have been among the highest for the year. It may appear that the intervention was successful, but the difference in the measurements between the two phases might have been produced by sampling error (normal fluctuations in the client's self-esteem), and not by the intervention.

We can use statistical analysis to determine the mathematical probability that any differences in the measurements of the target problem between an A phase and its subsequent B phase might have been caused by sampling error. Generally, if the differences are quite large, they are very unlikely to be the work of sampling error. However, it is not quite that simple. In determining if a difference is "large enough" we also have to factor in the size of the samples (how many measurements there were) in both the A and subsequent B phases because small samples are more prone to sampling error than larger ones. If there are only small samples of measurements, the differences in the A and B phases may have to be quite large to be statistically significant, that is, very unlikely to be the work of sampling error.

Any statistical comparison of A and subsequent B phases is based on certain somewhat questionable assumptions. They are:

1. The A phase consists of a random sample of measurements of the target problem.
2. The A phase is a reasonably accurate representation of the pattern of the dependent variable when the intervention is not present. (Sampling bias is not a factor.)
3. If the intervention were not introduced (no B phase), the same pattern of the target problem would continue.
4. Any difference between the patterns of the dependent variable in the A and subsequent B phases *may* (dependent on the research design employed) be attributable to the presence of the intervention during the B phase.

Selecting a Method of Statistical Analysis

As suggested previously, the first two assumptions are often not valid. Thus statistical analysis of single-system research data is of limited value. In addition, the sample (number) of measurements of the target problem is often small, and thus the analysis lacks statistical power. Even if the intervention is effective, finding statistical significance is unlikely. In less-common scenarios when the number of measurements is large (and the statistical analysis is thus powerful) findings of statistical significance can be equally misleading. It can lead us to make too much of an intervention that may make only a slight impact on the target problem. Nevertheless, providing some form of statistical analysis is increasingly becoming expected in reports of single-system studies, especially those that employ designs that can be described (somewhat loosely) as explanatory.

As in other types of research, two important factors in selecting a method of statistical analysis in single-system research are (1) the level of measurement of the dependent variable (the target problem), and (2) how its values are distributed. Thus, it must first be determined whether the level of measurement of the dependent variable is nominal, ordinal, or interval/ratio. (In fact, ordinal-level measurement of the target problem in single-system research is relatively rare.) If it is interval/ratio, a decision must be made as to whether the variable tends to be normally distributed around some central point (such as a mean) or not. Other factors, such as sample sizes (number of measurements that were made), or whether the number and variability of measurements in the two phases are comparable, also sometimes limit which tests should be used.

Two Widely Used Methods

Two statistical methods of statistical analysis, the two standard deviation method and the proportion/frequency method, are widely used among social work practitioners conducting single-system research. The popularity of these tests is attributable, at least in part, to the fact that they are (1) simple to use without benefit of a computer; and (2) easily understood.

The Two Standard Deviation Method. The **two standard deviation method** is often appropriate when measurements of the dependent variable are interval/ratio level. However, there is a second requirement that sometimes precludes its use. Measurements in the A phase (baseline) cannot appear to vary too widely and they should vary randomly around some central point (the mean of the measurements). Stated another way, the measurements should be relatively stable and normally distributed within the baseline phase. If the mean (for central tendency) and standard deviation (for variability) would be appropriate statistics to summarize the distribution of the measurements, the two standard deviation method is probably appropriate.

Understanding the underlying theory behind the two standard deviation method requires some knowledge of statistics. Like other statistical tests, it relies on the normal distribution (the hypothetical normal curve) and on the concept of sampling distributions. The areas of the curve allow us to determine the percent of times that a value that is a given number of standard deviations from the mean will occur because of sampling error or chance. The two standard deviation method also relies on the concept of rejection regions. A rejection region is an area of the normal curve where, if a value falls, it is possible to reject the null hypothesis. For a two-tailed research hypothesis, the rejection regions are beyond 1.96 standard deviations from the mean (either above or below it). Thus, a measurement that varies by as much as 2.0 standard deviations from the mean would occur rarely (less than 5 percent of the time). For a one-tailed research hypothesis, the rejection region falls beyond 1.58 standard deviations from the mean (but only either above or below it, depending on the direction of the hypothesis). Thus, a measurement that falls 2.0 standard deviation from the mean (in the predicted direction) would be an even rarer product of sampling error if a one-tailed research hypothesis had been used (the usual situation in single-system research).

How can we use the normal distribution and rejection regions when analyzing data with the two standard deviation method? It is a systematic process that requires little more than a calculator. If you can get a mean and a standard deviation (even if you are not totally clear about how you got them or what they mean), you can use the two standard deviation method. Here is how you would do it when using a one-tailed hypothesis:

1. Calculate both the mean and standard deviation for measurements *in the A phase only.*
2. Add two standard deviations to the mean to find the value that is two standard deviations above the mean of the baseline measurement. Subtract two standard deviations from the mean to determine the value two standard deviations below.
3. Draw a horizontal line for the mean and two bands (usually dotted lines) horizontally on the graph through the A phase and extended through the B phase. One band should be placed at the point two standard deviations above the mean, and the other point two standard deviations below the mean.
4. Decide which measurements (above the mean or below it) in the B phase would suggest that the intervention was effective.
5. Statistical significance ($p < .05$) has been achieved and the null hypothesis can be rejected if *either:* (1) the mean of all measurements *in the B phase* is outside the appropriate standard deviation band (the one either above or below the mean); or (2) any two consecutive measurements in the B phase fall outside the same standard deviation band.

As was previously noted, the measurements of the target problem are only two samples compiled at two different times (the A and B phases). Thus, we might expect them to differ somewhat, just because of sampling error. The difference in these two samples might be no more than the normal fluctuation of the dependent variable. Unless the difference is fairly large, statistical significance is unlikely to be achieved. The two conditions under which it occurs (step 5 above) using the two standard deviation method have been calculated by mathematicians using the rejection regions of the normal distribution and the laws of probability. They tell us when the difference is large enough that (mathematically) sampling error is an unlikely ($p < .05$) explanation for an apparent relationship between the intervention and changes in the target problem.

A hypothetical example may help clarify how the two standard deviation method works. Suppose that a school social worker, Katie, was counseling a 10-year-old child, Yolanda, who was very socially introverted. In the after-school program Yolanda would spend a short time interacting with the other children, and then ask to go to the school library to read. Katie wanted to learn if an intervention she planned to implement in her daily counseling (showing a series of brief videos portraying children happily playing together) might increase the amount of time that Yolanda spent interacting with the other children. So she decided to conduct a single-system research study.

Katie asked one of the adult supervisors to record how much time Yolanda spent interacting with the other children each day prior to leaving for the library.

She was timed for twenty-three consecutive school days. Katie did not offer the intervention (the A phase of the research) the first ten days. The measurements during this phase were (respectively): 16, 22, 19, 14, 19, 16, 19, 16, 18, and 13 minutes. During the next thirteen school days (the B phase), Katie offered her intervention. This time the measurements were: 18, 19, 25, 16, 25, 23, 28, 25, 18, 24, 24, 20, and 20 minutes. Katie recorded all of the measurements on a graph and then calculated the mean and standard deviation for only the ten measurements in the A phase. The mean was 17.20; the standard deviation was 2.48. She added two standard deviations to the mean of the A phase to find the location of the upper two standard deviation band. It was 17.20 + 2 (2.48) = 22.16. She subtracted two standard deviations from the mean to find the location of the lower two standard deviation band: 17.20 − 2 (2.48) = 12.24. She added the two bands that are shown in Figure 5.2, which is an example of a graph known as a Shewart chart.

Katie then computed the mean for all thirteen measurements during the B phase. It was 21.92, a little less than 22.16, so she knew she did not meet one of the requirements for a statistically significant relationship between her intervention and the changes in Yolanda's behavior. But she did meet the second one. There were at least two consecutive measurements above the upper two standard deviation band (days 20 and 21 and days 15 through 18). Thus, the change in the dependent variable that occurred when the intervention was introduced was very unlikely to have been produced by sampling error ($p < .05$). She had statistical support for the effectiveness of the intervention.

If, instead, the only consecutive measurements beyond a two standard deviation band had been below the lower two standard deviation point (below 12.24 minutes), Katie could not have claimed support for her research hypothesis. (She would have used a directional hypothesis that would have been supported only if the length of the desired behavior increased.) Of course, if this had happened, it

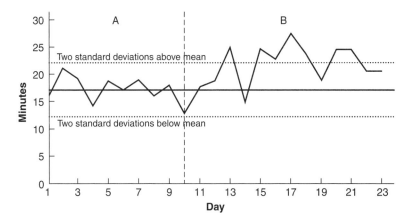

FIGURE 5.2   Single-System Study: Case 063 (Yolanda). Time Spent in Social Interaction

could be argued that the research still provided useful knowledge—it would suggest that her intervention was ineffective or even had a negative effect.

Because her design was only descriptive (AB), Katie would have to consider whether the positive change in Yolanda's behavior might have been caused by something else (threats to internal validity) other than her intervention. Perhaps, Yolanda experienced changes in her home situation somewhere about the tenth day, or simply made a friend in the after-school program sometime near the end of the baseline phase. Perhaps, it was only her growing relationship with Katie that resulted in increased confidence and a greater desire to spend time with her peers. These and other alternative explanations for the changes would still have to be considered before Katie could jump to any conclusions about the intervention's effectiveness. That's where logic and Katie's knowledge of Yolanda and of human behavior in general would be put to use.

The Proportion/Frequency Method.   In many single-system studies, the target problem is dichotomous, that is, some behavior or event simply occurs or it does not occur. When the dependent variable is only nominal level and dichotomous and there are a relatively large number of measurements in both the A and subsequent B phase (more than only a few in each), the **proportion/frequency method** is often useful. Assumptions underlying this method include:

1. Some desirable client behaviors or events (measurements of the dependent variable) occur some of the time, even during a baseline (A) phase.
2. If the intervention were not introduced after the A phase, these desirable behaviors or events would continue to occur about the same proportion of the time (the same trend would continue).
3. If desirable behaviors or events occur more frequently in the B phase than in the A phase, they *may* indicate that the intervention was effective.

Like the two standard deviation method, using the proportion/frequency method for determining if the relationship between the presence or absence of an intervention and changes in a target problem is statistically significant requires only a calculator and the use of the cumulative binomial probability distribution table. This table can be found in more advanced statistics books and in some research methods books.[4] The steps for using the proportion/frequency method are:

1. Construct a graph of the baseline (A) phase and subsequent B phase, or simply count up the number of desirable events or behaviors that occurred within each phase.
2. Determine the proportion of measurements in the A phase that reflect the desirable event or behavior (often, either "yes" or "no").
3. Count the number of desirable events or behaviors in the B phase.
4. Use a table of the cumulative binomial probability distribution to determine the minimum number of desirable events or behaviors in the B phase that is

required for statistical significance, given the number of measurements in the B phase.

When using the proportion/frequency method, the number of measurements in the A and B phases need not be the same. Thus, an A (baseline) phase need only last long enough to establish the usual pattern of the target problem, and a B phase can be scheduled to last as long as the social worker believes it might take for it to be effective.

Another example illustrates how the proportion/frequency method works. Suppose that Gwen, a social worker in a student counseling center was working with a student, Martha, who was in danger of being suspended for low grades. A major part of Martha's problem was that she often did not get up in time to attend her Tuesday morning history class and was failing it. Alarm clocks, wake-up calls from her roommate, and other usual methods did not seem to help. So Gwen wanted to see if an intervention (a review of her low-grade situation at the close of each Monday evening counseling session) might improve Martha's attendance at her Tuesday morning class. Gwen kept a record of her client's attendance over an eight-week period (while still offering her usual counseling) to form a baseline (A phase). During that time, Martha attended class three times (32.5 percent). Then she entered the B phase of her research, during which Gwen offered the intervention. Gwen constructed a graph of her research findings (Figure 5.3).

Martha attended class five times (62.5 percent attendance) during the B phase of the research. Clearly, this reflected some improvement in her attendance. Using a cumulative binomial probability distribution table, Gwen was able to determine that, with eight measurements in the B phase, and a proportion of attendance in the A phase of .325, Martha would have had to attend at least six sessions for the improvement in her class attendance to be statistically significant. Since the *p*-value

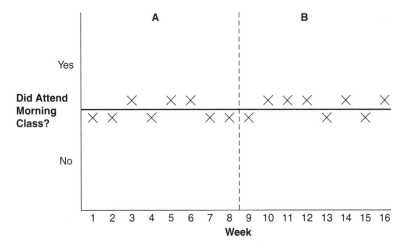

FIGURE 5.3   Single-System Study: Case 107 (Martha)

for her frequency of attendance during the B phase was greater than .05, Gwen was unable to reject the null hypothesis and conclude that her intervention had been effective. The difference between the A and B phases could have been the work of sampling error or her normal sporadic pattern of class attendance.

More Widely Known Statistical Tests

If you have studied statistics at all, you may already know and understand a number of statistical tests of inference that can be used in analyzing single-system research data. As long as their conditions for use are met, they may well do the job.

Cross-tabulation and chi-square.   If the target problem can only be measured at the nominal level (for example, rehospitalization/non-rehospitalization, attended group therapy/did not attend), some form of cross-tabulation analysis may be a possibility. There is some question about its suitability because the sample measurements (of the target problem) may not be regarded as independent as they are in a simple random sample. Nevertheless, the test is sometimes used.

Cross-tabulation involves the construction of a table with frequencies reflecting the number of times that each measurement of one variable was found with every measurement of the second variable. After cross-tabulation has been performed manually or by computer, the test most familiar to social workers, the **chi-square test** of independence can then be used. For example, if the dependent variable is *compliance with medication* (a yes or no measurement), chi-square would tell us whether the association between incidents of compliance and whether they occurred during an A phase or B phase is statistically significant.

Even if the measurements of the dependent variable are interval or ratio level but are badly skewed (do not approximate a normal distribution), cross-tabulation and the chi-square formula may be appropriate for data analysis. It would entail first using what is called the **median test,** really just a procedure for placing data into a cross-tabulation table. If performing analysis manually, there are seven relatively simple steps involved:

1. Arrange all of the measurements in order from lowest to highest to form an array.
2. Determine the median (midpoint) of the array of measurements.
3. For each measurement in the A phase, determine whether it fell below or above the median.
4. Repeat the procedure in step 3 for the B phase.
5. Enter the data into a cross-tabulation table.
6. Apply the chi-square formula to learn the p-value.
7. If $p < .05$, determine whether the disproportionately large frequencies are in the cells of the table that support the research hypothesis.

A cross-tabulation table for the median test would look like any cross-tabulation table except that the column headings would look like those in Table 5.1.

TABLE 5.1   Median Test Data: Number of Instances of Bullying by Day for the Johnson Middle School (Median = 6.4)

	NUMBER OF INCIDENTS		
Research Phase	*Above Median*	*Below Median*	*Totals*
A	21	11	32
B	11	21	32
Totals	32	32	64

$$X^2 = 5.06, df = 1, p < .025$$

The Two-Sample Independent *t*-Test.   The test sometimes can be used to analyze single-system data. The assumptions for its use are:

1. The measurements should be considered a random sample (which they often are not).
2. The data should be considered interval/ratio level and the distribution of the measurements in both phases should be "normally distributed."
3. The number of cases in the A and B phases should not be very different, nor should the amount of variability of the measurements within them.[5]

Despite these assumptions, *t*-tests are considered to be relatively robust. That means that they still provide quite accurate results even if all of these assumptions are not strictly met. The degree to which these assumptions can be violated without misleading the social worker or harming the credibility of any findings is a topic for an advanced statistics book. Before using the **two-sample independent *t*-test** for analysis of single-system data, it is probably wise to consult such a book or a statistician.

As in other tests used in single-system research, the two "samples" are the measurements in the A phase and those in the subsequent B phase. The mean of each sample of measurements is computed, and then the two sample means can be compared using the test's formula. Since it is quite complicated, a computer may be required. Generally, if the difference between the two means is quite large and in the predicted direction, it may be possible to reject the null hypothesis and conclude that the intervention was effective. However, as noted earlier, the size of the samples is a factor when determining if the difference is large enough to be statistically significant. It is part of the *t* formula.

Mann-Whitney *U*.   If it is concluded that the assumptions for using the two-sample unmatched *t*-test have not been adequately met, **the Mann-Whitney *U* test** is a good alternative. It is relatively simple to use (it only requires rank-ordering of measurements and simple arithmetic), and does not require a computer. It is a little more powerful than the median test or than chi-square, and is thus less likely to incorrectly conclude that sampling error is a likely cause for changes in the target problem (known as a type II error). The test has its own table of critical values (cutoff points for rejecting the null hypothesis). Directions for how it is performed and the table can be found in many statistics books.[6]

Statistical Significance in Perspective

In single-system research, a finding of statistical significance is of only limited assistance in concluding whether an intervention was effective. A statistical analysis that compares measurements of the dependent variable during an A phase with those during a subsequent B phase does not compare two random samples as they are normally defined. Thus, it is of limited use in telling us if the difference between the two sets of measurements is unlikely to be the result of sampling error. It certainly cannot tell us if the intervention caused any change in the target problem. The practitioner has to use his or her knowledge of human behavior, social work practice, and of the client or client system to speculate on what else may have caused it. As in all research, there is a list of "usual suspects." It is likely to include:

1. The way that the research was conducted (possible design flaws such as measurement error or sampling bias).
2. Other variables (rival hypotheses).
3. Threats to internal validity.

A finding of statistical significance also does not necessarily mean that any change in the target problem was "significant" in the more colloquial usage of the word. "Statistical significance" does not refer to magnitude or importance of the change. Especially when there are large numbers of measurements of the target problem, statistical significance often occurs even if the strength of the relationship between the intervention and the target problem is relatively weak. However, there are procedures to determine the magnitude of the effect that the intervention had. They entail computing **effect size,** a mathematical procedure described in some detail in many research methods and statistics books[7] and described in relation to the interpretation of statistical significance in program evaluations later in this book. Computing effect size can help the social worker put a finding of statistical significance in perspective. It can help to determine whether any change in the severity of a problem was a meaningful one from a practice perspective.

INTERNAL VALIDITY AND SINGLE-SYSTEM RESEARCH

If a research design consists of an A phase and a subsequent B phase, statistical analysis may provide support for a conclusion that sampling error did not produce a relationship between the intervention and a desirable change in the target problem. Computing effect size even may reveal that the magnitude of the change in the target problem was quite large. However, it would be premature to conclude that the intervention was effective. Some assessment must be made as to the degree to which the research design that was used was able to control for threats to internal validity.

Descriptive designs, those with only a small number of phases such as AB or ABA, do not offer good control of threats to internal validity. Some of the more complicated research designs mentioned earlier in this chapter are regarded as "explanatory." They do a more adequate job of controlling for other explanations of the apparent intervention success, especially threats to internal validity. As noted, they do this primarily by the use of multiple, alternating A and B phases. The assumption is, if desirable changes in the target problem consistently occur during all B phases and they consistently do not occur or occur less dramatically in the A phases, that is just "too much of a coincidence." It is probably safe to assume that nothing else but the intervention produced the changes.

In single-system research (as in outcome program evaluations—Chapters 10 and 11) the most common threats to internal validity take on specific forms. They require asking and determining the answers to certain questions related to the client and the activities of the social worker.

Two of the most commonly cited threats often present in basic research—direction of causation and instrumentation—are generally not issues in single-system research. Causation, if it exists, can flow in only one direction, from the independent variable to the dependent variable. It would not make sense to suggest that perhaps the target problem affected the intervention. Only the target problem can change; the social worker does not allow the intervention to vary in single-system research. Similarly, instrumentation cannot play a part in changes in the target problem. The social worker does not allow the measurement to vary. He or she measures the target problem in the same way or using the same data collection instrument throughout the research.

The other commonly cited threats are less easily dismissed, especially in pre-explanatory designs. How much of a threat each one poses is a function of such factors as the client or client system, the duration of the research, and the research design used. The forms that they can take in single-system research are:

1. *History.* This is a threat to internal validity in most single-system research. Over the course of the intervention, many events might have occurred that could have produced any desirable changes in the target problem. For example, the increase in a client's self-esteem may be attributable wholly or in part to the fact that she found a new partner, got a promotion, had her medication changed, or a hypercritical relative moved out of the home. Conversely, the apparent lack of success of an intervention could also be attributable to some outside event. During the intervention some event might have prevented it from producing a desirable change in the target problem (the intervention would have been successful had the event not occurred).

2. *Maturation or passage of time.* Especially if the client is a child or adolescent, maturation may help to explain desirable behavior changes such as better self-control or increased respect for authority, or undesirable changes such as adolescent rebellion or a decline in interest in school grades. The passage of time can easily explain desirable changes such as adjustment to losses or recovering from some trauma. For example, it is often difficult to know just how effective a bereavement group is. How much is the decline in client depression levels or an increase in social activities attributable to only the passage of time since the death of a loved one?

3. *Statistical regression to the mean.* If the baseline consisted of measurements of the target problem at its very worst, at a low point in its normal variability, then statistical regression to the mean may pose a threat. A social worker may have first contact with a client or client system when a target problem is most severe, bad enough to seek help or to be referred for help. Suppose a baseline is constructed during that time (as in an AB design). Then any apparent changes in the target problem during the subsequent B phase may not really be changes at all, only regression to the mean (to a pattern that is more typical of the severity of the target problem).

4. *Testing.* The repeated measurement of the target problem over time itself (rather than the intervention) may have produced improvement in it. Clients might have learned from the measurement instrument (testing) in some way that affected the target problem, or the testing may otherwise have positively influenced it. For example, after repeated measurements using the same instrument, a client may eventually surmise from it how she should behave in some social situation and adjust her behavior accordingly during a B phase. It was the testing (not the intervention) that produced the desirable change in client behavior.

5. *Selection bias.* There are usually two or more "samples" in single-system research—those measurements taken during the A phase(s) and those taken during the B phase(s). Relevant pre-existing differences between the A and B phase(s) might explain the difference in measurements of the target problem between A and B phases. For example, perhaps the social worker took all measurements of self-confidence within a baseline (A) phase while the client was unemployed and took all measurements in the subsequent B phase when he was working again. It might appear that the intervention increased the client's self-confidence. However, the "control group" (A phase) and "experimental group" (B phase) were not equivalent to begin with. They differed in an important way—the client's employment status.

6. *Experimental mortality.* Experimental mortality refers to loss of clients or research subjects in a way that produces an apparent relationship between the independent and dependent variables. For example, clients in a marital enrichment program who view the program as a waste of time are likely to drop out of the program. A measurement of the remaining clients' attitudes about the program would suggest that it is more successful than if all of its clients could have been surveyed. In single-system research, experimental

mortality could work in different ways. Remember, the *samples* compared in single-system research are the A and B phases. The *measurements* of the target problem within each sample are the equivalent of cases in other forms of research. Thus experimental mortality would have to be loss of *measurements* in a way that would affect the representativeness of one or both samples.

Suppose the single-system is a treatment group and the social worker is testing whether some intervention will decrease shyness among its members. The group could lose clients in a way that might affect the findings. For example, suppose the baseline (A) measurements of the treatment group's participation are taken early in the group's existence with all members present. However during the intervention, group members continually drop out of the group. Will they be a cross section of group members (in relation to shyness)? Not necessarily—they are most likely to be among the group's shyest members, and thus some of the highest measurements of shyness may be lost from the B phase. The shyness level of the group will decline during the B phase. But the appearance of intervention success in reducing group shyness may be the result of experimental mortality.

Now suppose the single-system is an individual client who is being counseled twice a week for clinical depression on an outpatient basis. There is only one client, so client loss cannot occur. However, loss of measurements can occur. During the B phase, the client is hospitalized for two weeks following a suicide attempt. No measurements of clinical depression can be taken for those two weeks. When comparing the measurements in the A phase with the remaining B phase measurements, the client appears less depressed in the B phase than in the A phase. The intervention appears to have been successful. However this may be an illusion produced by experimental mortality because measurements at the time that the target problem was most severe were not able to be included in the B phase.

In single-system research, experimental mortality and selection bias may operate a little differently, but they have a similar effect. Both can produce samples (A and B phases) that differ in some important way and thus affect the validity of a comparison of the two.

7. *Overlap of "treatments."* This a common threat to internal validity in single-system research. There are many ways that the overlap of treatments can make it especially difficult to determine just how much desirable change in the target problem is attributable to the intervention—I will mention only two of them. For example, if the intervention is an "add-on," clients may receive the usual help during A phases. Subsequent improvement in a B phase may be attributable either all or in part to what was offered during the A phases and continued into the B phase—the usual help offered.

Suppose the intervention is not an "add-on." It has been substituted for the usual help offered (perhaps in a BAB design). Clients may continue to practice some skill during the A phase that was learned as part of a previous intervention (B phase). The intervention was not completely absent; the A phase was not a true control group. Then when there is another B phase, the "success" identified in this second B phase may be attributable all or in part to what occurred in the previous A phase.

REPORTS OF SINGLE-SYSTEM STUDIES

After traditional, quantitative research studies are conducted, it is expected that a report will be written describing both the research methods and what was learned from them. It has a more-or-less standard format consisting of:

1. An introduction emphasizing the importance of the research and the broad questions addressed by the research.
2. A review of relevant literature, followed by hypotheses and/or specific research questions and operational definitions.
3. A methodology section (including any methodological limitations).
4. The major findings of the research.
5. Discussion of the findings.
6. Conclusions and recommendations for both practice and future research.

Because single-system research usually is conducted primarily for the benefit of the individual practitioner, full reports are not usually written. However, reports of especially interesting single-system studies are sometimes presented in staff meetings or other venues, such as conferences, where fellow professionals gather. They also are now appearing more frequently in our professional literature. The subjects in published reports range from individual clients to larger systems such as organizations and even communities. I believe this trend is a good one, even if the findings of the studies have little or no external validity. both helps to grant legitimacy to single-system studies as a form of evaluation research, and provides models of well-designed studies that readers can emulate.

When reports of single-system studies are published, they tend to look quite different from reports of other types of research. Primarily, they are more narrowly focused. They may consist of the following sections:

1. A description (de-identified for reasons of confidentiality) of the client or client system and the target problem.
2. A focused review of relevant literature with special emphasis on (1) what is known generally about the problem, (2) methods of intervention that have been used to address it in the past, and (3) methods that have been used successfully with similar problems. The literature is used to build a rationale for why the current intervention seemed to have potential for success and why it took the form that it did. The literature review also provides a justification (ethical, logistical, and so forth) for the research design that was used.

3. A methodology section stating precisely what the intervention was, how the target problem was operationalized, and how the research design was implemented.
4. Findings, presented in the form of a graph and, if appropriate, the results of statistical analysis of the data.
5. Discussion of the findings, with special emphasis on threats to internal validity.
6. If the intervention appears to have been successful, recommendations for replicating the research with other clients or client systems or for making changes in the research design that might result in more definitive conclusions about its effectiveness.

CONCLUDING THOUGHTS

Design variations are used to attempt to answer different questions, to attempt to control for threats to the internal validity of findings, and to avoid conflict with professional values and practice ethics. We looked at a few of the simpler designs with emphasis on when they are most appropriate. Some are considered exploratory, some descriptive, and some explanatory. We also examined some of the most common statistical methods for examining the possible effects of sampling error (chance) on relationships between the independent and dependent variables in single-system designs. They are limited, but somewhat useful in those designs that seek support for findings of association, or a cause–effect relationship, between variables.

The tests that were mentioned are among those most commonly used to analyze single-system data. While the list is by no means comprehensive, I would estimate that at least 75 percent of single-system research that uses statistical analysis uses one of the tests mentioned.

As stressed throughout this chapter and the previous one, the primary focus of single-system research is to objectively determine if some intervention of an individual practitioner produced a desired change in a problem experienced by a client or client system. That is consistent with a book on evaluation research. However, the methods of single-system research have other utility as well. It has been observed that they are sometimes required by funding organizations to verify the success of a program by documenting a certain number of "successful case outcomes."[8] While this practice would seem to lend objectivity to a program evaluation, I would question how accurately the data are likely to be reported if a program's funding is depending on it.

Single-system research is sometimes used in still other ways by social work professionals who rarely or never have direct contact with clients but whose work indirectly affects them. For example, supervisors or managers sometimes use single-system research to see if their intervention (perhaps how they interact with a staff member) will have a positive effect on his or her behavior or attitude toward clients. A manager might also design a single-system study to objectively evaluate whether some "intervention" (such as providing light refreshments) will increase the percent of professional staff members who are on time to the weekly staff meeting. Undoubtedly, the methods of single-system research are also used by some social work supervisors and managers to evaluate the effectiveness of other "interventions" that are even less closely related to client problems; for example, to get staff members to move toward a "paperless" office, or just to wash their coffee cups!

KEY TERMS

exploratory designs	compound intervention	median test
descriptive designs	two standard deviation method	two-sample independent *t*-test
explanatory designs	proportion/frequency method	Mann-Whitney *U* test
multiple-baseline designs	chi-square test	effect size

STUDY QUESTIONS

1. What can a descriptive design tell us about changes in the target problem that an exploratory design cannot tell us? Why?

2. When is the AB design most appropriate?

3. When would a design such as ABC, ACB, BAC, BCA, CAB, CBA be most likely to be used?

4. What is treatment carryover? Is it regarded as an indication that an intervention has been unsuccessful? Explain.

5. When would a design such as $AB^1B^2B^3$ be most appropriate?

6. What are three questions that can be answered using multiple-baseline designs?

7. What two "usual" threats to internal validity are not an issue in single-system research? Why are they not a problem?

8. When using statistical analysis, what two samples of measurements of the dependent variable are compared?

9. When using the two standard deviation method, what indicates that the relationship between the independent and dependent variables is statistically significant?

10. When would the proportion/frequency method be most likely to be used for statistical testing?

REFERENCES

1. Bloom, M., Fischer, J., & Orme, J. (2003). *Evaluating practice: Guidelines for the accountable professional,* (4th ed.). Boston: Allyn & Bacon, 400–427.
2. Ibid., 436.

3. Tripodi, T. (1994). *A primer on single subject design for clinical social workers.* Washington, DC: NASW Press, 109.

4. Rubin, A., & Babbie, E. (2001). *Research methods for social work* (4th ed.). Belmont, CA: Wadsworth/Thomson Learning.

5. Bloom, Fischer, & Orme, op. cit., 610

6. See, e.g., Abrami, P., Cholmsky, P., & Gordon, R. (2001). *Statistical analysis for the social sciences: An interactive approach.* Needham Heights, MA: Allyn & Bacon, 563.

7. See, e.g., Rubin & Babbie, op. cit., 527–532; or Weinbach, R., & Grinnell, R., Jr. (2004). *Statistics for social workers* (6th ed.). Boston: Allyn & Bacon, 95–96.

8. Unrau, Y., Gabor, P., & Grinnell, R., Jr. (2001). *Evaluation in the human services.* Itasca, IL: F. E. Peacock, 201.

. . . . .

CHAPTER SIX

TODAY'S PROGRAM EVALUATIONS: SOME COMMON ISSUES

Chapter 4 began the examination of single-system research by identifying some of the many characteristics that all single-system research studies have in common. When looking at program evaluations we are immediately impressed with how much they differ from each other. Even among evaluations that share a common purpose (for example, needs assessments or outcome evaluations) no two are ever exactly alike, even in those instances when an evaluation is loosely described as a "replication" of another, or when two programs are required by some outside entity to apply the same methods of evaluation.

Well, what do all program evaluations have in common? They all judge the merit, worth, or value of a program. In doing so, they examine one or more indicators of the success of a proposed, existing, or previously existing program. However, another commonality is that they must all wrestle with some difficult issues. These issues usually exist because of the sensitive political environment that characterizes most social programs. This chapter examines some of the issues that affect all program evaluations. The chapters that follow identify some that are unique to particular types of evaluation.

WHY ARE PROGRAM EVALUATIONS SOMETIMES REQUESTED?

Up to this point, I have been a little idealistic in looking at today's evaluation research and why it is conducted. It is easy to be idealistic when discussing single-system research. After all, despite ethical requirements that we evaluate our practice effectiveness (Chapter 1), very few supervisors or administrators require that social workers use single-system research for this purpose. So when it is used, it is generally because a social worker *wants* valid feedback—to know if what he or she did was effective with a given client or client system. Generally there is no ulterior motive for conducting single-system research except wanting to be a better practitioner—a knowledge-based one.

It is also fairly easy to be idealistic when discussing program evaluations in general and why we *should* conduct them. It is our ethical responsibility to judge the merit, worth, or value of programs and to make informed decisions about their futures. However, the real reasons why program evaluations are sometimes requested are not always so noble, and we need to be aware of them.

Undoubtedly, many program evaluations are requested because someone (a manager, a board of directors, or program staff) simply wants to know how to create the best possible program or to improve an existing one. Many needs assessments are requested to learn if a proposed or existing program is needed and, if so, what form it should take. Other program evaluations are requested because someone really is unsure of whether a program is effective and wants to know whether it is or not in order to make an informed decision about its future. Still others are requested simply to learn ways in which a good program can be improved. All of these are good, legitimate reasons for requesting program evaluations. Like good research of any kind, they seek knowledge to help in the process of decision making. However, we would be very naive if we thought those are the only reasons why program evaluations are requested. Some other reasons are far less legitimate, constructive, or ethical. What's more, they also provide ethical dilemmas for those people who are requested to conduct them and even for those who simply are asked to supply data for them.

To Find Justification for a Program

An administrator or board of directors may have already concluded that a particular program *is* needed and *will* be implemented. There are many reasons for making such a decision. It may entail yielding to political pressure from outside the organization. Or it may be that one powerful individual on the board just likes the idea of such a program, perhaps after learning about a similar one elsewhere, and thinks the organization should have one too. The goal of requesting the program evaluation would then be to find justification for the program. The evaluator might be told either subtly or directly to ignore any findings that suggest that the program is unneeded or otherwise not appropriate. However, to comply with such a directive would be unethical. No ethical researcher wants to be a part of research where unpopular findings will not be allowed to surface.

To Validate and Continue a Program

Sometimes program evaluations must be conducted—there is no choice. They are conducted because they are required for a program to continue to exist. That means there is a lot at stake—jobs, funding, reputation of the organization, and so forth. The mandatory nature of these evaluations and the consequences of receiving a poor "grade" can influence programs to "cheat" a little on them.

Accredited Programs.   Some programs (some of the more permanent ones) cannot operate unless they demonstrate certain characteristics. They need to become accredited and then periodically reaccredited. Typically, this process entails conducting a self-study reporting its findings, and then submitting to a site visit by persons outside the program. Is a cumbersome self-study process something that a program's staff would choose to do? Probably not. Can it be a constructive activity that often results in a better program? Yes, that happens quite frequently. However, the managers and staff of a program seeking accreditation or reaccreditation are sometimes far more interested in ensuring that the program continues than they are interested in using the accreditation process to improve their program.

Program managers sometimes do not want the self-study report to be an honest, valid indicator of the quality of the program, one that reveals all of the program's weaknesses as well as its strengths. Similarly, a program's staff members are unlikely to reveal major problems with the program or to reveal too many minor ones and thus jeopardize accreditation or reaccreditation. A program director seeking accreditation or reaccreditation for a program may be unlikely to present a completely honest picture of its functioning, unless he or she is absolutely certain that the program is a stellar one. What is sought instead is a description of the program in the best possible light. It identifies some problems, but only to enhance the report's credibility. The "problems" might even really reflect positively on the program. For example, a "problem" identified by a self-study might be, "Because of the program's reputation in the community, we have often had to put clients with acute needs on a three-week waiting list."

The deception is likely to continue into the ubiquitous site visit. When site visitors meet with staff, few if any staff members will air their grievances or share their concerns about the program—not if they wish to continue to be employed. (If there is a resident malcontent, she or he is likely to be assigned to work out-of-town for the duration of the visitors' visit.) Other groups (community leaders, clients, fellow professionals) are rarely picked to meet with the site visitors using random sampling methods. "Typical" representatives of these groups are likely to be people known to be favorable to the program. They are "friends," people who can be depended on to say all the right things and to describe how wonderful the program is.

What about the people who conduct accreditation reviews? Surely, they do their best to achieve honest, valid findings, right? Ideally, yes, but in reality, not necessarily. Site visitors and accreditation teams are often volunteers drawn from the staff of other similar programs, programs that are also subject to accreditation review. Their own programs will be reviewed someday, perhaps by one or more people employed by the program that they are reviewing. An informal **quid pro quo** has been known to occur—"I will overlook some program shortcoming and, in turn, some of the shortcomings of my program will be overlooked when my turn comes."

If one or more evaluators are employed by the accrediting body (the "national office"), they may also tend to overlook problems in a program. Accredited programs pay annual dues to their accrediting body, often a major source of income for the national office. In addition, it is desirable for a national accrediting body to have accredited programs in most, if not all, geographical regions. Unless a program has major flaws that cannot be ignored (for example, a major ethical violation or financial impropriety), there is often a tendency on the part of reviewers to "give them the benefit of the doubt." Thus, all too often, an accreditation review entails collusion between program staff members and evaluators, all of whom may have an investment in a program being accredited or reaccredited.

What I have just described sounds quite cynical about accreditation and reaccreditation reviews as program evaluations. Certainly not all of the problems that were described occur in all reviews, and none of them may occur in a given review. However, the pressure to become and to remain accredited can be great. It comes from many sources. Because of this pressure, otherwise skilled, ethical researchers may be tempted to make certain "compromises." When this happens, accreditation and reaccreditation processes become more an exercise in politics that one in ethical program evaluation.

Grant and Contract Funded Programs.   Programs with major external funding (usually time-limited ones) are also subject to periodic evaluation. Depending on the requirements of the funding source, evaluation may be regular and ongoing over the life of a grant or contract or may be mandatory only at, or near, its end (when renewal or extension for another specified period is sought). From the perspective of the program, the situation is similar to one in which accreditation or reaccreditation is sought. Unless the managers and staff have no desire for the program to continue or have already found funding elsewhere, they are likely to do everything possible to make the program look good. They are less likely to seek an honest evaluation of it. There are many ways that program staff can cause a program to appear better than it really is. They might entail hiding problems, misrepresenting data, losing records, and so forth. These methods cross into the realm of the unethical, and sometimes the illegal.

If program staff members conduct an evaluation, the likelihood of its being an honest one is diminished; the evaluators just have too much of an investment in the program's success. If outside evaluators employed by the funding organization are used (a common practice), an objective, valid, and ethical evaluation is more likely to occur. However, because they are not employees of the program, the evaluators must depend on staff members to orient them to it. They may not know which questions to ask or where to look for problems. Problems can be hidden or evaluators can be otherwise deceived.

Sometimes, evaluators are drawn from other programs supported by the funding organization, perhaps from similar programs in another state. On the surface, that would seem like a good compromise. The evaluator knows what to look for, yet is unlikely to try to cover up problems in the program that exist. However, with evaluators drawn from other programs, there is the potential for other difficulties. An evaluator may be a good administrator or a good program staff member, but he or she may lack the research skills necessary to conduct a good evaluation. It is also possible that an unfair, hypercritical evaluation may occur. An evaluator may try too hard to make the program look bad. Why? The evaluator may be competing for funding with the program being evaluated. His or her program may thus stand to gain at the expense of the program being evaluated. Even if this kind of "zero sum game"[1] does not exist, there may still be a tendency on the part of the evaluator to "run down" someone else's program in order to try to make his or her own program look better by comparison.

To Be Able to Respond to Criticism

Sometimes the real reason why a program evaluation is requested is not the reason stated. There may be hidden agenda. One reason why an evaluation may be requested is that it can make it easier for an administrator to respond to impending criticism or scandal. The goal is to reduce criticism of a program or to be able to better respond to its critics.

Many social programs (especially those in the public sector) operate in what can be described as a hostile task environment. Because their services or those they serve are unpopular (for example, income maintenance, work with people who are illegal aliens, work with sex offenders), many influential people and segments of the general public would like nothing better than to "expose" and discredit them. For example, they might wish to learn that clients are abusing the services offered, or that eligibility requirements for a tax-supported food stamp program are not being met. Suppose that there is a problem of this nature (some "irregularity" involving a small percentage of clients) and that an independent investigation is underway. The program manager has learned that its results will be the subject of a future newspaper article or a future segment on the six o'clock news. What can be done?

A manager in such a situation cannot prevent the "bad press" from occurring. However, it is possible to request a program evaluation designed to gain more insight into the problems in the program and to generate recommendations for correcting them. Then, when the "exposé" occurs, the manager can be interviewed and respond with something like this: "Yes we are aware of the problem and are very concerned about it. In fact, we have already begun a full-scale program evaluation to better understand how it was allowed to occur and to take the necessary remedial action to see that it cannot reoccur."

In theory, a program evaluation initiated to be able to respond to impending criticism can still produce some worthwhile findings that can improve the program and thus benefit its clients. However, evaluations initiated for this reason or similar "political" ones rarely are well planned or thought out. They tend to be "thrown together" quickly, because timing is so important. This reduces the likelihood that anything of value will be learned.

To Justify Planned Program Changes

Program evaluations are supposed to suggest changes, changes designed to improve programs. They are not supposed to provide justification for program changes that someone has already decided to make. However, especially if the changes are likely to be unpopular, that is exactly why some program evaluations are requested.

Personnel Changes.   A program evaluation is sometimes requested not to improve a program, but to "get the goods on" a person within the program, usually a manager. If the program is indeed being mismanaged and it is believed that it is being jeopardized by the manager's presence, conducting a program evaluation for this purpose may have some justification. However, suppose for example, that some members of the board of directors of an organization simply do not like the way a program is being managed or do not like its manager. They may want to fire the manager, perhaps because he or she has not been as responsive to their preferences as they would like, or the manager simply has a different managerial style than they are accustomed to seeing. Yet, the program appears to be successful, and the manager is well-liked by subordinates within the program. The board might request an **administrative audit,** a kind of program evaluation that focuses on how well managed the program is, and which identifies areas of mismanagement. The evaluation is almost certain to identify some weaknesses of the manager (everyone has them), especially if the evaluator is told in advance why the evaluation is being conducted and told where to look for problems. Then they can be used to justify firing or demoting the manager.

There is nothing inherently wrong with administrative audits or other evaluation methods that place heavy emphasis on an individual staff member's performance. They can be useful in themselves, or as one component of a broader program evaluation, but only *if* they are conducted with an open mind and designed to provide data for improving a program. For example, they can be used to identify problems that a manager is having so that the manager can get needed assistance or to help a board of directors decide *if* a manager needs to be replaced. However, if a decision has already been made to fire or demote an individual and the real purpose of an administrative audit is to merely find documentation for the decision (while ignoring any evidence to the contrary), the decision to conduct the evaluation is not an ethical one. Besides, if the reason for the evaluation is quite transparent (as is often the case), its findings are unlikely to convince those staff members who like and respect the manager that the change is a good one. More likely, they will only become more resentful of the change than they would have been if the "charade" of an evaluation had never been conducted. The evaluation can also cause staff members to mistrust and be skeptical of the findings of other program evaluations, including those conducted for all the right reasons.

When evaluations are used to justify predetermined personnel actions, ethical questions exist for just about everyone. The evaluator can easily be in a "no win" situation. Suppose a potential evaluator discovers that such a hidden agenda exists before an agreement has been reached or a contract signed to conduct the evaluation. He or she can (and should) just refuse to conduct it. But if an evaluator learns that there is a hidden agenda after starting an evaluation (a fairly common occurrence), he or she can still refuse to provide anything other than a fair, complete evaluation. This would be the correct, ethical response. However, it would undoubtedly antagonize the person or groups who requested it, and would make it unlikely that the evaluator will be called on again. Others outside the organization may learn of what happened (probably in a distorted version) and avoid using the evaluator. Fearing these and other possible repercussions, some evaluators might simply give the individual or group what they want. That would be a breach of research ethics.

Even staff members who are asked simply to provide certain, selective data are put into an ethical bind. They can refuse to provide damaging information and risk the anger of their bosses, if not their jobs. Or they can provide it as directed and have to live with the fact that they played a part in an unethical use of the evaluation process.

Situations in which program evaluations are used to justify personnel actions are fairly common, especially in cases where staff may be unionized or cannot be easily fired or demoted without adequate cause. A program evaluation such as an administrative audit can provide an organization with supportive evidence if a fired or demoted employee files a lawsuit against the organization or its leaders, or files a complaint with a labor union or a group such as a Human Affairs Commission. However, the use of one can also backfire—it can be used as evidence that people in the organization were "out to get" the employee. It is understandable that people in human service organizations would want to try to protect themselves against accusations of discriminatory personnel practices—they can be very embarrassing for an organization dedicated to fairness and justice, even if they have no basis in fact. However, there are better, more ethical ways than misusing program evaluations to justify the decision to fire or demote someone, for example, by performing regular performance evaluations and through the process known as "progressive discipline."

Program Modification. Sometimes administrators of an organization may request a program evaluation to justify making program changes that appear to be needed. For example, a program may appear to be "top heavy" (too many managers and not enough direct service workers) or its supervisory structure may seem ineffective. Suppose the administrator of the organization where an internally funded program resides perceives the program to be overstaffed or overfunded, while other programs and the organization as a whole are struggling. Based on the administrator's limited observations, the program has a budget surplus or its staff members seem to have too much free time. Assuming any of these perceptions is accurate, in the ideal world, the director of the program might volunteer to "help out" other programs by offering to shift some of the program's funds, sharing some of its travel money, or by loaning staff to other programs. In the real world, this would be less likely to happen. Program directors often get possessive about "their" program and its resources and would rather hide their surpluses or spend them unnecessarily than give them up. Thus, the organization's administrator might request a program evaluation, part of which might be a budget audit, a review of the program's accounting system, or an analysis of the job descriptions and salaries of its staff members. The goal of the evaluation would be to examine the program's resources and to justify reallocating those that appear to be excessive. Any "surpluses" thus identified would be used to justify budget cuts for the program that might free up resources for use in other programs or for the organization's general operating expenses. (Of course, if the program's funding originates outside the organization, such a shift in resources would probably be impossible, and there would be no value (to the administrator) in conducting such an evaluation.)

Conducting an evaluation to justify changes in a program that may be over-funded or otherwise appears to be inefficient may be very legitimate. If the reason is pretty much out in the open (no duplicity), and the results are presented and used honestly and fairly, this can be a good use of a program evaluation. There is nothing inherently unethical about this practice, even though staff within the program may bitterly resent it. If the evaluation results in a leaner, more efficient program and improvement in other programs as well, it can produce a "win-win" situation for the organization.

When might an evaluation designed to justify changes in a program be unethical? There may be no evidence that the program needs to be changed. The evaluation may be performed simply out of jealousy or to harass the program, to try to raid its resources, or for some other self-serving reason. Or, as is the situation when an evaluation is used to justify a planned personnel action, if the person requesting it has already decided what he or she plans to do, is not open to changing his or her mind, and will only selectively use the results of the evaluation to justify it. ("I've made up my mind, don't confuse me with the facts!") In these instances, what could be a legitimate reason for a program evaluation has been perverted.

To Justify Program Termination

Sometimes, the administrator or the board of directors has concluded that a program must go. The program might even be an effective one and a popular one among staff members. However, it may be very unpopular with some segment of the general population and may thus threaten the organization's relationship with the community or its sources of funding. Examples might be programs that dispense birth control devices to single adolescents, resettle certain refugee groups, or that seek to reintroduce people with mental illness to the community by lodging them in group homes. For whatever reason (legitimate or not) and despite the good the program is doing, it has become a liability for the organization and for its other programs. It is a political lightning rod. Perceiving this to be the case, a program evaluation might be requested hoping to find one or more "legitimate reasons" (ones that staff members cannot dispute) why the program should be discontinued, thus attempting to defuse any resentment about its discontinuation.

Is this an appropriate use of a program evaluation? It might be, but only if (1) the evaluation examines both program effectiveness *and* the sources of resistance to the program, (2) the evaluation is conducted objectively and data are not selectively reported, and (3) those people who request it remain open to changing their opinion about the program and its future pending the findings of the evaluation. However, if the decision has already been made that the program must go, an evaluation would waste valuable resources and would accomplish nothing. It might only increase resentment among those people who provided data that were apparently ignored. If nothing learned through a program evaluation will reverse the decision to terminate a program, it would be better to simply "bite the bullet" and announce its termination, explaining why it is necessary for the good of the organization.

OTHER ETHICAL ISSUES

The questionable reasons for requesting program evaluations that were just described present a variety of interrelated ethical issues. A common denominator in many of them is that they seek to use program evaluations to justify some decision that has already been made. They are not designed to judge the merits, worth, or value of a program and to improve a program in some way. It is probably safe to say that people who use evaluation research in these ways are often using it unethically, even if the decision might be the correct one. That is *not* how program evaluations are supposed to be used. In addition, program evaluations are time consuming and expensive—they are a wasteful use of an organization's resources in order to accomplish a job that could be better and more ethically accomplished in some other way.

A second ethical issue that comes up when a program evaluation has a hidden agenda relates directly to the person conducting the evaluation. What should he or she do in situations where the purpose of the evaluation is suspect? Ethically, the evaluator should either refuse to conduct an evaluation that is requested for the wrong reasons, or conduct it but present the findings objectively, whether or not they meet the requirements of those who sought the evaluation. But what if the evaluator is employed within the program or is an employee of the organization? It is very difficult to refuse a request from the boss. If the evaluator sought is not an employee of the organization, the ethical response is a little easier—it is to refuse to conduct anything other than a complete, objective evaluation. However, in the real world, refusing to conduct a slightly biased evaluation might only mean that someone else will do it. That person may have fewer ethical concerns relating to it and might be even more inclined to compromise the evaluation's objectivity. Once again, there is no easy answer to an ethical dilemma.

Sometimes, it is not too hard to *know* what is ethical or unethical. However, in the real world where political and pragmatic concerns often also must be addressed, what to *do* is not always so obvious or so simple. The reason we describe a situation as an ethical dilemma is that there is no simple way (and sometimes, no right or wrong way) to resolve it.

It is easy to say that the ethical way to conduct a program evaluation should always entail conducting the evaluation as objectively as possible, presenting findings honestly and openly, and "letting the chips fall where they may." Our own (NASW) code of ethics describes sixteen ethical responsibilities of social workers who participate in evaluation and research. Most of them relate to protection of research participants, an issue that was discussed in relation to single-system research in Chapter 4 and that will come up again in later chapters. However, one standard (Standard 5.02n) clearly relates to deliberate misrepresentation of research findings. It states that, "Social workers should report evaluation and research findings accurately. They should not fabricate or falsify results and should take steps to correct any errors later found in published data using standard publication methods."[2] The standard is quite clear. We can say with certainty that it would be unethical for a manager, an evaluator, or someone else to deliberately misrepresent a program's success or otherwise distort the findings of an evaluation in order to save his or her own job or to otherwise profit from it. However, beyond that, things get a little murky.

For example, suppose that a program manager must demonstrate a program is effective in order to secure another round of outside funding. The program is having some successes, but by purely objective standards, it has not achieved its projected outcomes. However, the program is making changes, and the manager honestly believes that, with some more time, the program will be a very good one. Should the data be manipulated a little or some of it omitted to portray the program in a somewhat better light? Would that be unethical? Based on the NASW standard, it would appear to be. However, the manager might argue that many other ethical requirements for professional practice relate to the best interests of our clients. What about the program's clients? If the program were to be discontinued, its clients will no longer be served. What about its staff members, who might lose their jobs and experience major personal problems if the program were to be discontinued? Wouldn't attempting to save the program by manipulating the data a little just be a way of the manager advocating for the program's staff?

An issue always has (at least) two sides to it, usually with a compelling argument for each. Now look at the other side of this issue—why the data *should* be presented fairly and completely, even if it jeopardizes the future of the program, its clients, and its staff. It relates to the evaluator's responsibility to others. Does the manager have an ethical responsibility to the organization that provided funding for the program? Yes! What about the people who donate money to the funding organization, expecting that it will be used in the most productive way? Yes, the program is accountable to them too. What about clients in general? They deserve the best we can offer them. Perhaps, if the program is discontinued based on an honest evaluation, the money that would have been used to continue to support it can be used to support some other, more effective social program instead.

This ethical dilemma can be resolved. The manager can conduct an honest, objective evaluation of the program *and* include data to indicate that the program is improving, and with more time can be likely to achieve its objectives. This approach may or may not save its funding, but the evaluator will have done what is ethically correct. Often, a compromise solution of this type can be achieved. It only involves a little more thought and a little more work than an unethical response to the dilemma.

Program evaluations create many ethical dilemmas. Because there is often so much at stake (funding, jobs, reputation, and so forth), some ethically questionable practices will inevitably occur. It is important that we recognize the issues involved and come to decisions that we can live with as professionals.

PROGRAM COMPONENTS AND THEIR MEANINGS

Chapter 3 observed that today's program evaluations focus on a program's effectiveness and efficiency. This is done by carefully examining certain program components, those characteristics that both provide a program with its unique identity and also suggest the degree to which it will be or has been successful. In the context of program evaluation, several familiar terms are used to describe a program's key components. Chapter 9 will show how they can be used in combination to reflect the degree of integration of a program (the "logic model"). The discussion now illustrates each of the program's key components using a common example, an after-school program for children who would otherwise be alone in the home.

Inputs

Inputs are the resources expended for a program. Every program has its costs. Often, inputs are a combination of resources contributed from outside the organization and from the organization that houses the program. The input that comes from the program's organization is often referred to as the "match," and reflects its commitment to, and willingness to share in, the expenses of the program. Many inputs of a program are reflected in its budget; some are less easily expressed in monetary terms. Many are tangible; others are less tangible.

Some inputs are standard in all programs; others are unique to a program or at least to a particular kind of program. Examples of inputs in all programs would be funding, staff (paid and volunteer), and facilities—a program needs money and people to run it and it has to be located somewhere. When we get much beyond those three, inputs tend to depend on the program. For example, in one after-school program, inputs might include art supplies, printed educational materials, transportation, first-aid materials, and parent volunteers. In another after-school program, computer software and sports equipment might constitute additional inputs, but art supplies, transportation, and parent volunteers might not.

Constraints

Very few, if any, programs are totally free to do whatever they wish. Their **constraints** take many forms, including laws, mandates, regulations, rules, procedures, or funding requirements. They share a common characteristic—they limit the nature and extent of a program. In a less rigid way, the mission of the organization in which a program is housed is often another constraint. A program needs to provide services that are consistent with the organization's mission. For example, if the organization seeks to serve low-income families, our after-school program cannot be offered free of charge to just anyone. However, we might be able to open it to a limited number of children from more affluent homes on a pay-for-services basis, if we can justify the decision on the basis that their fees (an input) would help subsidize the cost of the program and thus make it available to more low-income children.

Many programs must meet licensure requirements. The requirements for becoming and remaining licensed are constraints. In an after-school program, there might be requirements regarding staff-child ratios, provision of meals, presence of a registered nurse or other health care professional, credentials of the program director and other staff members, and so forth. Other constraints related to health and safety might include requirements related to room temperatures, availability of potable drinking water, isolation of children with infectious diseases, and so forth.

In a program evaluation, we do not evaluate a program's constraints—they constitute a "given." However, fairness dictates that a program's services, what it offers or does not offer, its accomplishments, and so forth should be evaluated within the context of the constraints under which the program operates. Thus, good program evaluations often tend to qualify any judgments of a program with reference to its constraints.

Activities

A program's **activities** are what a program's staff does. It is how it uses its inputs to try to produce desirable outcomes. Activities are implemented in such a way that, it is believed, they will address some problem of the program's clients, either directly or indirectly. Those activities designed to directly serve clients are its services (defined earlier). However, some other activities (especially those offered by managers and administrators) may be designed to support staff members who offer those services and the program in general. They only indirectly serve clients. For example, a program's director may be involved in activities such as public relations, fund raising, or recruitment of volunteers. While these activities are not client services per se, they make services possible and increase the likelihood that they will be successful. Thus, they are a focus of a program evaluation.

In our after-school program example, activities of the program might include individual counseling, social-skills-building groups, tutoring, educational field trips, or planned recreation. However, other important activities that are not direct services to clients would include publicizing the program in a variety of settings, screening of applicants, seeking corporate donations, and holding Friday afternoon meetings for staff to voice their concerns about the program.

Outputs

Outputs are the products of program activities. Outputs can usually be quantified. They may be the number of units of service delivered, the number of clients served, the number of educational pamphlets distributed by a program, and so forth. Outputs can be used to suggest the efficiency of a program or to compare the efficiency of two programs. The more outputs a program can produce (per monetary unit) the more efficient the program. For example, if program A serves 100 clients at the same cost as program B which serves 50 clients, program A (at least on the surface) appears to be twice as efficient as program B. Or, if we look only at outputs, a program that had no budget increase but served 20 percent more clients this year, had a better year. Historically, outputs have been the primary indicator of program success, and as Chapter 9 shows, that has been, and continues to be, a problem. Outputs in our after-school program might be the number of children who actively participated in the program, the number of field trips completed, the number of individual counseling sessions offered, or the number of children who received tutoring services.

Outcomes

Outputs alone are no guarantee of program success or value. For example, just because a certain number of clients completed a program, that does not guarantee that they have benefited from it. The degree to which a program achieved its desired outcomes is what really suggests whether a program has been successful. In most programs, a central outcome objective is some benefit for clients who complete the program, often a change such as a reduction in or elimination of some problem that they have. In programs that serve clients whose main problems cannot go away or reflect improvement (for example, people with Alzheimer's disease or those who have a terminal illness) change of some form may still be a realistic outcome objective. For example, a desired outcome of the program might be improvement in some aspect of quality of life, such as increased independence or increased participation in family activities. If even an outcome like that is not realistic, an outcome objective might be to reduce or slow the onset of negative changes in the program's clients, for example, to maintain the current level of client functioning for an extended period of time, or to slow the rate of clients' decline in functioning. Or, it might be the prevention of some problem for all or most of the people the program is designed to benefit, for example to reduce unwanted teen pregnancy or to reduce the spread of sexually transmittable diseases.

Outcomes are the degree to which a program has benefited those who are supposed to be its beneficiaries, generally its clients. They are the primary yardstick by which program success *should* be measured. Examples of outcomes are changes in behavior, knowledge, attitudes, skills, values, conditions, and so forth. In our after-school program example, outcomes would be the degree to which children who participated in the program benefited in some specific ways from their participation, the degree to which some present or potential problem diminished because they were enrolled. Obvious examples might be better grades or improved social skills.

Outcomes are sometimes classified as short-term, intermediate-term, and long-term. **Short-term outcomes** are how clients (or sometimes a larger system, such as a community) benefited directly from a program. For example, in an after-school program, other short-term outcomes might include having a safe place to be while parents are at work, having a quiet place to complete homework, learning "cooperative play," positive use of free time, or learning positive alternatives to handling conflicts. **Intermediate-term outcomes** often entail continued growth and application of learning following program completion. In an after-school program, intermediate-term goals might be continued grade improvement, use of positive alternatives in conflict situations, or continued growth in use of social skills. **Long-term outcomes** are the ultimate effects of a program that participants may carry through life. Like intermediate-term outcomes, documenting success in achieving long-term outcomes requires follow-up of participants over time (after they leave a program) and is more difficult. In an after-school program, long-term outcomes might include maintenance of good grades, completion of high school, admission to a college of choice, avoidance of substance abuse problems, lack of legal difficulties, and a high level of social functioning.

Impacts

Impacts are sometimes synonymous with long-term outcomes. In describing how a program affected its clients over time, this is probably correct. However, the impact of a program can extend beyond those effects experienced by just those clients who participated in a program. For example, some programs, while helping a limited number of individual clients, can still manage to affect how members of society perceive their problem. A program also can affect other programs within an organization, other similar programs within the community, its staff, and so forth. Impacts can be either positive or negative. For example, an after-school program could reduce the need for parent-teacher conferences, could increase attendance at school social activities, could reduce the number of children in nearby religious instruction programs, or could cause a problem of staff morale among those not offered employment in it.

It is important to note that, while some impacts of a program are more or less predictable, some are not. Despite the best planning efforts, some unexpected impacts almost always occur. This should not surprise anyone who understands systems theory. No program operates in a vacuum. Its implementation will invariably impact on the larger system in unpredictable ways, and not all of them will be desirable.

Indicators

As a group, outcomes (especially intermediate and long-term ones) can be difficult to measure, certainly more difficult than outputs. They often cannot be measured directly, so we use the next best thing, indicators. **Indicators** are the measurements of behaviors, attitudes, and so forth that suggest to what degree program outcomes have been achieved. In evaluation research, the term indicator is used similarly to the way it is used in basic research. The degree of reliability and validity of an indicator is always a major issue. When they are used in a given situation or with a given group of people and how they are used, both affect the credibility of any conclusions of an evaluation.

For example, in an after-school program, short-term indicators might be percent of homework completed—that would be a valid, straightforward indicator. However, indicators of, for example, knowledge of cooperative play or of positive alternatives for conflict resolution would be "softer," measured perhaps in the form of staff observations of children's behaviors. Similarly, the ability to find a valid indicator of achievement of intermediate and long-term outcomes would vary. For example, high school or college graduation rates would be good indicators of academic success. However, "avoidance of negative behaviors" would be more difficult to operationalize. And, of course, with the passage of time, it would be increasingly difficult to prove that it was the program and not something else that produced the desired outcomes reflected by the selected indicators.

Further Clarification

Most social workers understand what constitutes an input; they know or can identify the resources (financial and other types) that are expended for a program. However, there often is confusion about exactly what an outcome is, and specifically, how it differs from an activity or and output. Because these are such important distinctions, perhaps a familiar example, a BSW or MSW degree program, would be helpful.

Examples of *inputs* into a BSW or MSW program would be its facilities, faculty, students, funding (from tuition, grants, contracts, and so forth), and clerical staff. *Constraints* would come primarily from the requirements of the social work accrediting body, the Council on Social Work Education. However, the program would also be constrained by the rules and requirements of the college or university of which it is part. For example, there may be requirements that a course must meet a certain number of contact hours for each credit hour awarded, that a certain percentage of courses must be taught by full-time faculty members, or that only certain professors may teach certain level courses. Examples of *activities* would be course offerings, student social events, field experiences of students, student library research, and study groups. Examples of *outputs* would be number of courses taught, number of graduates produced, number of faculty publications authored, or amount of grant money received. *Short-term outcomes* would reflect primarily the changes that the program produced in its graduates, for example, graduates who possess certain knowledge, values, and skills that they are believed to have lacked when they entered the program. Longer-term outcomes might relate to career advancement of graduates. *Indicators* of these might be its graduates' scores on licensure exams, or the program's reputation among administrators who employ its graduates: a "softer" indicator. *Impacts* might include how the presence of the program has changed the employment market for social workers, how it has affected other social work programs, or how it reduced the severity of various social problems within the community or region.

Later chapters return to the difficulty of determining just "what is what" in evaluating programs. I will also show why, for example, evaluators focus primarily on inputs in one type of program evaluation, activities in another, and outputs in a third.

SOURCES OF KNOWLEDGE
FOR PROGRAM EVALUATIONS

Professional literature contains numerous reports of program evaluations. They exist in journal articles, research reports, and monographs. Especially if they are unfamiliar with the type of program they are about to evaluate, evaluators often rely on them to serve as a reference point. They help formulate questions about a program and what data are needed. For example, an evaluation report of a similar program that was successful might suggest what services should be present, how they should be used, or what staffing patterns should exist. Or, they might suggest what is adequate funding for a particular type of program, or what is a desirable staff-to-client ratio. This knowledge can then be used to determine what needs to be learned about the current program in order to evaluate its quality.

How do program evaluators attempt to answer their questions about a program? Like any research, they collect and analyze data. The primary data source in single-system research (Chapters 4 and 5) is the client or client system. Only the method for compiling it (self-report, personal observation, reports of others, and so forth) can vary. However, in program evaluations, evaluators collect and compile data from a variety of sources using a variety of methods. That is how we attempt to learn about the merit, worth, or value of a program.

We would not expect to get a true "reading" about the potential for success of a proposed program if we only asked professionals about it. Similarly, an evaluation of an existing program would have little credibility if, for example, it relied only on client records or only on staff attitudes. Either data source would have a valuable perspective to offer, but the perspective is likely to be less than accurate. If we are to arrive at the truth about a proposed or existing program, we can do it best by using many data sources (sometimes asking the same questions) and then identifying areas of consensus and disagreement. Then, through a process of sorting out and synthesizing, an evaluator attempts to create an accurate picture and, where applicable, a valid measurement of a program's true worth. This process is sometimes called "convergent analysis"[3] in the program evaluation literature. It is similar to what other researchers call "triangulation," which involves "using several different research methods to collect the same information."[4] The process is designed to address the problem of systematic error[5] that can occur if only one data source is used.

There are many potential sources of knowledge for use in program evaluations. Some are most appropriate for use in certain types of program evaluations; others make a valuable contribution to all evaluations. We will look at some of the most commonly used ones.

Evaluator Observation

People who conduct evaluations often want to form their own impressions of a program without being biased by the impressions of others. Usually, prior to collecting other data, they may just want to observe a program, to get a general "feel" for it. This can be accomplished in a very structured way, known as **systematic observation,** for example, by measuring and recording the number of minutes that clients spend in a program's waiting area. Observation can also be far less structured, for example, by chatting with clients over lunch at some activity of the program to get a general idea of their level of satisfaction with the program or to learn how they hope to benefit from participating in it.

When firsthand observation is used as a data source, the evaluator may identify himself or herself as an evaluator or may choose to employ a little deception, perhaps by allowing clients and staff to assume that he or she is a client, if that is possible. The evaluator may choose to participate fully in client activities (such as social gatherings or group sessions) or to participate in only some of them. Of course, ethical issues may occur if any of these methods is used; they will need to be addressed. For example, clients might reveal attitudes about a program to a person they believe to be a fellow client that they would not reveal to someone else. Was this information acquired ethically or just ingeniously? Could it have been acquired in some other way that did not entail deception? What about "voluntary informed consent" and confidentiality issues? After all, the clients were unwitting participants in the research. There is no simple answer to the question of whether deception of this type is a violation of research or practice ethics. However, we can say with certainty that an evaluator doing something similar would have to be very careful not to reveal what exactly the clients said or who said it, because they might potentially be harmed by these revelations.

The proposed use of evaluator observations (especially those involving deception) can be a "red flag" for evaluation designs that must be approved by an Institutional Review Board (IRB). To gain approval for its use, the evaluator might have to convince the IRB members that the deception is absolutely essential to the evaluation, that it is relatively harmless and offers no threat to individuals providing information, and that any necessary debriefing of participants will take place. The appropriate use of this data source (and others that will be mentioned) are discussed in the guiding principles for evaluators that can be found on the web site of the American Evaluation Association or in recent issues of the *American Journal of Evaluation.*

Confidential Interviews

Evaluators often rely on confidential, one-on-one interviews with staff, clients, or other people associated with a program to obtain candid assessments of the program. Their purpose in conducting the interview is not concealed; there is little or no deception involved. When using one-on-one interviews, evaluators assume that participants are more likely to express their true feelings about some aspect of a program than if they are asked about the program in front of others who have a vested interest in the program's success.

Confidential interviews often rely on several planned, open-ended questions to acquire data. For example, an evaluator might ask several staff members in private what they consider to be a program's greatest strengths or weaknesses. Or, a client might be asked, Would you recommend this program to a friend? followed by, Why? or Why not? A community leader might be asked to describe how the program is viewed within the community. Of course, such inquiries will only produce valid data if the people being interviewed are confident that their confidentiality will be respected. Besides, to do otherwise would be unethical. It would violate the NASW Code of Ethics Standard 5.02l which states, "Social workers engaged in evaluation or research should ensure the anonymity or confidentiality of participants and of the data obtained from them."[6] Furthermore, as Standard 5.02m states, "Social workers who report evaluation and research results should protect participants' confidentiality by omitting identifying information unless proper consent has been obtained authorizing disclosure."[7]

Generally, because of issues related to confidentiality, information obtained in confidential interviews tends to appear only in very general form in research reports. For example, it might be observed that "Staff interviews revealed some concerns about the amount of administrative support being offered" (never, "Mary Jones said the boss is always on the golf course when we need him.") However, once having learned of a possible problem within a program in a one-on-one interview, the evaluator often collects data relating to it from other sources that will either confirm its existence, or indicate that it is not founded. Similarly, fairness would dictate that if a special strength of a program is described in a confidential interview the evaluator should also collect additional data to attempt to see if it can be documented.

Program Records

Programs generally keep extensive records for a variety of reasons. Sometimes they are kept specifically as data for use in a future program evaluation. More often, they represent secondary data, that is, data that were collected for some other purpose such as client records or personnel files. In analyzing them, an evaluator seeks only the answers to questions relevant to the evaluation. For example, if a confidential interview with a staff member reveals a concern that clients are being seen for extended periods of time in a crisis-intervention program, an analysis of client records could determine if this is indeed a widespread problem or merely one staff member's impression. Or, if percentages, tables, and graphs have not been compiled, an evaluator could examine case records to see if clients being served seem to reflect the desired socioeconomic, gender, age, or ethnic diversity.

The demographic characteristics of clients and data on other variables such as number of client contacts, number of missed appointments, or length of participation in a program that are found in client records may be quite accurate. However, they may also be inaccurate. This may occur because of sloppy record keeping (perhaps because the data have never been used in the past) or deliberate misrepresentation (for example, if payment for services is received based on number of services offered, the number may be deliberately exaggerated by the use of duplicate counts). Other data may be even less trustworthy. Especially if the desired outcome of a program is something that is vulnerable to subjectivity in measurement (for example, improved self-esteem, enhanced family functioning, increased communication among family members), program records are not a very reliable indicator of whether such an outcome has been achieved with a given client or group of clients. Why not? Like other forms of secondary data, client records are compiled for reasons other than to provide valid data for evaluation. What is contained in them may simply not contain all the necessary information to determine whether an outcome has been achieved. In addition, client records may also contain deliberate omissions because of the need to protect clients (should records be subpoenaed) or, as was noted previously, because a more complete accounting might reflect negatively on the program or on the professional who keeps the record. Of course, in programs designed to address medical or psychiatric problems of clients, recently passed legislation (HIPAA) may preclude the use of client records altogether by evaluators, because they contain individually identifiable health information.

Personnel records are another potential source of evaluation data. They can help an evaluator to evaluate staff credentials or determine if salaries and benefits are adequate. They can provide an indicator of staff stability or of rapid and suspicious staff turnover. They can also suggest whether staff performance evaluations are conducted in a timely and appropriate manner, or if other expectations of a well-managed program have been met.

Budgets and accounting records can be another valuable resource. Expenditures can be examined, either in the form of a budget audit or in a less-structured way. Records of the receipt and disbursement of in-kind donations to a program (such as furniture, clothing, and so forth) should have been kept, and can be examined. Timesheets of paid staff members and volunteers, travel reimbursement forms, and even phone records can be revealing and are a good source of data reflecting the efficiency of program operation. While not possible in some program evaluations, in others (for example in programs where there are concerns about waste or even misconduct) review of budgets and accounting records can be an important component of a program evaluation.

Social Indicators

Another data source for program evaluations is social indicators. Unlike organization records (which are sometimes kept specifically for use in program evaluations), social indicators are always regarded as secondary data. Generally, social indicators are data that are drawn from an entire population, such as a city, county, or state and reflect certain aspects of the health and welfare of its citizens. They are aggregated from reports and statistics submitted to some central office, often as required by law. For example, a state health department might accumulate data from each of its district or county offices and construct an annual report on the incidence of such social problems as sexually transmittable diseases, low birth weight births, and deaths attributable to various causes. Similarly, a county department of social services might collect and summarize annual incidence data on, for example, child abuse and neglect, children in foster care, or adoption disruptions.

A major advantage of social indicators is their availability. They are in the public domain and are often accessible on the Internet or in widely distributed written reports. However, the utility of social indicator data for program evaluations is often limited. They may not contain what is needed; they often are not specific enough to the client or client group that a program seeks to serve. Thus, they are often of minimal help in making decisions regarding a potential or existing program. For example, they may help to tell us that a school dropout prevention program is serving a cross-section of high school students in the community. They may also tell us that the most recent high school dropout rate in a specific school district was 40 percent. However, that number will in no way tell us that the program was the reason why the rate dropped from 42 percent in the previous year. When combined with some of the other data sources described in this chapter, more definitive answers can be found.

Key Informants

A **key informant** is someone who is especially well-informed about the problem that a program seeks to address and the best ways to address it. Knowledge could have come from professional education or from work experience. Or, it could come from the fact that a person simply has just been exposed to the problem on a regular basis, perhaps because it affected his or her family or friends. For example, if we were evaluating an after-school program, key informants might include teachers, staff of similar programs, guidance counselors, child-protection workers, psychologists, activity therapists, parents, or clergy who have worked with these children. Key informants are especially valuable data sources for evaluations of proposed programs. Their insights into a problem, and their knowledge of programs that have addressed it, can be very helpful for avoiding mistakes that other programs have made.

When using key informants as a data source, an evaluator hopes to tap into their knowledge and expertise. The job of selecting key informants requires making judgments. The evaluator has to determine (1) Is an individual *really* knowledgeable about the problem and its solution (as opposed to the fact that they simply should be); and (2) Can they be relied on to be open and helpful (as opposed to pursuing some personal agenda). For example, not all child-protection workers are very knowledgeable about child neglect issues—they may work exclusively with cases of child sexual abuse. Or, a counselor in another after-school program may be very knowledgeable, but may be so convinced of the correctness of how her program is designed that she may be unable to provide valuable suggestions or provide insights for another program that may have somewhat different goals, objectives, or methods of intervention.

Focus Groups

Data for an evaluation can also be obtained by bringing together a small group of people to discuss certain questions or issues about a program in a focus group. A **focus group** consists of people who are more similar than dissimilar, but may still contribute different perspectives on a program. For example, a focus group could consist of staff members of a program or of some current or potential clients.

A focus group may be formed because its members share some other characteristic as well. For example, parents of children in an after-school program might be selected for a focus group because they have been among its most verbal critics. They might be encouraged by the evaluator to express their concerns and to propose improvements that might be made in the program. Or, a mixture of parents who are critics and parents who have made positive comments about it could be deliberately brought together in a focus group to try to identify areas of consensus and disagreement about the program's strengths and weaknesses.

Perhaps, a good focus group would comprise parents who might benefit from the after-school program but have not enrolled their child. The evaluator could lead a discussion to try to identify what participants perceived to be obstacles to enrollment—cost, transportation, misunderstandings about the program and its goals, and so forth. The group might also ask parents what changes would be needed to convince them to enroll their child. Some would suggest a change; others might disagree with it. Some changes could possibly be implemented; others would be impractical. Some consensus could be achieved, but areas of strong disagreement could also be identified.

The assumption underlying the use of focus groups is that people participating in them are likely to be open and honest when they are in a group of people similar to themselves and who may share their impressions and beliefs. However, sometimes the opposite effect can take place. The presence of the others and what they say can shape an individual's impressions and opinions, or at least how he or she expresses them. Certain group phenomena can occur. For example, in a focus group composed of critics of a program (staff or clients), a kind of "feeding frenzy" can occur. Participants may compete with each other to come up with the most derogatory comment, even though they may not really feel that negatively about some aspect of a program. Or looks of shock or dissatisfaction from a few group members can quickly stifle future expressions of feeling or attitudes.

Obviously, leading a focus group requires considerable skill. The group leader must keep the group "on-track" and productive. It cannot be allowed to degenerate into, for example, just a forum for complaining about a program or a place to verbally abuse other focus group members. At the same time, members must not feel overly controlled, or that their opinions and perceptions are not respected or are being manipulated by the group leader.

There is yet another problem with the use of focus groups. Unless an evaluator is familiar with a program and its environment, he or she may have to rely on a program manager or organization administrator to identify and invite people to participate in them. This can result in focus groups that are "stacked," and may reduce the value of a focus group for helping to answer questions about, for example, staff morale, client satisfaction, or program effectiveness.

Community Forums

An evaluator can collect data on a proposed or existing program by convening a **community forum** or other public gathering. To a limited degree, this venue can contribute a community perspective on a program. It is used most frequently when an existing or proposed program is controversial or appears to lack community support. A community forum can be effective for identifying problems that a program may have in its community and why it may meet resistance. However, data collected cannot be construed as a cross-section of community opinion. Sampling bias is almost always present at community forums. The group that attends is likely to be overrepresented by the program's critics, its staunch supporters, and others who have a strong vested interest in it. The "middle" group, consisting of those people who hold neither extreme position, is likely to be underrepresented.

While community forums can be a useful source of data in a program evaluation, they also can be an inefficient use of an evaluator's time and resources. (Focus groups can provide community input at far less cost.) For most people, community forums are not popular events; people usually have other things they would rather do. They invariably conflict with other scheduled events. It is not unusual to schedule a community forum, invite the media, and have only a handful of people show up, some of whom do not even live in the community.

Surveys

Surveys remain a popular way to acquire data for a program evaluation. In evaluating a proposed or existing program, an evaluator may attempt to acquire answers to a number of standardized questions by mail, phone or, increasingly, e-mail or fax. All of these methods are relatively inexpensive and can yield large amounts of data, but each also has its problems. Mailed surveys have notoriously poor response rates—it may be necessary to mail out 400 surveys to get 100 completed ones returned. However, even 100 responses could be very useful, except for the problem of response bias. Suppose we wanted to survey community members about their opinions of a program. If we received 100 completed surveys they would contain a disproportionate number from people who (1) hate the program; (2) love the program or have a vested interest in it; and (3) inexplicably enjoy completing surveys, whether they know anything about the program or not.

Telephone or electronic methods of data collection also have limited utility, invariably containing sampling bias. Phone surveys, unless the participants have a strong investment in the program (for example, they are staff members or present clients) can be rendered virtually worthless because of unlisted numbers, increased use of cell phones, and the use of caller ID to screen calls. The result is an inability to reach potential participants who might have a valuable perspective to offer, and an overrepresentation of those with a lot of time on their hands. The data thus acquired cannot be considered representative of opinions about or impressions of a program.

As mentioned earlier, client-satisfaction surveys have special problems as a data source. They tend to be overwhelmingly favorable, perhaps in part because (1) those clients who complete and return them are disproportionately those most involved in and positively predisposed toward a program; and (2) a combination of gratitude, fear, and pleasure because someone actually cared enough to ask their opinion of the program.[8] Do you want your program to look good?—Use a client-satisfaction survey!

Even though they are not good measurements of program success, client-satisfaction surveys are still widely used and are often a requirement of the organizations that fund social programs. (This may be a long-term response to the consumer movement discussed in Chapter 2.) Despite their shortcomings, there are some ways to increase their value somewhat. For example, if the same instrument is used repeatedly within the same organization, over time a baseline (the usual satisfaction level for a certain type of program) can be developed. Then, it is at least possible to know whether a specific batch of client-satisfaction surveys reflects an evaluation of the program that is "high," "average," or "low."

It is also a good idea to have a mixture of fixed-alternative and open-ended items in a client-satisfaction survey. For example, in addition to scales or yes/no items, it might be useful to ask, How would you describe this program to a friend? or, Describe how this program has changed your life. The open-ended items can provide either a verification or nonverification of the client's responses to the fixed-alternative items. They also give the client or former client a chance to say what he or she *really* thinks about the program in his or her own words. That sometimes offers some unique insights!

Client-satisfaction surveys are probably most useful in evaluations that occur early in a program's life cycle. They can help to identify program strengths, and can sometimes point out areas of dissatisfaction that can be corrected in order to increase client participation or otherwise improve the program. Later, the utility of a client-satisfaction survey as an indicator of program quality or success is questionable at best. As observed earlier, client satisfaction simply cannot be assumed to be synonymous with the achievement of a program's desired outcomes or the true merit, value, or worth of a program.

Statistical Analysis

Statistical analysis of data from a program is not a data source per se; it is how we make sense of data such as those found in records. It can sometimes tell us some things about a program that the other sources cannot. There are several ways that statistical analysis can be used to answer questions in a program evaluation. First, it can be used to identify certain trends or characteristics that might not be otherwise evident within program data. Suppose that an evaluator wishes to answer several questions about the characteristics of clients served by a program, such as their ages, years of education, and so forth. If the program is a large one with many clients, it would be difficult to visualize whether the program is serving those people for whom it was intended from client records or from making personal observations about its clients. However, descriptive statistics such as means and standard deviations (or medians and interquartile ranges) could be computed to identify the "typical" age, education level, and so forth and to suggest how much variation in these variables exists within the program's clients. (They would actually be called "parameters" rather than statistics because they would be compiled on the entire population of clients served by the program.)

It would also be possible to use correlation analysis to learn the strength and direction of a relationship between two variables such as a program's client ages and education level or its staff's salaries and years of experience. It could tell an evaluator, for example, that older clients tend to have less formal schooling and may not benefit from some program materials, or that staff with many years of work experience are not paid much more as a group than new graduates (a potential personnel problem).

Statistical tests are very useful in evaluating program outcomes. They can help us to estimate the characteristics of all clients in a large program from measurements of a small sample of clients. They can also tell us the mathematical probability that any improvement in a problem among clients could have been produced by sampling error, that is, whether it is statistically significant. Thus they can help in making informed decisions about a program's effectiveness, much as they are used (Chapter 5) to help to inform us as to whether a specific intervention with a given client or client system might have been effective.

CONCLUDING THOUGHTS

This chapter examined a number of issues and concepts that relate to program evaluations. Later chapters focus on others that are specific to different types of program evaluations.

Program evaluations are no longer just optional; they are usually mandatory, and the evaluation must produce certain results if the program is to survive. While that is desirable overall, it also causes problems. Although program evaluations still are used to try to improve programs, it would be naive to suggest that this is the only reason why they are conducted or the only way that they are used. This chapter examined some other common reasons for, and uses of, program evaluations that either border on the unethical, are just plain unethical, or at least produce ethical dilemmas. Certain common denominators seem to run through these "other" reasons for a program evaluation—they are often self-serving and they are designed to get results that will help to justify a decision rather than to assist in decision making.

This chapter also defined and illustrated certain key terms that are central to program evaluations today. They will be used frequently in the chapters that follow.

Finally, this chapter examined some of the most frequently employed sources of data (and one method for analyzing it) that are used for drawing conclusions in conducting program evaluations. Some are used regularly in one type of evaluation, but less frequently in other types. Some are used in all types of evaluation but assume different forms in one type or another. Later chapters return to their specific usage.

KEY TERMS

quid pro quo	outcomes	systematic observation
administrative audit	short-term outcomes	key informant
inputs	intermediate-term outcomes	focus group
constraints	long-term outcomes	social indicators
activities	impacts	community forum
outputs	indicators	surveys

STUDY QUESTIONS

1. How does the need for some programs to be accredited, or to continue to be funded, sometimes result in a lack of accurate findings when they are evaluated?

2. How are program evaluations sometimes used to justify decisions that have already been made? Why is this wrong?

3. What social work ethical standards relate to conducting program evaluations that are self-serving?

4. What ethical issues does a potential evaluator face when asked to conduct a program evaluation in which there is one or more hidden agenda for wanting to evaluate a program?

5. What ethical issues does an evaluator confront when firsthand observation of programs is used as a source of data?

6. How do program activities differ from program outputs? What is the relationship between them?

7. Why are program outcomes a better indicator of program success than program outputs?

8. Who might be considered a key informant for a proposed program that is designed to address the problem of rural homelessness?

9. Who might constitute a useful focus group for a proposed program that is designed to address the problem of rural homelessness?

10. When are community forums sometimes useful in program evaluations? What is their major limitation as a data source?

REFERENCES

1. Emerson, R. (1962). Power Dependent Relationships. *American Sociological Review, 27,* 31–41.

2. National Association of Social Workers. (1999). *Code of ethics.* Washington, DC: NASW Press.

3. Royse, D., et al. (2001). *Program evaluation: An introduction.* Wadsworth, CA: Brooks/Cole, 67–69.

4. Rubin, A., & Babbie, E. (2001). *Research methods for social workers.* Belmont, CA: Wadsworth/Thompson Learning, 189.

5. See, e.g., Singleton, R., Straits, B., & Straits, M. (1993). *Approaches to social research.* New York: Oxford University Press, 116–117; or Weinbach, R. & Grinnell, R., Jr. (2004). *Statistics for social workers* (6th ed.). Boston: Allyn & Bacon, 78.

6. National Association of Social Workers. (1999). *Code of ethics.* Washington, DC: NASW Press.

7. Ibid.

8. For an excellent summary of research on client-satisfaction surveys, see Royse, D. et al., op. cit., 197–198.

CHAPTER SEVEN

NEEDS ASSESSMENTS

When we hear the term program evaluation, we are most likely to think about an evaluation to see if a program was effective—an outcome evaluation. However, good program evaluation is an ongoing process. It starts when a program is only being considered, before a definite decision about actually implementing it is made—with a needs assessment.

NEEDS ASSESSMENTS FOR PROPOSED PROGRAMS

We are the only county in the state that doesn't have this kind of program.

Everything about that program makes sense. Let's do the same thing here.

The problem is growing every year. We need this program and we need it now.

It should be obvious why, even if correct, these statements are insufficient justifications for establishing a program. They suggest why programs that seemed promising have failed: they were based on impressions and assumptions, not on empirical evidence. They also suggest why needs assessments are so important to program success.

Ideally, no new program should be implemented without first conducting a needs assessment. However, as some authors note, that is often not the case. "Needs assessments (and the foundations they form) are often ignored in favor of 'knee-jerk' political agendas and reactions to emerging social crises."[1] Some of the reasons for not conducting a needs assessment before offering a program have some legitimacy; they relate to time and cost. However, frequently someone just thinks a needs assessment is unnecessary; they believe (erroneously) that nothing would be learned from it.

As the term suggests, one reason for conducting a needs assessment for a proposed program is to find out if there is a need for such a program. However, that is only the beginning. In fact, most needs assessments determine rather quickly that a perceived problem is a real one and *some* program is needed to address it. The observations and judgments of professionals who proposed the program usually are confirmed. Once the need for a program has been established, then the real work of the needs assessment begins: learning how the program should be designed in order to maximize its potential for success. A needs assessment is a planning tool; it "helps to plan a feasible, effectively targeted program."[2]

Only rarely are needs assessments conducted without at least a beginning model of a program in mind. Often, a proposed program has already been designed. However, even when the program model is fully developed and contains considerable detail (as in instances when a program already offered elsewhere is being proposed for another location or with another client population), that program is never considered to be "set in stone." Invariably, a needs assessment suggests some needed changes, often to address the unique characteristics of the clients the program will serve, the organization in which it will exist, and the community in which it will be located.

Sometimes the findings of a needs assessment suggest that a proposed program is needed and, with a few modifications, it could be effective. However, examination of the data also reveals that the program cannot be offered. This happens most often because of budgetary or political concerns. For example, data may suggest that to operate the proposed program effectively would be very expensive and might thus create a negative impact on other valuable programs within the organization. Or, perhaps the program might create too many enemies and harm the overall image of the organization within the community. The ultimate decision to offer a program is a complicated one that, as in other forms of program evaluation, requires making sense of data drawn from many sources.

Role of the Evaluator

All evaluators of programs (even only proposed ones) function as researchers, unlike single-system research in which the individual conducting the research remains first and foremost a social work practitioner. However, any additional role that an evaluator of a program assumes differs depending on what type of program evaluation is being conducted.

Needs assessments are sometimes "contracted out" to outside researchers who design and conduct them. However, they are more likely to be completed by an organization staff member or a team already on the payroll. The evaluator functions with what is described as **staff authority.**[3] This means that he or she is supposed to design the needs assessment, collect necessary data, make recommendations about the program, and even attempt to convince the people who requested the study what decision or decisions should be made. But the evaluator's authority stops there. Whoever requested the needs assessment has ultimate authority to decide whether a program will exist, what form it will take, how it will be implemented, and who will manage it.

There are many reasons why the recommendations of an evaluator might be ignored or "overruled." The decision to not go ahead with a recommended program may be based on facts not known to the evaluator (for example, an administrator's insights into funding, timing, or political issues). Conversely, the findings of a needs assessment might produce clear evidence that a program is unnecessary or that, while needed, if implemented it might not be successful. Yet the program is implemented anyway, perhaps because the administrator is under political pressure to offer it. Fortunately, ignoring or overruling the findings and recommendations of a needs assessment does not happen too often. When it does, it can be demoralizing to the evaluator and gives the impression that the needs assessment was only a waste of time and resources.

While a good knowledge of research methods and statistical analysis is certainly helpful when conducting a needs assessment, it is less essential than, for example, in an outcome evaluation. What are important characteristics for people conducting needs assessments? Creativity, flexibility, interviewing skills, knowledge of social work practice, and knowledge of the community (and its power structure) where a proposed program might be implemented can be helpful. Having connections and personal friendships with those in the community and in related programs elsewhere would be additional assets.

Conducting a needs assessment also requires evaluators to have the ability to make changes in the research "as they go," something that would be less important or even undesirable in other types of program evaluations. In a needs assessment, evaluators collect widely differing types of data, some planned and some unplanned. Some of it may be conflicting. Ultimately, the evaluator needs to step back and make sense of it all. Thus, the ability to organize and interpret data and to conceptualize what it all means, primarily by "pulling diverse sources and types of information together"[4] is a very important quality for evaluators. In short, the role of the evaluator is that of a knowledgeable social worker who is also a good **researcher/synthesizer.**

Central Research Questions and Hypotheses

In a general sense, all research is about answering questions and testing hypotheses, verifying whether what we believe to be true is really true. Program evaluations are no exception; they attempt to answer many questions about a program. Much of the work of an evaluator is determining just which questions to ask.

In any type of program evaluation it is also possible to identify the central research questions and central hypothesis or hypotheses. In a needs assessment, research hypotheses usually are implicit rather than stated and tested directly.

In a needs assessment of a proposed program, the central research question is, Is the proposed program needed and, if so, what form should it take? The central research hypothesis may be, The proposed program is needed. If so, this would be considered a directional hypothesis, because it suggests that if the proposed program were implemented (the independent variable) there would be a reduction in the problem it would address (the dependent variable).

In a needs assessment, support for a central research hypothesis comes from many sources. Statistical analysis of data rarely entails the use of tests of statistical inference. Support for the hypothesis is much more likely to take the form of graphs, frequency distributions, and measures of central tendency and variability.

They are used primarily to describe, summarize, and communicate the most dramatic features of what was found. Occasionally, correlations between variables may be reported, if they provide insights into issues regarding a proposed or existing program. For example, it might be useful to report that, "Among the 100 potential clients surveyed, there was a fairly strong ($r = -.51$) negative correlation between age and amount of financial assistance required in order to participate in the program."

Specific Research Questions

There are many, diverse research questions in a needs assessment for a proposed program. Some questions (such as those in Box 7.1) help to shape many needs assessments; others are unique and relate directly to the program under consideration.

The questions in Box 7.1 (and other similar ones) suggest the way that a needs assessment should be approached. Needs assessments can be characterized as both exploratory and descriptive. As in all good research, an open mind is required.

BOX 7.1

**RESEARCH QUESTIONS FREQUENTLY ASKED
IN NEEDS ASSESSMENTS FOR PROPOSED PROGRAMS**

- Is the problem a real one? What appear to be its causes?
- If the problem is real, how severe or widespread is it? Who appears to suffer most from it?
- How adequate are existing programs for addressing the problem?
- What additional services appear needed?
- Would the proposed program be able to offer the needed services?
- What would be reasonable objectives for the program?
- What would be the budgetary and staffing requirements of such a program?
- What additional sources of funding may be available?
- What organizations and individuals would be supportive of the program? Who would be opposed to it and why?
- How might the program's existence affect other programs both inside and outside the organization?
- If offered, what potential clients should it target?
- What are potential referral sources for the program?
- How should the program be marketed in order to make it attractive to potential clients?
- What logistical obstacles to client participation exist? How could they be overcome?
- What would be a realistic time frame for implementing the program?
- What activities would have to be completed for the program to become operational?
- How and when should the program be evaluated?

Conducting a Needs Assessment

Every needs assessment is unique, just like every other type of program evaluation. However, planning and conducting needs assessments usually follow roughly the same steps. They are displayed in Box 7.2. Notice how many of the steps entail planning prior to actually collecting any data.

An Example: A Needs Assessment for a Proposed Program

While it is possible to describe various types of program evaluations in general terms, it may be helpful to get a little more concrete at this point. I will introduce an example of a program here, describe how a needs assessment of it might look, and continue with the same example in the next three chapters.

Here is the scenario. A private, not-for-profit family service agency currently offers both family counseling and private adoption services. During the past three years, there has been a decline in requests for adoption services. Furthermore, about twenty couples and other potential adoptive parents who were clients of the

■ ■ ■ ■ ■ ▬▬▬▬▬▬▬▬▬▬▬▬▬▬▬▬▬▬▬▬▬▬▬▬▬▬▬▬

BOX 7.2

CONDUCTING A NEEDS ASSESSMENT

1. Determine and specify the general purpose of the research. What knowledge is sought and for what reason (usually to make some decision or decisions)?
2. Determine and specify the time parameters for the research. When will it begin and at what point must the findings be available for decision making?
3. Determine what additional resources and personnel will be available to conduct the research.
4. Specify the questions that the research will attempt to answer.
5. Determine what data will be required.
6. Determine how much of the needed data are available from secondary sources and how much will need to be collected as original data.
7. Identify the best sources for collection of new data and the best methods to collect them.
8. Estimate how long data collection for each method is likely to take.
9. Develop a timeline for data collection.
10. Determine what role each person will play in data collection.
11. Find or develop any needed data collection instruments.
12. Collect both secondary and original data.
13. Organize, analyze, synthesize, and interpret all available data.
14. Identify any gaps in data, and fill them if possible.
15. Summarize the research in report form and present and distribute it to those who will use it for decision making.

agency, and had been approved for adoption, terminated services because they became impatient while waiting for a child to become available. In a follow-up call, it was learned that twelve of the couples are now new parents. Their children were adopted from Russia, China, Romania, and South America. Following numerous phone conversations and e-mails with her colleagues who are directors of similar agencies around the country, the director concluded that an international adoption program might be a good thing. However, she recognized that to attempt to offer such a program without first conducting a needs assessment would be unwise. She assigned a team of three staff members to plan and conduct it, providing one day per week release time and a fairly generous budget to cover expenses. They were to explore the feasibility of developing an international adoptions program and to come up with a recommendation as to whether such a program should be implemented. They were given four months to complete the research.

What follows is but one example of how the team might have tackled the job. It is meant to show how a needs assessment might be planned and conducted; it is not meant to suggest necessarily the best or the only way to do it.

Identifying Needed Knowledge. The first meeting of the team without the director present was essentially a brainstorming session. It relied on what team members already knew about international adoptions, both professionally and personally. Although they knew they would have to revise it over time, they began to compile (in no particular order) a long list of questions that they believed the needs assessment would have to answer in order for the director to make an informed decision. After sharing the list with the director, they added a few more at the next meeting, deleted some, and revised others. Ultimately, the list consisted of the following questions:

1. What other local organizations are already offering international adoption services? Is there a need for another international adoptions program in the area? Are international adoptions on the increase, or on the decline?
2. How pleased are staff and administrators with existing programs? Would they support or resist another program in the area? How much help could they be expected to offer in getting a program established?
3. Would a program require the hiring of additional staff or could it be implemented with current personnel? Would it require specialized skills such as foreign language fluency or cultural competency not already existent within the agency?
4. Should such a program have international adoption "specialists" or should all adoption workers be involved in both international and domestic adoptions? What additional staff training costs might be involved?
5. What is the approximate total cost of adopting a child from a foreign country? How do costs vary by country? What is a typical fee paid to the adoption agency?
6. What resources (such as employee assistance plans) are available to assist parents in paying for the expense of an international adoption?

7. How large is the "pool" of potential adoptive parents who would be willing to pay the cost of an international adoption who are not already working with another organization?

8. What do parents who have adopted internationally see as the biggest hurdle to adoption? Would they do it again? Why or why not? Would they be willing to work with other potential parents to facilitate the process?

9. What are the state and federal licensing requirements for offering such a program? How much cost and time would be required to become licensed?

10. What international contacts would have to be established? Would they require travel and out-of-country time for agency staff on a regular basis?

11. How do current government immigration quotas limit the number of children available for adoption? Are quotas likely to increase or decrease within the current international political climate?

12. What initial start-up costs would be involved? At what point could the agency expect the international adoptions program to be financially self-supporting?

13. Is there an adequate supply of children available to meet the demand of potential adoptive parents?

14. What countries offer the most likely source of children? What requirements do they have—age of parents, marital status, health status, economic situation, and so forth that might limit the number of potential adoptive parents? Which children are most frequently made available—boys, girls, babies, older children, special needs children?

15. In what counties are opportunities for adoption "opening up"? Where are they "shutting down" and why?

16. What is the usual length of time required for adoptive parents to complete their application, become approved, and receive their child? How does it vary from country to country? What travel requirements, if any, exist?

17. In what countries have unethical practices (for example, children being forcibly taken from their parents and "sold" for adoption, or bribery of local officials) been practiced in the past? How might this impact the reputation of the agency?

18. Do children adopted from some countries seem to have a more difficult time adjusting to North American culture than others? Why? What do parents need to provide to ensure that they grow up with a knowledge of and appreciation for their heritage? What services should the agency provide to assist parents in this task?

19. What are some common postadoptive problems that children and their families face and what services would need to be provided to address them? Would parents be likely to avail themselves of the services, if offered?

20. What venues should be used to "market" the program and what costs would be involved?

21. What is the general attitude of the community toward international adoptions?

22. Is there support for international adoptions among social workers and others working in adoptions in both the public and private sectors? Is there resentment, and if so, why?

23. How supportive would the agency's own staff be of establishing such a program if they know all that it entails? What sources of resistance would likely be encountered?

Determining What to Do First.   At their next meeting, relying on their knowledge as social workers and (to a lesser extent) on their knowledge of research methods, the team members tried to reach some consensus on how best to get the answers to their questions. Alongside each question, they listed several sources of data that could be used to answer it. Then they went back through their list and attempted to cut back on their potential data sources in order to stay within budget and time constraints, while still getting all the perspectives necessary to get a good answer. After revising their list, they decided on a number of "minimum" data requirements for answering each of their research questions. They are displayed in Box 7.3.

Working within Time Constraints.   As they looked back over both their questions and how they tentatively planned to answer them, it became obvious to team members that some could be answered rather quickly and easily. Others would take more time, and would require data collection and synthesis from several sources. Some answers would be based on facts that could be compiled; others would necessarily be more subjective.

Given their time constraints, the team began setting up a timeline reflecting a tentative sequence of events. They went back over their list again, first identifying those questions that would take longer to answer and thus required that they begin the process of answering them as soon as possible. For example, measuring community support for the proposed program would require more time and observation and the use of several different venues. Others, it was decided, could wait, because getting an answer would be relatively simple. For example, a phone call to the state department of social services or a single personal interview at some later juncture could provide the needed information about state licensing requirements. In some instances, if an attempt to get the answer to a question were made too soon, the answer might change before the report of their findings was to be written. Because up-to-date answers are essential, there would be little value in seeking an answer to the question months earlier. For example, political upheavals or a health epidemic (such as the SARS virus outbreak in 2003) might affect whether international adoption was possible in a given country at any given time.

Once the team members had identified what they needed to know, how they would attempt to learn it, and had determined the general sequence of events for data collection, they had constructed a preliminary draft of their research design. In a needs assessment, that is generally enough to begin data collection. Almost certainly, the design would have to be revised, perhaps many times. For example, they might find some data or key people to be unavailable. They might uncover other unanticipated questions that require an answer and thus need to be added to their list. They might encounter some diametrically opposed perceptions held by key informants that would require the use of one or more additional data sources in order to learn which one is accurate. They might have to make any number of

■ ■ ■ ■ ■

BOX 7.3

EXAMPLES OF QUESTIONS AND DATA SOURCES IN A NEEDS ASSESSMENT FOR AN INTERNATIONAL ADOPTION PROGRAM

1. *What other local organizations are already offering international adoption services? Is there a need for another international adoptions program in the area? Are international adoptions on the increase or on the decline?*—Review of area agency directory of human service organizations, phone calls to key informants, confidential interviews with prospective parents who did not use existing programs, confidential interviews with select administrators, social indicators.

2. *How pleased are staff and administrators with existing programs? Would they support or resist another program in the area? How much help could they be expected to offer in getting a program established?*—Focus group of professionals in existing programs, confidential interviews with administrators.

3. *Would a program require the hiring of additional staff or could it be implemented with current personnel? Would it require specialized skills such as foreign language fluency or cultural competency not already existent with the agency?*—Focus group of professionals in existing programs, confidential interviews with administrators.

4. *Should such a program have international adoption "specialists" or should all adoption workers be involved in both international and domestic adoptions? What additional staff training costs might be involved?*—Focus group of professionals in existing programs, confidential interviews with administrators.

5. *What is the approximate cost of adopting a child from a foreign country? How do costs vary by country? What is a typical fee paid to the adoption agency?*—Focus group of professionals in existing programs, survey of parents who have completed foreign adoptions.

6. *What resources such as employee assistance plans are available to assist parents in paying for the expenses of an international adoption?*—Focus group of professionals in existing programs, phone calls to personnel offices of major employers in the community.

7. *How large is the "pool" of potential adoptive parents who would be willing to pay the cost of an international adoption who are not already working with another organization?*—Review of agency adoption records, phone calls to key informants.

8. *What do parents who have adopted internationally see as the biggest hurdle to adoption? Would they do it again? Why or why not? Would they be willing to work with other potential parents to facilitate the process?*—Survey of parents who have completed foreign adoptions.

9. *What are the state and federal licensing requirements for offering such a program? How much cost and time would be required to become licensed?*—Telephone call or personal interview with person in charge of licensing adoption programs.

10. *What international contacts would have to be established? Would they require travel and out-of-country time for agency staff on a regular basis?*—Focus group of professionals in existing programs.

11. *How would U.S. immigration quotas limit the number of children available for adoption? Are quotas likely to increase or decrease within the current political climate?*—Review of Bureau of Citizenship and Immigration Services (BCIS, formerly INS) policies on the Internet, confidential interviews with administrators.

12. *What initial start-up costs would be involved? At what point could the agency expect the international adoptions program to be financially self-supporting?*—Confidential interviews with administrators.

13. *Is there an adequate supply of children available to meet the demand of potential adoptive parents?*—Search of the professional literature, confidential interviews with administrators.

14. *What countries offer the most likely source of children? What requirements do they have (age of parents, marital status, health status, economic situation) that might limit the number of potential adoptive parents? Which children are most frequently made available (boys, girls, babies, older children, special needs children)?*—Focus group of professionals in existing programs.

15. *In what counties are opportunities for adoption "opening up"? Where are they "shutting down" and why?*—Focus group of professionals in existing programs, Internet search of news services.

16. *What is the usual length of time required for adoptive parents to complete their application, get approved, and receive their child? How does it vary from country to country? What travel requirements, if any, exist?*—Survey of parents who have completed foreign adoptions, focus group of professionals in existing programs.

17. *In what countries have unethical practices (for example, children being abducted from their parents and "sold" for adoption, or bribery of local officials) been practiced in the past? How might this impact the reputation of the agency?*—Internet search of news services, confidential interviews with administrators.

18. *Do children adopted from some countries seem to have a more difficult time adjusting to North American culture than others? Why? What do parents need to ensure that they grow up with a knowledge of and appreciation for their heritage? What services should the agency provide to assist parents in this task?*—Focus group of professionals in existing programs.

19. *What are some common postadoptive problems that children and their families face and what services would need to be provided to address them? Would parents be likely to avail themselves of the services, if offered?*—Focus group of professionals in existing programs, survey of parents who have completed foreign adoptions.

20. *What venues should be used to "market" the program and what costs would be involved?*—Focus group of professionals in existing programs, confidential interviews with administrators, review of the professional literature.

21. *What is the general attitude of the community toward international adoptions?*—Focus group of professionals in existing programs, key informants, evaluator observations, confidential interviews with administrators.

22. *Is there support for international adoptions among social workers and others working in adoptions in both the public and private sectors? Is there resentment, and why?*—Review of the professional literature, focus group of public and private adoption workers.

23. *How supportive would the agency's own staff be of establishing such a program if they know all that it entails? What sources of resistance would likely be encountered?*—Focus group of staff, confidential interviews with key staff members.

other adjustments as they went along. In a needs assessment, such changes are both inevitable and desirable. They should be made whenever indicated. After all, a needs assessment is not explanatory research. The evaluator is not concerned about, for example, the introduction of confounding variables. Changes in the design of a needs assessment will not damage the credibility of its findings; they will only enhance it.

Making Sense of It All.   The team members had set a deadline for data collection—three weeks before the report was due. When the date arrived, they took what they had and evaluated it in relation to each of their questions. The data included notes from private interviews, literature reviews, and Internet searches, copies of e-mail messages, summaries of focus group discussions and conversations with key informants, and data collected from the survey that had been mailed to a sample of parents who had volunteered (in response to a newspaper advertisement) to complete a questionnaire about their experiences. Some knowledge gaps were still found; they had to be filled. Team members were able to do this through some follow-up phone calls and e-mails to people who had supplied data and by initiating a few new contacts. Then they divided up the work of writing a draft of their report. It was organized using the outline presented in Box 7.4.

BOX 7.4

**A POSSIBLE OUTLINE FOR A REPORT OF
A NEEDS ASSESSMENT (NEW PROGRAMS)**

Executive Summary
  I. The Background and Purpose of the Research
  II. The Research Questions
  III. Sources of Data and Methods of Data Collection
  IV. Tentative Answers to the Research Questions
  V. Conclusions: Why a Program Should (or Should Not) Be Implemented
  VI. Proposal for a Program
     A. Staffing and Budget Requirements
     B. Implementation Procedures and Strategies
        1. List of Tasks to Be Completed
        2. Timeline for Completion
     C. Relationship to Other Programs
        1. Within the Agency
        2. Within the Community
     D. Evaluation*
        1. Formative Evaluation Timetable
        2. Outcome Evaluation Timetable
Appendices

*Outside consultation may be required.

The report contained a brief **executive summary** prior to the body of the report. It was a three-paragraph abstract of the full report. The body of the report contained some data (such as annual international adoption figures and the number of children housed in orphanages and awaiting adoption). They were presented in brief tabular form. Longer tables, the results of some statistical analyses (reflecting associations or correlations between variables measured in the adoptive parents survey), and narrative summaries of focus group discussions were included as appendices. Much of the first part of the body of the report was written in narrative form. However, because the team was recommending that an international adoptions program should be implemented, it also included a proposal for a program as part VI (Box 7.4). That part of the report relied more on numbers and figures (for example, it included a proposed budget and a timeline for program development).

The draft of the report was presented to the director one week prior to its due date. She reviewed it and made numerous comments and asked questions in the margins, primarily in relation to statements that were unclear or where conclusions did not seem to follow from the data presented. Then the team met for the last time and made the necessary revisions to the report. One member did a final "edit" to ensure that it was written in a consistent style, and then it was submitted. The director later shared the report with her board of directors for their reactions and input.

NEEDS ASSESSMENTS OF EXISTING PROGRAMS

> We conducted an extensive needs assessment for this program before it was implemented ten years ago, and the problem certainly has not gone away.
>
> The program is well-known and has been nationally recognized.
>
> The program clearly has outlived its usefulness. It is expensive to operate and needs to be shut down.

Statements like these, spoken with a voice of authority, have sometimes been the impetus for making decisions about the future of existing social programs. For example, they have been used to justify making no changes in a program, or to simply eliminate a program with only the flimsiest of evidence. Too often, the decision was the wrong one. A needs assessment might have prevented a costly error.

Indicators That a Needs Assessment May Be Appropriate

A needs assessment can be useful at most any time in the life cycle of an existing program, but it is most likely to be used when someone (often someone in a position of influence) has questioned the continuing need for the program, at least in its current form. Needs assessments can inject some objectivity into decisions about the future of the program.

Needs assessments of existing programs are most likely to occur when certain warning signs have appeared. How can we tell that a needs assessment of an existing program might be informative? Perhaps fewer clients are taking advantage of a program, or the program does not seem to be serving the people it was intended to serve. Perhaps staff morale is low and/or staff members complain that the program no longer seems to be as effective as it once was. Or, resistance to the program in the community seems to be growing. A needs assessment could help us to learn what is happening or has happened and would help us to decide what to do about it.

Changes That Occur

If a program was needed and effective in the first place, it should continue to be needed and relevant, unless some important change has occurred. More often than not, when warning signs are present, that is exactly what has happened. What kind of changes may cause us to question the continuing need for a program, at least in its present form, and thus precipitate a needs assessment? I will mention only a few of many possible examples. They frequently are interrelated, that is, a change in one area often leads to changes in one or more of the others.

Changes in the Community.   The community in which the program exists may appear to have changed in some important way. A program, for example, an appropriate one for families with young children, may no longer be needed as residents of the neighborhood have "gentrified." Or, it may have targeted homemakers in one-wage-earner families, but both parents in many families are now fully employed. Or, it may have addressed the problems of low-income families, but the neighborhood has become fashionable again and more affluent people have moved back. In short, it may be a good program, but not what the community needs or wants.

Changes in "the Competition."   In business, competition is always a threat. It threatens the very existence of a business. The presence of other programs seeking to address the same problem is usually not a threat to a human service agency in the same way that it is in the corporate sphere. However, increased or decreased "competition" from other organizations and programs with similar goals and serving the same client base can impact a program and thus can be an indication that a needs assessment would be useful. When new programs and services appear, a central research question might be, Should our program be modified to avoid duplication of services? Or, Can we now safely scale back our program and find a better use for the resources that will thus be conserved?

When other programs and services disappear or are cut back, the central question would be different. It might be, How much do we need to expand in order to fill the void left by the other programs? Or, it might be, Which of the services that are no longer available could be subsumed by our program within its mission, and which should be left for other programs to offer?

Any changes in the competition might suggest the advisability of a needs assessment. Even if the amount of competition remains about the same, other programs may change their focus, for example, from a focus on treatment to one of prevention. In this case a needs assessment might indicate whether a program should and can make similar changes and, if so, how should they be accomplished. Or, if they are not perceived as desirable, what changes in the current program still should be made to help the program to interface with the other, modified programs.

Changes in Understanding of the Problem. As other, more traditional research studies are conducted, we learn more about a problem—especially its manifestations and origins. Sometimes, what is learned causes us to "re-think" a program and to try to find out if it is still appropriate, given what we now know about the problem. The mental health field provides some very good examples of how this can occur. Based on medical research during the late twentieth century, we now understand many forms of mental illness in a very different way than we did twenty or thirty years ago. As more diagnoses are found to have genetic and chemical origins, many mental health programs (especially those with a strong psychoanalytical treatment philosophy) have had to undergo major revisions or have been terminated altogether. Services now include far less emphasis on traditional "talk therapy," and focus instead on helping patients maintain their health through medication compliance. Our perception of the optimal "treatment relationship" with clients has been modified along with the nature of services offered. Those programs that have successfully made the transition have frequently employed needs assessments prior to making changes, much as they would have had the old program never existed. Some very basic questions have been addressed, for example, Is there still a need for our program? and, If so, what changes must be made to make it more relevant to the problem as we now understand it?

Changes in Intervention "Technology." **Intervention technology** is not the same as information technology and does not relate (at least not directly) to computers. It is our knowledge of the best way to treat a problem. Sometimes our understanding of a problem and what causes it changes little over time, but we learn what interventions are (or are not) effective in addressing it. This is most likely to occur following one or (more likely) several program outcome evaluations that have either (1) demonstrated the effectiveness of services very different from ours, or (2) demonstrated the ineffectiveness of services like ours for addressing a problem. Then, a needs assessment can help us to address such central questions as, If we offer the service that has proven most effective, will clients be receptive to it? Or, Should the new service be offered along with the old one or in place of it?

Sometimes changes in what is considered to be "state-of-the-art" intervention technology are imposed on us rather than something we learn from experience or even believe to be desirable. A program may need to conduct a needs assessment to learn how much it needs to change in order to continue to remain credible or continue to receive financial reimbursement based on current beliefs and policies regarding "what works best." For example, during the last few years of the twentieth century, welfare reform and the replacement of the old AFDC program with Temporary Assistance for Needy Families (TANF) created a new "prescribed" intervention for the problem of financial dependency. It changed from cash assistance to provision of certain time-limited services as child care, and job training and education—services designed to help clients locate and get good paying jobs. By 2003, over half of federal welfare spending was no longer going to provide cash to needy families. It was going for the other services instead.[5] Programs in the public sector and those in the for-profit or not-for-profit sectors who depended on contracts with the public sector for payment for their services could have benefited from a needs assessment designed to learn how to make their programs more responsive to this development and to avoid the loss of federal reimbursement.

Changes in Funding.   If a program receives a large funding cut, a needs assessment can help to determine what services can be eliminated or scaled back while doing the least damage to the program and its chances for achieving its objectives. In the less common scenario in which funding increases, a needs assessment can help to answer the central question, What would be the most productive use of the increased funding for increasing the likelihood that the program will achieve its objectives?

A related situation that may suggest the advisability of a needs assessment is changes in reimbursement for services. Some programs depend heavily on contracts for outside reimbursement for services, for example, through a contract with the local department of social services to provide a certain number of "billable hours of service" or to serve a certain number of clients. Any changes in the formula for reimbursement by the contracting agency can represent a major threat to the funding of the program. When these changes occur, decisions must be made regarding such important program issues as who can continue to be served or what services can continue to be offered, given the amount of funding that the program must have to survive. Such decisions can be made most equitably and with the least disruption to the program with data from a needs assessment.

In programs that depend on third-party reimbursements from HMOs or other health insurance providers such as Blue Cross/Blue Shield, any major changes in reimbursement policies can suggest the need for a needs assessment. In the 1990s, efforts at cost containment resulted in changes that virtually eliminated reimbursement for long-term mental health counseling or long-term evaluation of mental illness. A greater emphasis on brief evaluation, crisis intervention, and outpatient services has meant that many programs offering more traditional, long-term health services needed to evaluate whether they were still needed (and could remain financially solvent) or what changes in their services were required for them to continue.

Changes in Mandates.   A **mandate** may come in many forms, but they all represent a requirement that a program must meet. They may originate in some branch of the federal, state, or local government. They may take the form of laws, amendments, executive orders, or some other carefully worded statement that, for example, dictates hiring practices, working conditions, methods for protection of client confidentiality (such as HIPAA), and so forth. Or, they may be simply the requirements of a private foundation (often reflecting its mission and the values of the individual or group that donated money to establish it) that provides funding for a program.

If a program is receiving outside funding, it must comply with certain mandates and requirements. If they change, the program must adapt or risk losing its funding. The best way to learn how to adapt is often by conducting a needs assessment. When this occurs, often the central research question is, How can we make the necessary changes to be in compliance with the new mandate while not jeopardizing the program's potential for achieving its objectives?

Role of the Evaluator

The role of the evaluator in a needs assessment of an existing program is essentially the same as in a needs assessment of a proposed program—a researcher. The evaluator can be an outsider, or someone employed within the program or the larger organization. Whichever is the case, his or her role is to use whatever data sources and methods are necessary to learn if the program is still needed and, if so, what changes are indicated.

Central Research Questions and Hypotheses

In a needs assessment designed to evaluate an existing program, the central research question would be, Is the program still needed and, if so, does it need to be modified? Of course, if it is concluded early in the course of a needs assessment that a program is no longer needed (a rarity), a second central research question might be, What would be the best way to phase out the program?

The implicit hypothesis in a needs assessment of an existing program would usually be, The program is still needed in some form. However, in less common situations in which evidence has accumulated that the program may have become obsolete or unnecessary, the implicit research hypothesis might be, The program is no longer needed. Thus, it would be predicted that the program and the incidence of the problem are no longer related.

Specific Research Questions

The specific research questions in the needs assessment for an existing program relate directly to the changes that are perceived to have occurred. They are designed to determine if they are real, and if so, how they may have affected the need for the current program. If it appears that the program is still needed but requires revision, questions will relate to the appropriateness of any revisions that are being considered and how successful they might be.

General Characteristics

Needs assessments of existing programs share many of the same characteristics as needs assessments conducted of programs that are only being considered. For example, they use a wide range of methods of data collection and rely heavily on the evaluator to make sense out of data that take many forms. Conclusions are necessarily subjective and take the form of recommendations, rather than definitive answers.

There are also some notable differences. A needs assessment of an existing program tends to be more narrowly focused and is thus generally smaller in scope. Funding to conduct it often must be drawn from the existing program budget. The program is unlikely to have the luxury of being able to grant released time to one or more staff members to conduct it. Because it is most likely to be conducted in response to some change that has occurred (such as those just mentioned), answers are often sought to only one or a few specific questions directly related to that change. They will influence decisions that sometimes (as in the case of changes in funding or in mandates) must be made almost immediately. The decisions cannot be postponed pending more data collection, because the financial stability of the program, jobs of its staff members, or the well-being of its clients is often at stake.

A program that has been in existence for a while has "learned" over time. In some instances, its staff members have confirmed what was suggested by an earlier needs assessment; in others, they have found it to be incorrect. A good program manager takes note of what has been learned and already has made necessary adjustments as the program matured. So, by the time a subsequent needs assessment is conducted in response to some change, much of what was unknown prior to the program's implementation (for example, the demographic characteristics of its clients, attitudes of community leaders toward the program, staffing needs, budget needs) is now known. There is no need to assess these "contextual variables" again, unless there is reason to believe that the change that has occurred has somehow affected them. That makes it possible to devote limited time and energies to addressing the central research question or questions.

Reports of needs assessments conducted on existing programs tend to be shorter and more "to the point" than those of programs only in the planning stage. Sometimes they consist of simply a series of research questions and their respective answers, with documentation for the answers presented in response to each question (or included as appendices). The documentation is likely to consist of a mixture of descriptive statistics, quotations from key informants, and narrative summaries of focus groups or community forums.

CONCLUDING THOUGHTS

Whether conducted in relation to a proposed program or an existing one, needs assessments are performed to improve decision making. They can help us to avoid costly mistakes and the inefficient use of limited resources.

There is no one best way to conduct a needs assessment. Each is designed as a unique entity, relying heavily on common sense, our knowledge of practice, and our knowledge of research. The example of the needs assessment for a proposed international adoption program reflects my ideas, experiences, and preferences for getting the job done, but is in no way an exemplar of the right way to do it. I would be surprised if readers did not find fault with something I proposed and did not think there would be a better way to accomplish it. Such a difference of opinion is only natural, and is one reason why needs assessments often are conducted by a team or committee rather than an individual. Often, someone else really does have a better idea.

Needs assessments, as was noted, are exploratory and descriptive in nature. A design for a needs assessment is supposed to be flexible—more flexible than in, for example, an outcome evaluation. Changes during the process of data collection invariably occur, and that is OK. In a needs assessment, the evaluator is only trying to obtain the most accurate picture possible. The best way to do that is often unclear until the data collection is already underway.

Unlike some other types of program evaluation, the evaluator in a needs assessment is not greatly concerned about introducing confounding variables or threats to internal validity. The findings of all needs assessments are necessarily subjective and are assumed to contain some degree of measurement error.

Needs assessments often draw much of their data from confidential interviews, focus groups, or key informants. The people in these groups cannot be considered a random sample, as they contain "some conscious or unconscious bias."[6] The groups are comprised using what can best be described as purposive sampling, since they are designed to select "unique cases that are especially informative."[7] Members are chosen because it is assumed that they possess some knowledge or insights that can be helpful in making a decision about the program. Diversity of opinion is often desirable, often at the expense of sample representativeness. Thus, needs assessments are, at best, a good estimate of reality. They produce better, more informed decisions, decisions based on more than simply what appears logical or what common sense suggests. However, no one could ever claim that they will ensure that a decision based on a needs assessment will always be the correct one. Only time can tell us that.

KEY TERMS

staff authority	executive summary	mandate
researcher/synthesizer	intervention technology	

STUDY QUESTIONS

1. What is the role of the evaluator in a needs assessment? How does it differ from the usual role of a researcher?

2. What are some personal attributes that are desirable for a person conducting a needs assessment?

3. What do we hope to accomplish from conducting a needs assessment of a proposed program?

4. What are some reasons why an administrator might decide not to implement a program that a needs assessment has identified as needed?

5. What are some of the most common sources of data in needs assessments? Why do they produce what can be described as just an "estimate of reality"?

6. In what ways does the report of a needs assessment differ from the usual format of a research report?

7. What are some indicators that it might be desirable to conduct a needs assessment of an existing program?

8. What are some recent changes in *intervention technology* (our knowledge of the best way to treat a problem) that might cause us to question the need for an existing program in its current form?

9. What are some recent changes in state and federal mandates that might suggest that a needs assessment of an existing program in your area should be conducted? Explain.

10. What are some of the major ways in which a needs assessment of a proposed program differs from a needs assessment of an existing one?

REFERENCES

1. Nugent, W., Sieppert, J., & Hudson, W. (2001). *Practice evaluation for the 21st century.* Belmont, CA: Brooks/Cole, 32.
2. Ibid.
3. Weinbach, R. (2003). *The social worker as manager: A practical guide to success* (4th ed.). Boston: Allyn & Bacon, 209–211.
4. Nurius, P., & Hudson, W. (1993). *Human services: Practice, evaluation, and computers.* Pacific Grove, CA: Brooks/Cole, 188.
5. Pear, R. (2003, October 13). Welfare spending shows huge shift. *The New York Times on the Web.* http://www.newyorktimes.com.
6. Fortune, A., & Reid, W. (1999). *Research in social work* (3rd ed.). New York: Columbia University Press, 214.
7. Neuman, W. L. (2004). *Basics of social research: Qualitative and quantitative approaches.* Boston: Allyn & Bacon, 138–139.

CHAPTER EIGHT

EVALUATIONS TO IMPROVE PROGRAMS

A needs assessment (Chapter 7) can help us to determine whether a proposed program is needed and, if so, what form it should take. An outcome evaluation (discussed in Chapters 9–11) can help us to learn if a program has been effective in achieving its objectives. That covers the two ends of a time-limited program's life cycle. But what about a program that is underway, but not yet at the point that it would be fair to try to arrive at conclusions about its effectiveness? This chapter examines some common types of evaluation activities that occur during the middle phases of a program's life cycle. They all share one goal—program improvement.

COMPLETING UNFINISHED BUSINESS

In the ideal world, programs develop like this: A tentative **program model** is constructed. It describes what is believed to be the problem, what potential clients the program will serve, and how the program plans to approach addressing the problem. Then a comprehensive needs assessment confirms the need for such a program and suggests ways that the program model should be modified, based on what was learned. Then a revised program model is constructed. It is consistent with the overall mission of the organization. The model contains a clear description of the program's anticipated inputs, activities, outputs, and outcomes. There are clear goal statements and carefully worded program objectives that state precisely what the program hopes to accomplish and by when. The program is implemented with everyone knowing what they are doing and why. It all fits. Does it happen this way in the real world? Sometimes, but not always.

Even when a good needs assessment has been conducted and it has been used to construct a program that seems to have good potential for success, it is not unusual for the program to get underway with many important planning tasks not completed. Sometimes, this occurs because of poor management or simply a lack of appreciation for the importance of conceptualizing just what the program is all about. But it also may occur because of time pressures. For example, funding for the program may be available only if it is "up and running" by a certain date. If not, the program may have to wait for another year (and there may be no guarantee of funding then). Or, the need for the program may appear to be so great that the decision is made to start it now and complete the rest of the task of conceptualizing the program after it is underway. After all, it is rationalized, every program encounters some "surprises," unanticipated events or phenomena that may require modifications in the program model. Why not just finalize the model after the program is operational?

Identifying Problems in Program Models

If there is any indication that a program is operating without a complete, well-articulated, and well-integrated program model, the situation must be corrected. However, first it must be learned exactly what is missing or inadequate. This is accomplished by something called **evaluability assessment.** It is a procedure for discovering whether a program is ready to be evaluated. Often, it identifies gaps and other problems in a program's model, thus making it possible to correct them. Once an evaluability assessment has been conducted and necessary changes made, it then becomes possible to evaluate it using the methods in this chapter and those that follow. As Unrau, Gabor, and Grinnell state, "evaluability assessment can expose areas of the program's conceptualization and/or organization that interfere both with the delivery of its services and with the program evaluation effort itself."[1] The procedure generally involves a "team effort" on the part of program staff and the program's stakeholders designed to identify gaps in the program model or components of it that are illogical, not clearly articulated, impractical, unrealistic, and so forth.

Probably the most common problem that evaluability assessments identify is a lack of clearly articulated goals and objectives. While the two terms are often used together, the distinction between goals and objectives is important in program evaluations because the achievement of a program's *objectives,* specifically outcome objectives, not its *goals* is a major focus of outcome evaluations (discussed in Chapters 9–11).

Goals.   A program's **goals** are more specific than a mission, but not as specific as a program objective. A goal may be unique to a program or it may be one that is shared by other programs that seek to address the same problem. Goals are sometimes described as "what a program would hope to accomplish." Sometimes that description is accurate; sometimes it is less accurate. What a program would hope to accomplish is often idealistic and unattainable. Ideally, the goal of many programs is to eliminate a problem altogether. But many problems such as family violence or substance abuse will not be eliminated in our lifetimes and will probably never be eliminated. In some cases, the elimination of a problem may never be achieved because societal values or political forces stand in the way. For example, homelessness or poverty are problems that no program realistically can hope to eliminate, although it might be theoretically possible to accomplish it because the necessary resources exist. In fact, programs that address such problems are unlikely to even make a measurable dent in them. Thus, in many programs the real goals of a program tend to be more limited and realistic than what the program would hope to accomplish.

Consider the possible goals of an international adoption program, the hypothetical example from Chapter 7. They might be only somewhat more specific than its mission statement. For example, the mission might be "to advocate for and unite children in foreign nations and their potential adoptive parents." A goal might be, "to provide loving homes for unwanted children now living in orphanages in countries throughout the world." Or, because such a program (unlike most other social programs) would really have double beneficiaries (adoptive parents and children), it could also be, "to provide children from foreign nations for couples and individuals who seek to become parents through adoption." Either goal is attainable, but only in a very limited way. Certainly the program would not be able to provide a home for every child who meets the description or to meet the needs of every potential parent who seeks a child. There are just too many of both groups. In addition, children in some countries will be unavailable for political reasons. Others will have such severe special needs that it may not be possible to find parents willing or able to adopt them. Immigration quotas will also limit the number of adoptions that can be completed each year. And, even among those adoptions that are completed, will every home be "loving" as the first goal states? Unfortunately, probably not.

The fact that the goal of a program is only attainable to a limited degree does not mean that it is not useful. Goals (like missions) help to keep a program on track and to provide guidance to program staff. They "provide the focus, orientation and direction needed to harness the combined energy and activities of a staff so that chaos and confusion are minimized and clients' needs are served by the program."[2] So, for example, the first goal of our international adoption program would inform staff that the potential for a "loving home" might be a more important criterion to apply when conducting adoption studies than the education levels, ages of prospective parents, or the fact that one potential parent might have a disability. Or, the second goal would suggest that a single person or a gay or lesbian couple might be considered acceptable parents.

Both examples of possible goals relate to clients and how the program would hope to serve them. However, programs sometimes have other goals that may seem more self-serving. For example, another goal of the international adoption program might be, "To have the program fully self-supporting from client fees by the end of the third year of its operation." There is nothing wrong with such a goal; it is perfectly legitimate. After all, unless the program can become financially self-sufficient in a few years it might have to close down. It cannot continue to be a drain on the rest of the agency's budget. Of course, no social program should have *only* outcome goals that even appear on the surface to be designed to benefit the agency or its employees. That would make for very poor public relations. The clients served should be the program's prime beneficiaries, and at least some of the program's goals (such as the previous ones) should reflect it.

Objectives.   Program **objectives** tend to be more specific and more easily measurable than goals. They describe the outcomes that a program seeks, and whenever possible, the time at which it is hoped they will be accomplished. They often entail changes in its clients' behaviors or some other reduction in the problem that the program is designed to address. Thus, they describe how, it is believed, clients who complete the program will be better off than before they entered it. College students tend to be familiar with outcome objectives—examples of them are on the course syllabus distributed at the beginning of a class. They tell how a student should be different following course completion than he or she was before taking the course. Specifically, course outcome objectives state the knowledge, values, and skills that a student can be expected to possess following successful completion of the course.

In an international adoption program, some objectives might be less focused on client changes than in other programs where clients have a problem such as substance abuse, family violence, or are "dysfunctional" in some other way. Examples of the program's objectives might be:

1. "To provide a viable option for those prospective adoptive parents who may not qualify for domestic adoption services because of one or more demographic characteristics."
2. "To provide a viable option for those prospective adoptive parents who, for various reasons, might prefer to adopt a child from a foreign country over a domestic adoption."
3. "To have successfully placed forty children from foreign orphanages in loving homes by the end of the second year of the program's operation."

The first two objectives are may still sound somewhat vague, more like a goal or even a mission. However, they would be reasonable objectives for such a program. With a little thought and planning, it would be possible to determine whether the program had successfully achieved them. The third objective is more specific and contains time parameters. It is more typical of what objectives tend to look like in well-designed programs. It would be consistent with the program's goal of moving toward financial self-sufficiency.

Of the three objectives above, the second is probably the most controversial. But then, international adoptions itself is a controversial issue. Some people suggest that it is contradictory to principles of social justice. For example, international adoptions may exploit family poverty and gender discrimination. They can violate a child's right to his or her cultural and ethnic identification.[3] Furthermore, the second objective would seem to grant legitimacy (for whatever reason) to choosing to adopt a child from, say China or Russia over one in North America (perhaps, one with special needs) who is also in need of a loving home. That also is controversial and can introduce the specter of racism or elitism. So, should the second objective be an outcome objective of the program? Yes, if it is in fact consistent with the agency's mission. The controversial issues surrounding international adoptions should have been identified and discussed as part of the needs assessment for the program. Once having decided to implement the program (knowing it would be controversial), it would be best to be up-front about what the program hopes to accomplish. Besides, as the second objective is written, it seems consistent with social work values. Providing additional options to our clients (and allowing them to choose among them) is generally consistent with good social work practice.

The achievement of a program's objectives should be its central focus. All of the programs' activities should be related to it, either directly or indirectly. When goals and objectives are not clearly stated, some of the activities of a program may seem to lack purpose and direction. Conflicts can arise over whether a task is necessary or desirable. The question, Just why are we doing this? may be difficult to answer.

When there is a lack of clearly stated goals and objectives, there is also a second problem. It will be difficult, if not impossible, to conduct an objective outcome evaluation at some later date. How is it possible to learn if a program has been successful in achieving its objectives if they have never been clearly articulated?

Addressing the Problem

Whether a program model lacks clearly stated goals and objectives or is found to have one or more other problems in its conceptualization, the procedure for correcting the problem is much the same. It entails a careful examination of the program as it currently exists and then making necessary adjustments in the program and its model so that they reflect a better "fit." Sometimes this task falls solely to the program manager; more often it is delegated to a task force of the program's staff. Stakeholders may also be invited to participate.

Newer Programs. When a program has not been around very long (and especially if a needs assessment was completed prior to its start-up), it is relatively easy to complete its program model. The program will not have had much opportunity to "drift." Most likely, a few individuals will be able to sit down together for a few hours, examine the program thus far, and construct well-articulated goals and objectives that are appropriate for it. The process will result in few program changes.

Older Programs. If a program has been in existence for a few years or more and if its model was never clearly articulated in the first place, the task of completing its program model becomes more difficult. Without a clearly articulated program model, the program may have headed off in many different directions. It may have responded to various crises or forces such as client demands or political pressure. It is likely to lack unity and coherence; its goals and objectives may appear to be quite diverse, sometimes even conflicting.

Even if a program began with a clear purpose and its goals and objectives were unspecified but generally understood, the passage of time is likely to have produced important changes. The conditions that existed (for example, the severity of the problem, its pool of potential clients, its treatment philosophies, the needs of its clients) may have changed since the program began, and the program may have (and generally should have) adapted to these changes. Thus, beliefs about the programs goals and objectives that were once valid may now be obsolete. For example, consider a program designed to meet the needs of people who are HIV-positive that was implemented in 1990. At the time, AIDS was viewed as a terminal illness affecting primarily gay men and intravenous drug users. The major need of clients was to cope with their impending deaths. Now, because of medical research and progress in extending life, the needs of people who are diagnosed as HIV-positive are more similar to those with other long-term, chronic illnesses than to those who are terminally ill. And, of course, HIV-AIDS is now known to be a problem of people of both genders, all ethnic groups, all sexual orientations, and so forth. If the program has remained responsive to clients and their needs, it will necessarily have undergone numerous changes. Its goals and objectives should have changed accordingly.

Even if the need for an older program has not changed, change is still likely to have occurred. It can happen unintentionally and imperceptibly. Over the course of time, programs sometimes just tend to "drift" away from the way that they were originally conceived. Changes in staff can contribute to this. As staff members leave and are replaced, the new members bring with them their own preferences, experiences, biases, and beliefs that affect the program and how it functions. Changes in funding also can produce changes. Funding losses can cause a program to scale back, or increased funding can provide opportunities for services and other activities that were not originally planned.

Specifying the components of a program that has been in existence for a number of years must be accomplished with reference to what is, not what was supposed to be or what once was. "Fleshing out" the program model of a program that has been around for a while is an inductive process, the same approach used in qualitative research. It entails looking carefully at many aspects of the program that have evolved, its activities and services in particular, and determining what seem to be the various components of the program model. Certain questions are frequently asked. For example:

- What problem does the program appear to be addressing?
- How many clients does it serve?
- What are their demographic characteristics?
- What activities characterize the program?
- To what end do services seem to be directed?
- What outputs does the program produce?
- What about the program seems inappropriate or out of place?

Program evaluations that seek to complete the model of an older program almost invariably lead to changes in the program. That is to be expected. As programs drift, they begin to be less integrated. An evaluation reveals what changes are required to make the program more efficient, and to help it to function better as a unified system. The evaluation can suggest the need for changes in any part of the program. Sometimes, the original, implicit goals and objectives need to be first identified and then deleted in favor of others. The evaluation, after determining what appear to be the original goals and objectives of the program, may suggest that they are no longer appropriate. For example, a demographic description of the program's current clients may suggest that the old goals are no longer realistic or are otherwise inappropriate for them.

Some program components may be found that exist for no apparent reason, or for the wrong reason (for example, a staff member's personal preference). When examined, they just do not fit well with the rest of the program. For example, an activity group that is popular among both staff and clients may not contribute to the achievement of any of the program's apparent objectives in any way. If so, the group probably should be discontinued. It can be replaced by another service that promises to better contribute to their achievement.

There is likely to be a back-and-forth juggling and revising until everything about the program "fits" and is clearly articulated. The product that eventually emerges (a complete program model containing clear outcome objectives) makes it possible to conduct an outcome evaluation (Chapters 9–11) to learn if the program has been successful.

PROGRAM MONITORING

Even well-designed programs with a logical, fully-developed program model seem to have a life of their own. They can easily head off in new directions, or fail to move in anticipated ones. They require monitoring to keep them on track. **Program monitoring** is an ongoing activity. It is also an important part of program evaluation.

Role of the Evaluator

Monitoring is conducted internally, that is by people within a program rather than by an outside evaluator. Most often the responsibility for program monitoring falls to the program's manager. Monitoring is a normal management function—what manager would not want to keep up with what is happening within his or her program? Thus, unlike some of the other types of program evaluation that we will examine, the evaluator does not assume a new or different role. The evaluator remains, first and foremost, a manager. There is one notable exception, however. Some very large programs (in which monitoring is a full-time job) hire a "quality control" person whose only role is that of program monitor. In some programs that receive major outside funding, there is now a requirement that the program have a quality control specialist.

Central Research Questions and Hypotheses

The central question in program monitoring is, Are program activities being accomplished as intended? The implicit research hypothesis is, Program activities are being accomplished as intended. The monitoring is designed to determine whether this is indeed the case.

Specific Research Questions

There are always a number of research questions in program monitoring. They relate to the program design and the degree to which any variations from it have been allowed to occur. Research questions may vary over the course of the program. As problems are identified, new questions are often added to learn if they have been addressed. Some questions may also be dropped over time as they are answered satisfactorily.

Monitoring Issues

Monitoring, like other forms of evaluation, entails collecting data and, in a less-formalized way, processing it. When I refer to processing here, I am referring to compiling data and descriptively analyzing it, not using tests of statistical inference. That does not mean that computers cannot be used to store data (they often are), or even to aggregate it in a way that it can more easily be interpreted (such as through frequency distributions or graphs). However, the primary activity of monitoring is collecting data about a program and using it to fine-tune the program.

Of course, monitoring varies from program to program. Developing the best monitoring plan for a given program requires addressing certain questions. They include:

Who Assumes What Role?   Whoever assumes the ultimate responsibility for monitoring (manager or quality control specialist), assistance is generally available. The day-to-day tasks of monitoring often can be delegated to others. It is a good idea to involve staff at every level and as many stakeholder groups as possible. This can help to give everyone a sense of shared ownership in the monitoring process. Regular, unobtrusive data collection by many people should occur over the full life of the program. It should be an integral part of the program model. When this happens, data collection is just part of the everyday routine, and staff members who participate in it do not speculate too much on possible ulterior motives for why it is being collected.

How Much Data Should Be Collected?   Data collection for monitoring purposes should be sufficient to form impressions and make certain judgments about the program and its functioning. It should help the evaluator to identify major potential or emerging problems early enough that they can be corrected before they become too costly. But it does not need to spot and suggest corrective action for every little glitch in the program. That usurps the role of others and leaves the manager or others vulnerable to charges of micromanaging.

Data collection should never be so extensive that it hinders the functioning of the program and its staff members. It should not elicit comments such as, "We have no time to serve our clients; we spend most of our time keeping records!" In short, the answer to the question, How much data should be collected? is, No more than is needed.

What Data Should Be Collected?   It is the program that is being evaluated, not personnel within it. Thus, the kind of data collected should be about the program and its functioning, not about its staff members. The data should not give the impression that the evaluator is trying to "get the goods" on anyone or even on any part of the program.

As a general rule, the most relevant data to collect would be those related to the program's inputs, activities, outputs, and outcomes. The demographic characteristics of clients served is pretty standard. Other common ones would be amount of services provided, client retention in the program, referral sources, staff turnover, and where the program is relative to its budget.

Most of the data collected as part of monitoring evaluation are also those that are generally required for use in an outcome study. Collecting them on an on-going basis as part of monitoring can save having to dig for them later when access to some of them may have been lost.

Whose Data Are They, and How Should They Be Aggregated and Stored?   The data belong to the program and its staff. With the exception of those few that might be related to personnel matters (such as salaries), they should be stored in a place where they are available to program staff. If professional staff members have personal computers, they should be able to access program data from their own work stations; if not they can be kept in files readily accessed. Periodically, data should be aggregated and shared in staff meetings or in written or electronic reports. This can be performed by an administrative assistant or anyone else capable of doing it.

Besides the manager, other staff members may use the data from time to time (while maintaining appropriate confidentiality) to assist in making day-to-day decisions that they have the authority to make. For example, a review of demographic descriptions of client characteristics may result in changes in day care or transportation support provided.

Responses to Monitoring

The most obvious response to monitoring is to address problems as they are identified. For example, if a program is overspending its budget, spending cuts may have to be made or additional program funding acquired. Or, if referrals to the program are dropping off, networking efforts and marketing of the program may need to be increased or modified. By constantly monitoring a program, damage control can be kept to a minimum. Problems can be addressed before they cause major difficulties for the program.

Sometimes managers conducting program monitoring are too focused on problem identification. They are so busy pouring over data to detect problems that they fail to see where good things are happening in the program and to compliment and reward those who are helping them to occur. Providing compliments and showing appreciation for the work of subordinates is always good management practice. However, from an evaluation perspective, identifying program strengths is a valuable exercise for another reason. It is just as important as spotting and addressing problems. Learning what is working or where a program appears to be successful can lead to a program doing more of the same—and, thus, can increase the likelihood of the program being successful overall.

FORMATIVE EVALUATIONS

> We already have a two-month waiting list for our services.
>
> Our staff seems to have more than enough to do.
>
> The program seems to have attracted a very experienced group of professionals.

In the past, observations like these have sometimes been the basis for determining how a relatively new program seems to be functioning. They may indicate that the program is doing just fine, moving toward achieving its objectives. Or, they may not! A long waiting list could reflect all kinds of problems related to program start-up or an inefficient intake system, and, of course, we can only speculate on why the program is so popular with clients. A busy staff could be an indication that the other activities of staff (for example, record keeping, meetings, correspondence) are interfering with service delivery. The fact that a staff is experienced may be a plus, or it could be a warning of a potential problem—perhaps, preconceived ideas about how the program should function. Staff members may be set in their ways and resist adapting to the new program, and its philosophy, and the program model.

There are now better ways to evaluate a relatively new program. The type of program evaluation that is most associated with programs in their early stages is the formative evaluation. Like program monitoring, **formative evaluations** are conducted primarily to "fine tune" and improve programs after they have been implemented, but before they are at a stage where an outcome evaluation (also called a summative evaluation) might be appropriate.

Monitoring and Formative Evaluations

The distinction between program monitoring and formative evaluations sometimes gets a little blurred. This is attributable in part to the fact that some programs contract to have a formative evaluation performed, yet they really are requesting some monitoring as well. For example, they may want the evaluator to collect relevant data over an extended period of time as the program matures (which is a lot like monitoring). Another factor contributing to the confusion is that in conducting a formative evaluation the evaluator relies on many of the same data that are routinely collected as a part of program monitoring. For example, client counts and characteristics, sources of referral, and client attrition often are important indicators used in conducting a formative evaluation.

A certain amount of overlap between program monitoring and formative evaluations is inevitable, given the shared primary purpose (program improvement) of these two types of program evaluation. However, there are some important interrelated differences. They can be very helpful for understanding what a formative evaluation is (and what it is not):

1. Monitoring is conducted primarily to assess program fidelity, that is, Are the intended activities occurring in the intended way and by the intended people? In contrast, a formative evaluation is conducted to learn if the intended processes are in place *and* if they seem to be achieving the intended outcomes or at least have the potential to achieve them. It is designed to learn which processes are working best and which may not be working as well or not working at all.

2. Generally, monitoring is a function of, and conducted by, managers (agency employees). A formative evaluation is most often conducted by an outside evaluator hired specifically for this purpose. While both program monitoring and formative evaluations rely on many of the same data to draw conclusions, they may be interpreted differently in a formative evaluation than in program monitoring. The outside evaluator has less personal investment in the program and its success than its manager, who is likely to have been heavily involved in planning for it. The outside evaluator is likely to identify problems in the program that its manager is more likely to miss or ignore. In program monitoring, the manager may have certain blind spots about "my program" or may only choose not to see certain problems developing. In addition, staff are probably less likely to reveal problems with the program to their boss (and risk his or her displeasure or defensiveness) than to an outside evaluator.

3. With monitoring, the person conducting the evaluation generally has the authority to make changes in the program (and makes them) based on the data that are collected. In a formative evaluation, the evaluator collects data and recommends changes to the program manager, but the manager ultimately decides whether to implement the recommended changes.

4. Scheduling of and budgeting for a formative evaluation often are part of the program model. Unless stipulated by a grant or contract agreement, the manager generally decides who will conduct it. However, after hiring the evaluator, the manager only provides certain input (often communicating what he or she especially wishes to know about the program's functioning) and assists the evaluator. Creation of the actual design of the evaluation usually is left to the discretion of the evaluator—the expert on evaluation.

5. Monitoring is (or should be) ongoing over the life cycle of a program. Data collection for it is often part of the program model. A formative evaluation is generally conducted over a limited period of time. It seeks to evaluate the status of a program at some point in its life cycle, usually early in its existence.

(However, sometimes conducting formative evaluations can take a relatively long time.)

6. Program monitoring is conducted strictly for the benefit of the program and the agency where it is housed. Its findings are not designed to be shared with anyone outside the organization. A formative evaluation is also conducted for the benefit the program, but its findings may be shared with others, for example, the government agency or charitable foundation providing major funding for the program. Formative evaluations are now mandatory for many programs receiving outside funding. In the contract signed by all parties there is a written requirement that a report of a formative evaluation must be submitted by a prescribed date. Sometimes the design for the evaluation is even specified. Thus, unlike those of monitoring, the results of a formative evaluation sometimes place a program's continuation in some jeopardy if they are critical of the program's progress.

Role of the Evaluator

In a formative evaluation, the evaluator generally is an "outsider," that is, not a regular employee of a program. Evaluators conducting formative evaluations function like consultants in many ways—becoming knowledgeable of the program, identifying strengths and weaknesses, and making recommendations for how it can be improved. However, if the results of the evaluation are to be shared with people outside the program (such as those who provide its funding) to assist them in making decisions about the program's future, an evaluator also has another role: fact finder. The evaluator is expected to see if the program is doing what it promised, is cost efficient, is on schedule, and so forth. This expectation can result in managers and staff sometimes attempting to hide problems that exist within the program, thereby limiting an evaluator's ability to function as an effective consultant.

Central Research Questions and Hypotheses

In a formative evaluation, one central research question is, How is the program doing so far? The central research hypotheses are implicit, not stated or tested through rigorous inferential statistical analysis. However, there are two central hypotheses in most formative evaluations. They are, (1) The program has been implemented as planned, and (2) The program is progressing satisfactorily toward the achievement of its objectives. Or, the two hypotheses could be combined and stated as one: The program is operational and making satisfactory progress.

Specific Research Questions

A formative evaluation, like any research, seeks answers to a number of specific questions. Some of them are common to all formative evaluations, others are unique to the program being evaluated. Unlike an outcome evaluation which seeks feedback, a formative evaluation seeks **feed-forward**. What is the difference? Feedback seeks answers to questions like, Did this program work? or, What did its clients think of it? In contrast, feed-forward is designed to evaluate a program while it is still early enough in its life cycle to make changes and correct problems before it is too late. Both types of information are valuable, but for different purposes. Feedback helps us to do better the next time, while feed-forward helps us to make improvements now. In a college course, a professor can obtain feedback by reviewing the student evaluations completed at the end of the course. But he or she can obtain feed-forward by formally or informally asking students how the course is perceived by them and asking for suggestions for change after only a few weeks into the semester. In a similar way, in formative research evaluation the evaluator asks, How is the program doing so far? but also, What changes need to be made to the program?

All program evaluations are selective. They focus on certain limited aspects of the program. In a formative evaluation, the focus is primarily on the status of services and the support system present for them. Thus, the activities and perceptions of professional staff, administrators, and clients often receive considerable attention. In conducting a formative evaluation, the evaluator hopes to learn what services are being offered, what do clients and staff think about them, and what administrative activities seem to support or obstruct service delivery. What is learned can then be used to make needed changes in the program in order to increase the likelihood that the program's objectives will be achieved.

What are some of the more specific questions that formative evaluations commonly seek to answer? If the program is still quite new, they might include those in Box 8.1. If the program is a little more "mature" and has been offering services for some time, some of the questions in Box 8.1 may still be appropriate.

BOX 8.1

**COMMONLY ASKED QUESTIONS IN A
FORMATIVE EVALUATION OF A NEW PROGRAM**

- What components of the program are not yet implemented?
- Is the program at its anticipated stage of development?
- How many clients have been served to date?
- Is the program fully staffed with qualified people?
- Are personnel practices within acceptable guidelines?
- Are expenditures appropriate for the program's stage of development?
- How well known is the program in the community?
- Are there any common misconceptions about the program and its services? Who holds them and why?
- How well have sources of client referral been developed?
- What obstacles to planned activities have been encountered?
- What do staff members like, or not like, about the program?
- How do staff members perceive support for the program, both within it and within the agency and community?

BOX 8.2

**COMMONLY ASKED QUESTIONS IN A FORMATIVE
EVALUATION OF A MORE "MATURE" PROGRAM**

- How long has the program been fully operational?
- Do services offered seem to have the potential to contribute to achieving program objectives?
- Does the program seem to be making good progress toward achieving its objectives?
- Are activities and services still consistent with the program model?
- Is the program serving the clients for whom it was intended?
- Is the program visible and respected within the human services community?
- How much attrition has there been among clients and among staff?
- Do staff members perceive that they receive the appropriate amount of autonomy for decision making?
- Do staff members perceive that administrative support is adequate?
- Does it appear that the program is "overbudget" or that there were other financial miscalculations?
- How satisfied are staff and the program's stakeholders with the program?
- How satisfied are clients with the program?

However, others designed to evaluate the viability of the program and to see if it is operating as intended might require answers. Box 8.2 contains some research questions that are frequently asked in a formative evaluation of a more mature program.

Data Sources

As in a needs assessment, support for the implicit research hypothesis or hypotheses comes from many sources. Some of them (for example, number and sources of referrals, budget expenditures, or staffing patterns) can be quantified and displayed using graphs, tables, and descriptive statistics. They are used primarily to describe services, activities, and outputs to date. Some associations and correlations between variables may also lend support for the research hypotheses. However, many conclusions about the current status of the program (for example, those based on personal observations of the evaluator, confidential interviews, and focus groups) can only be supported by narrative descriptions and summaries.

While, as described earlier, client-satisfaction surveys have dubious value in most types of program evaluations, formative evaluations are a notable exception. Satisfaction surveys often can be quite valuable, not so much as an indicator of whether the program is achieving its objectives, but more for their capacity to identify obstacles to client full participation in the program. For example, a satisfaction survey may reveal that clients perceive that the program is not sufficiently accommodating because it does not provide child care or has limited evening hours in which working clients can participate. Or it may reveal that the program is perceived by clients to be elitist or favor one group of clients over another because of some component of the program itself. Often, once these "dissatisfiers" have come to the attention of the program's manager, relatively minor changes can be made to address them and full client participation can be increased.

What clients reveal about what they like about a program in a satisfaction survey can also be helpful. It might be revealed that the program is producing some unintended additional benefits, an indication that few changes should be made. Or comments may suggest that the program is vulnerable to being abused. For example, a parent education program may appear to be primarily providing free babysitting or time off from work; clients are not using it for the purposes intended. Then, changes in the program can be instituted to reduce the likelihood of abuse and to increase the likelihood that it will produce the desired outcomes.

Methods for Conducting Formative Evaluations

Sometimes a standard already exists that can be applied for conducting a formative evaluation. Perhaps the program is only one of many similar programs offered throughout the country by organizations that have a national affiliation. Over time, it has been learned what a program of this type should look like, and how it should function if it is to be successful. Standards have been developed. (An example might be the Healthy Families program offered by many state chapters of the national organization, Prevent Child Abuse America.) If this is the case and the specific program is a relatively new one, the focus of a formative evaluation would be pretty much a "given." The evaluation would examine the program with reference to the standards, identifying where things are going well (that is, are consistent with the standard), and where changes may need to be made.

If no standards already exist, as is more often the case, a formative evaluation requires more creativity. Sometimes an experienced evaluator who has evaluated similar programs can do the job alone. Other times, an evaluation team may do a better job of developing an evaluation design that covers all of the important questions and issues. The team may consist of several evaluators who have become experts at conducting evaluations. Or it may be a team of individuals who are not professional evaluators, but bring a variety of valuable perspectives to the assignment. For example, the team (sometimes referred to as a "blue ribbon panel") may be composed of people who bring a variety of perceptions of and interests in the program. Such a team might include:

- a member of the program's professional staff
- a member of the program's support staff
- a representative of the community who is not a client
- a board member
- a staff member from a related program who interacts with the program (for example, he or she makes referrals to the program)
- one or more clients of the program

Unless one or more of these individuals has some experience in conducting a formative evaluation, the team may seek out some paid or volunteer consultation services. Additional expertise sought could be in any area where the team acknowledges it is lacking, for example, in research methods, program management, personnel issues, or medical and legal issues.

An Example: A Formative Evaluation for a New Program

Again using the example of an international adoption program in a family service agency, this program began nine months ago, is licensed, is conducting home studies with prospective adoptive parents, but has not yet placed a child for adoption. Thus, the program is still not yet fully operational. (This situation is a little unusual since, after nine months, at least some client "successes" would be an expectation in most other programs.)

In addition to most of the questions listed in Box 8.1 (modified as required to fit the program), there are always other questions in a formative evaluation that are specific to a given program and its unique characteristics. Box 8.3 contains examples of what some of these might be in a nine-month-old international adoptions program, along with the data sources that could be used to answer them.

The questions in Box 8.3 are by no means a comprehensive list. As the data collection for a formative evaluation takes place, other potential indicators of how the program is functioning to date would emerge. They, in turn, would suggest some new questions. They could be added to the list and their answers sought. That is a common occurrence and a perfectly acceptable one in a formative evaluation. Modifications in the evaluation design are made whenever it is believed that they will help to produce a more complete picture of the program and its functioning.

Because establishing an international adoption program faces so many bureaucratic obstacles and takes so long, a formative evaluation after only nine months of its existence could probably produce only a very tentative conclusion about whether the program is likely to be successful in achieving its outcome objectives. All that might be learned is whether everything is in place, or is getting in place, as it should be so that the desired outcomes of the program *can* occur when the time comes.

Some people might suggest that a formative evaluation of a program of this nature might better be delayed until, say after the second or third year of its operation. However, an opposing argument would be that to delay a formative evaluation that long might cheat program managers of feed-forward information when it is most needed. It might not provide it soon enough to make necessary changes in the program. For example, what if the fee schedule for clients had been set too low? A formative evaluation after the second or third year might be too late to save the program from major financial difficulties. Why wait? It is possible to get a pretty accurate description of the financial situation of the program's clients much earlier and, at the same time, to identify other problems that the program has begun to encounter.

BOX 8.3

EXAMPLES OF QUESTIONS AND DATA SOURCES IN A FORMATIVE EVALUATION OF AN INTERNATIONAL ADOPTION PROGRAM

- *What international connections have been established? In what countries? How soon are children likely to be released for adoption?*—Confidential interviews with program managers and selected staff.
- *What is the perception of the program among community leaders?*—Key informants, evaluator observations.
- *Are clients receiving enough assistance from staff members in completing all requirements for adoption?*—Client-satisfaction survey, focus group with selected clients, confidential interviews with selected staff members.
- *How satisfied are clients overall with the progress that is being made?*—Client satisfaction survey, focus group with selected clients.
- *What legal and/or logistical obstacles remain to be overcome?*—Group interviews with program managers and selected staff.
- *What unanticipated expenses has the program encountered? Does the program budget appear adequate to continue to meet them?*—Confidential interviews with program managers and review of financial records.
- *Is the fee structure for clients appropriate, given the economic status of those who have applied and the sources of assistance that are available?*—Program records, confidential interviews with key staff.
- *Does the program appear to be on schedule for meeting its objective of being self-supporting by its third year of operation?*—Confidential interviews with program managers and review of financial records.
- *How has the program been received by other agencies who offer international adoption services?*—Focus group of personnel from other agencies, evaluator observations.
- *How does the program appear to have affected other agency programs?*—Confidential interview with agency director, focus group of staff in other programs.
- *How supportive have managers been to staff as they make mistakes and learn to function in a different kind of program?*—Focus group and confidential interviews with staff.
- *Are staff members satisfied with the progress that the program has made to date? What is the morale level of staff?*—Focus group and confidential interviews with staff, evaluator observations.

As a general rule, fine tuning of a program is best accomplished as soon as the data are available to indicate where it is needed. That is why most formative evaluations are conducted early, or at least not beyond midway, in the life cycle of a program.

PROCESS EVALUATIONS

Stating exactly what a **process evaluation** is (and is not) can be somewhat difficult. There is considerable disagreement as to whether a formative evaluation and a process evaluation are indeed different, or whether they are only different labels for the same type of research (like outcome evaluations and summative evaluations). One recent book mentions process evaluations, but it fails to even mention formative evaluations in its typology of program evaluations.[4] Other authors suggest that formative is just a way to describe one characteristic of a process evaluation; in other words, formative is only an adjective used to indicate the purpose of a process evaluation, an evaluation of a program that is "in-process" or underway (as opposed to a summative evaluation).[5] Other authors clearly perceive them as different. They identify some subtle as well as some substantive differences.[6] I have taken the latter position, that they are indeed different in some very important ways. The text that follows will expand on those differences, much as was done in differentiating between monitoring evaluations and formative evaluations earlier in this chapter. However, it will be a little more difficult here because, while most writers agree about what both monitoring and formative evaluations are all about, there is much less consensus about what a process evaluation is.

Formative Evaluations and Process Evaluations

Like a formative evaluation, a process evaluation is conducted when the program is underway, but is not yet far enough along to conduct an outcome evaluation. Another similarity is that both types of research are used primarily to improve the program rather than to pass judgment on it. That is about where the similarity ends. What appear to be some important differences?

1. A formative evaluation is a necessity for any program. While a process evaluation is often desirable and can provide some valuable insights about a program, it is not always necessary, especially for programs that seem to be producing the expected outcomes.
2. A formative evaluation has a relatively narrow focus; it is primarily the status of services and the support system available for them. A process evaluation examines a program somewhat more broadly. It is more like a "systems analysis" of a program, with an emphasis on processes. It is concerned with how the program works overall and how it got where it is today, and less with where it is at the time of the evaluation.
3. A formative evaluation is conducted relatively early in the life cycle of a program. It seeks to learn how the program is doing so far and, whenever possible, if it is on track for achieving its objectives. A process evaluation can be conducted any time during the life cycle of a program, but it is usually conducted closer to the end of a program. It often is conducted when a program is winding down, sometimes as a preparation for an outcome evaluation. It can provide data that are useful for the outcome evaluation, if they are not already available through program monitoring. Sometimes a process evaluation is conducted when it is apparent that a program will not achieve its objectives. Then, it is used mostly to try to uncover why and how the program failed, to identify where the flaws were in a program that "should have worked."

4. A formative evaluation is designed primarily to improve an existing, developing program. A process evaluation examines a program to learn how it can be more effective if offered again, or to guide others who may undertake to design similar programs. It can tell them what they might encounter in the way of problems and can point out mistakes that they should avoid.

5. A formative evaluation looks at the present status of a program; it seeks to learn how the program compares with where it should be in its development. A process evaluation looks backward to see if, among other things, a program ultimately evolved as planned.

Role of the Evaluator

The role of the evaluator in conducting a process evaluation is a combination of systems analyst and detective. In situations where the program is on the verge of failing and it is too late to do anything about it other than conduct a post mortem, we might add "coroner." The evaluator usually has some hints, but no preconceived notions of what he or she will find. The evaluator sets out to understand the program fully, to "get the facts."

All of the usual sources of data described in Chapter 6 can be used in process evaluations. However, agency records and confidential personal interviews are especially useful. Both sources can be very helpful for learning "what really happened," especially when dealing with politically sensitive issues.

In a process evaluation, it may be necessary to try to attempt to reconstruct the past, going back several years to try to understand what happened in the program and why it happened. For example, confidential personal interviews with long-term employees might reveal the motivation and management style of the program's original director and might help the evaluator to understand some of the decisions that he or she made. Or, they might reveal how personnel preferences and biases of staff members might have altered the nature of services that were originally part of the program model. Or, a meeting with a group of key informants might help the evaluator to understand how early marketing of the program prevented it from ever being accepted within the community. In many ways, conducting a process evaluation is a lot like doing historical research. The evaluator tries to understand the present situation of the program by understanding its historical antecedents.

Central Research Questions and Hypotheses

The central research question in a process evaluation is, What occurred and why did it occur? The implicit research hypothesis is, Something occurred that affected the program's ability to achieve its outcomes.

Specific Research Questions

Certain specific research questions occur frequently in process evaluations. They include some variation of those in Box 8.4. If the evaluator has some suspicions

■ ■ ■ ■ ■

BOX 8.4

COMMONLY ASKED QUESTIONS IN A PROCESS EVALUATION

- How did the program come into existence in the first place? What sources of support or resistance were present? How were they addressed?
- What was the program model, and was it implemented as planned?
- What was done to increase support for the program in the agency and in the community?
- How was the program marketed? What potential client groups were recruited?
- Did the program succeed in serving those potential clients for whom the program was designed?
- What additional services to clients might have increased its likelihood of success?
- Why have some clients left the program prematurely?
- Who was instrumental in implementing the program? Was its implementation delayed and, if so, why?
- What problems in implementation might have influenced the eventual success of the program?
- Was there adequate planning for the program?
- Did management carry out all necessary management functions in a timely manner?
- Was the program monitored well and were changes made in response to data as they were aggregated?
- What changes occurred over time that were unplanned and inconsistent with the program model?
- Did the program succeed in recruiting and retaining competent professional and support staff? Was staff turnover a problem?
- What group norms, traditions, and patterns of interaction among staff and between staff and clients seem to have become established?
- What personnel problems have existed? How healthy is the program's "organizational climate?"
- How well has the program collaborated with other related programs in sharing information, making and receiving referrals, and so forth?
- Was the program budget adequate to meet program objectives? What changes in funding over the course of the program may have influenced the potential for its effectiveness?
- What indicators should be used to provide a fair outcome evaluation of the program?
- What should be done differently if a similar program were to be undertaken?

about why a program has struggled or what obstacles to its success may have existed, the research questions may be more specific and more narrowly focused from the outset. And, of course, there will always be some specific questions that are unique to a given process evaluation and the nature of the program that it seeks to evaluate.

Often, individuals such as staff members think they know where a program's strengths and weaknesses lie and want to share their impressions with the evaluator. This can be helpful in that it allows the evaluator to devote more attention to some areas and less to others. However, there is a potential pitfall in doing this. Too much attention to what others (who probably have not looked at the program objectively) have identified as either strengths or weaknesses of a program can create a mindset for the evaluator and lead him or her to draw the wrong conclusions. There may be a tendency to simply confirm the "helpful" insights of the other individuals, thereby lending credence to what might be nothing more than their biases or helping them to pursue their own agenda (for example, to get the program manager fired for mismanagement). Good evaluators listen politely, but prefer to draw their own conclusions.

CONCLUDING THOUGHTS

This chapter looked at those time-honored methods that evaluators use to improve programs, but are not used to draw conclusions about program effectiveness. Evaluability assessment and program monitoring were discussed because they (1) entail the application of research methods, and (2) are used to improve programs. To me, that makes them part of program evaluation. However, some people do not regard either as a type of program evaluation per se. Some other efforts at program improvement that currently occur within programs were deliberately not included (for example, strategic planning and total quality management) because, while they may entail some research and data collection, they are related more to strategies of management than to program evaluation. They also contain certain elements of "faddism" that may not stand the test of time. Other similar approaches have come and gone, often with scant evidence that they really led to program improvement.

Perhaps more than in any other chapter, the reader has been "treated" to some very controversial positions. For example, I have presented what "works for me" in understanding certain evaluation activities, when they occur, and how they differ from other evaluation activities. Other authors would present the material differently, and would eagerly debate some of my conceptualizations, which is the way it should be. That is how some of the confusion and ambiguities that exist within the literature of evaluation research (and there are many) may ultimately get resolved. Perhaps, someday we will all know, for example, if formative evaluations and process evaluations really are all that different.

The issue of timing (when to conduct each type of program evaluation) is among the most controversial. For example, there is no consensus about when to conduct a process evaluation, probably because there is so little consensus about what it is. Some authors take the position that "a process evaluation can be conducted any time"[7] in the life cycle of an operational program. Others say that it entails monitoring and measuring but state that "ideally, a process evaluation occurs before, or at the same time, as an outcome evaluation."[8] Still others suggest that it takes place during the development of a program.[9] None of these positions is totally consistent with the descriptions in this chapter. Figure 8.1 summarizes what I have proposed about the timing of different types of program evaluations.

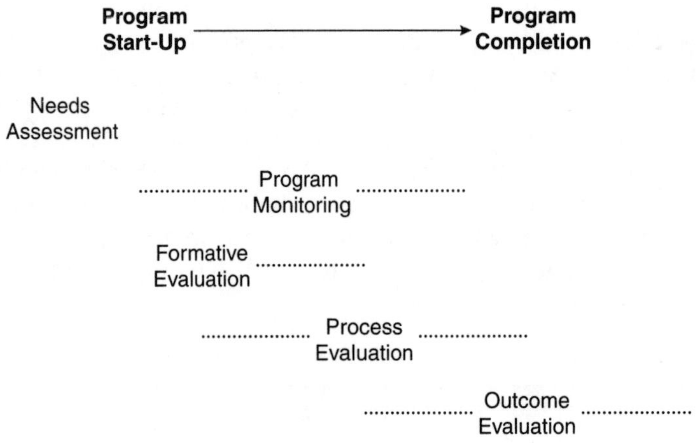

Program ——————————————→ **Program**
Start-Up   **Completion**

Needs
Assessment

.... Program ....
                    Monitoring

Formative ....
Evaluation

.... Process ....
                    Evaluation

.... Outcome ....
                    Evaluation

FIGURE 8.1   A Proposed Timeline for Evaluating Time-Limited Programs

Figure 8.1, like any conceptual model, has its limitations and requires qualification. It is designed for a program that is time-limited (as many are), that is, one that has a limited life cycle such as is the case with most grant-funded programs. It would not be appropriate for conceptualizing the timing of various forms of program evaluation in a program that is a permanent, well-established, integral part of the organization with its funding clearly identified as part of the agency's annual budget. For example, in a permanent program, a needs assessment could also be conducted most any time that significant changes have occurred and questions have been raised as to whether it is still needed in its present form (Chapter 7). Such a program has no foreseeable end. Thus one or more outcome evaluations might be conducted over time. As long as the program is "mature," that is, it is reasonable to expect that it should have produced the desired outcomes, an outcome evaluation could be undertaken.

KEY TERMS

program model	objectives	feed-forward
evaluability assessment	program monitoring	process evaluation
goals	formative evaluation	

STUDY QUESTIONS

1. What is a program model? Why are program models sometimes incomplete when a program is implemented?

2. How do goals and objectives differ? Provide an example of a goal and an objective for an AIDS awareness program that demonstrates this difference.

3. What are some reasons why it is important for a program to have clearly stated goals and objectives?

4. Who is most likely to monitor a program? What is the primary activity of program monitors?

5. When is a formative evaluation most likely to be conducted? Who is most likely to conduct it?

6. What are the major reasons why formative evaluations are conducted?

7. What is feed-forward, and how does it differ from feedback? Why are both useful to a program?

8. Why are client-satisfaction surveys more useful in formative evaluations than in other types of program evaluations?

9. How does the role of the evaluator in a process evaluation differ from the role of the evaluator in a formative evaluation?

10. How can a process evaluation of a program that has apparently been unsuccessful be useful?

REFERENCES

1. Unrau, Y., Gabor, P., & Grinnell, R., Jr. (2001). *Evaluation in the human services.* Itasca, IL: F. E. Peacock, 67–69.
2. Royse, D., et al. (2001). *Program evaluation: An introduction.* Belmont, CA: Brooks/Cole, 126.
3. Hollingsworth, L. (2003). International adoption among families in the United States: Considerations of social justice. *Social Work, 48*(2), 209–217.
4. Nugent, W., Sieppert, J., & Hudson, W. (2001). *Practice evaluation for the 21st century.* Belmont, CA: Brooks/Cole, 32–34.
5. Unrau, Gabor, & Grinnell, Jr., op. cit., 69–71.
6. Royse, et al., op. cit., 116–117.
7. Ibid., 116.
8. Unrau, Gabor, & Grinnell, Jr., op. cit., 70.
9. See Ginsberg, op. cit., 96; or Weiss, C. H. (1998). *Evaluation* (2nd ed.). Upper Saddle River, NJ: Prentice-Hall.

■ ■ ■ ■ ■

CHAPTER NINE

OUTCOME EVALUATIONS: AN OVERVIEW

80 percent of clients who completed the program described it as either "very help-ful" or "helpful."

The program served 12 percent more clients than it did the previous year.

Among the clients who completed the program, there was a statistically significant increase in knowledge about the problem.

In the past, statements like these have been used to provide proof of program suc-cess. If they are in fact correct, any of the above statements *may* help to suggest that a program has been successful. However, it should be obvious by now that, in themselves, they are very inadequate indicators of program effectiveness or of the overall merit, worth, or value of a program. Besides, each is flawed in some impor-tant way. Clients who complete a program are almost always satisfied with it. The number of clients served is an output; it is not an indicator that the program nec-essarily achieved the desired outcomes. And, an education program will almost certainly produce a statistically significant change in client knowledge if it is mea-sured when clients have just completed the program.

Sometimes it is very evident that a program is not working or is even making a problem worse. Then additional evidence may not be required. The decision is made to "pull the plug" on the program immediately to avoid additional waste of resources or harm to its clients. But, more typically, a program either completes its life cycle or, in a program that is designed to be a permanent component of an orga-nization, there comes a time when it is appropriate to ask if the program has been successful. Then no single indicator of program effectiveness is sufficient. A com-prehensive outcome evaluation (also known as a "summative evaluation" or an "outcome assessment") is conducted.

As is the case in all program evaluations, an outcome evaluation has to be designed to fit the program. However, there are certain features that outcome eval-uations share in common, and they are the focus of this chapter. Chapters 10 and 11 focus on differences among outcome evaluations.

GENERAL CHARACTERISTICS
OF OUTCOME EVALUATIONS

Some characteristics of outcome evaluations distinguish it from other types of program evaluations. However, because many of the same research methods are used, much of what follows will sound familiar.

Purpose

In general, the purpose of an outcome evaluation is the same as all program evaluations—it is to judge the merit, worth, or value of a program. However, an outcome evaluation is designed to produce more definitive answers about the worth of a program than, say, a formative evaluation. The findings and recommendations of an outcome evaluation are used to answer questions and make decisions about the future of a program. For example, Should it be continued? If so, how can it be improved? or, If not, how can it be discontinued in a way that is least traumatic to the organization and the program's clients?

An outcome evaluation can employ different criteria for assessing a program's success. The criteria used tend to be those that its stakeholders view as important indicators of program success—what they hoped it would accomplish. Some evaluations focus primarily on whether a program has been effective in achieving its objectives. Others attempt to learn if one program was more effective than another one designed to address the same problem. Still others seek to learn if a new program was just as effective as an older one, but at a lower cost.

Benefits

The findings of evaluation research generally have limited external validity. No two programs (their staff, setting, and so forth) are identical. In addition, every program's clients are unique. They are not a random sample of people with a given problem, and thus only limited conclusions can be drawn about whether a type of program is effective with a particular type of problem. In fact, the participants in a human service program often are little more than a convenience sample, and any assumptions about their being representative of all people who share their problem would be unjustified.

The way that people become participants in a program often involves a selection process that ensures that they are almost certainly not representative of clients with a given problem. For example:

- They may have been referred to the program by other professionals who, in the course of offering them other services, became aware that they had a certain problem.
- They may have requested to participate in the program because they recognize that they need the help it offers.

- They may have been pressured to be in the program by family members or friends.
- They may have been court-ordered to participate in the program.
- They may have been selected for the program from a pool of existing clients because their problem is especially severe.
- They may have been selected for the program from a pool of existing clients because they appear highly motivated to work on their problem.
- They may have been selected for the program from a pool of existing clients because other methods of intervention have been unsuccessful in addressing their problem.
- They may be all of the clients with the problem that the program can recruit or identify within a limited time.

Like other types of evaluation research, the primary beneficiaries of an outcome evaluation are its stakeholders. However, they are not the only ones who benefit. Despite the ways in which clients are selected to participate in programs, outcome evaluations are more likely to make a contribution to our professional knowledge base than the other types of program evaluations that we have examined. Because of the uniqueness of programs and their clients, many findings cannot be generalized. But others can, and they may be useful to other professionals who are not in any way associated with a given program.

How might this happen? Suppose that an outcome evaluation determines that a program has been successful in addressing the needs of a specific group of clients who have some problem. The report of the research is published or otherwise disseminated. Its findings include a detailed description of the program. An administrator who is considering developing a similar program might use these findings to determine whether such a program is desirable or even feasible within his or her organization or community. If it appears that it is, they could also be useful for designing the new program, one tailored to the unique characteristics of its potential clients. For example, they could be used for determining how long the program should last, what fees should be charged, what staff will have to be hired, what additional training they will require, or what facilities will be needed. They could be especially useful in constructing a realistic budget for the new program.

An outcome evaluation that reports on a program that was ineffective can be just as informative. An outcome evaluation of a failed program can cause others to question the effectiveness of certain services for addressing a problem and to better understand the problem and what may be contributing to it. This often happens when an evaluation reveals that the intervention produced certain sought-after changes in its clients, but there was no change in the problem itself. For example, an outcome evaluation of an educational program designed to reduce adolescent use of the drug "ecstasy" might reveal that adolescents who complete the program have a significantly improved knowledge of the medical effects of the drug. However, they continue to use it with the same frequency. An administrator planning to implement a similar program could use this finding to suggest changes in the kind of services her program should offer.

Role of the Evaluator

A program's future very often is determined by the findings of an outcome evaluation. Thus, the evaluator is both a researcher and a judge. The latter is an especially uncomfortable role for many social workers. They generally do not enjoy judging the work of their colleagues or recommending a decision that may cost people their jobs or result in the curtailment of services that clients need. Outcome evaluators often are more likely to be feared and disliked than evaluators who conduct other kinds of program evaluations. Even if an evaluator recommends program continuation but also recommends some substantive changes in a program, he or she may meet with defensiveness and resentment from program managers and staff. Nevertheless, what is expected of the evaluator in an outcome evaluation is (1) provide an unbiased assessment of the program's value using both quantitative and qualitative research methods as indicated, and (2) make evidence-based recommendations about the future of the program. Of course, the role of evaluator is not always difficult or unpleasant. If the program is a good one, it may entail compiling evidence of its effectiveness, providing positive feedback, and suggesting some minor changes to make the program even better.

Central Research Questions and Hypotheses

As suggested earlier, there are many ways to arrive at conclusions about the merit, worth, or value of a program. They are reflected in various research questions and their answers. A description of the general plan for conducting an outcome evaluation can often be communicated using standard research design terminology and symbols. Some of the designs that are common in outcome evaluations (such as those that will be described in Chapter 10) can determine *if* the program's objectives were achieved, but they are not as useful for determining whether it was the program or something else that caused their achievement. Other designs (such as those that will be described in Chapter 11) can do both. However, they still may not provide definitive answers about a central focus of an outcome evaluation: determining a program's overall value. That often requires the application of social work practice knowledge.

In outcome evaluations, both central research questions and central hypotheses are often stated. Whenever appropriate, the hypotheses are tested using statistical tests of inference. A common central hypothesis in an outcome evaluation is, The program was effective. Variations might be, The program was valuable, or The program made a major impact on the problem. All of these are directional hypotheses—they not only state that a program will have made a difference in the problem that it sought to address, it also will have affected it in the desired direction. Even if the evaluator suspects in advance that a program has not been effective or as valuable as it might have been, it is usually a good idea to use the directional hypothesis, that is, The program was effective. To do otherwise might suggest that the evaluator pre-judged the program to be a failure and may have only sought support for his or her biases. Besides, if the data ultimately suggest that the program did not achieve its objectives or was otherwise not very valuable or successful, that will be demonstrated by the lack of statistical (and other) support for the directional hypothesis.

A variation in the directional research hypothesis would occur if a program is being compared with some other program or programs, for example, an older program that addresses the same problem and shares the same outcome objectives. Then the central research question would be, Was the program more effective at meeting the objectives (or more valuable) than the other program(s)? The directional hypothesis would be, The program was more effective (or was more valuable or had a greater impact on the problem) than the other program(s).

Perhaps, it is believed that a program may be only as effective in achieving the desired outcome objectives as some other, better-established program or one that is more expensive, longer, or otherwise is less desirable. Then the central research question would be, Do the programs produce the same effects (outcomes)? The central research hypothesis would be, The programs are equally effective (or equally valuable). Support for the research hypothesis would be found if data analysis fails to find evidence that the variables are related, that is, that one program produces better results than the other one. Statistical support would come from a finding that the null hypothesis *cannot* be rejected.

Sometimes, a nondirectional central research hypothesis might be more appropriate in an outcome evaluation. For example, when previous programs have been ineffective, the evaluator may only wish to learn if a program made a difference at all, either a positive or a negative one. Then the research question would be, Did the program have any effect on the problem? The nondirectional research hypothesis might be, The program had an effect on the problem. Obviously, it is rare that an outcome evaluation would actually discover that a program made the problem worse, but it can happen, especially if an outcome evaluation is the first program evaluation conducted on a new program. However, if program monitoring or a formative evaluation are conducted, destructive programs are usually discovered early and either terminated, or changed to make them more effective, before an outcome evaluation would ever be conducted. If the program is believed to have been improved based on earlier evaluations, usually a directional central research hypothesis would be used rather than a nondirectional one.

Nondirectional hypotheses would be somewhat more common in situations where two or more existing programs are being compared and there is no clear indication as to which program may be the more effective. Then the central research question would be, Which program was more (or most) effective (or valuable)? The central research hypothesis would be the nondirectional, One program was more effective (or valuable) than the other(s).

Specific Research Questions

While specific research questions are unique to a given program, its goals, and its objectives, they are most frequently a variation of the central research hypothesis. They are only a little more specific and include references to the indicators of program effectiveness or efficiency that will be used in the evaluation.

EVALUATION FOCI

As noted, outcome evaluations often tend to focus on program outcomes and the degree to which they have been achieved. Chapter 6 described and defined what generally is meant by the term outcome. To review, an outcome is the degree to which some problem has been affected by the program, how its clients or some larger social system have benefited from it—in short, its degree of success.

In an outcome evaluation, there are other common indicators of the merit, worth, or value of a program that are commonly examined. They tend to relate to a program's goals. We will look briefly at some of the more universal ones.

Were the Intended Clients Served?

Every program targets a specific group of clients. However, not every program is successful in reaching them. For example, a day care program may have been designed to serve low-income single parents, but it may end up serving those who could easily make other arrangements for their children. Part of the outcome evaluation process entails examining demographic data that describe the program's clients to see whether they match those of its intended clients.

A problem of serving the wrong group of people should have been identified prior to an outcome evaluation through monitoring or by a formative evaluation. However, an outcome evaluation can determine whether the problem remained the same, got worse, or was successfully addressed by, for example, changes in marketing, new standards for admission to the program, the establishment of new referral networks, and so forth.

What Unintended Effects Occurred?

Even the best-planned program, based on a thorough needs assessment, is bound to encounter some surprises. Frequently, the program and its presence produce some side effects that no one could have anticipated. Some may be desirable; others may be undesirable. Some are relatively trivial; some are more substantive. The unintended effects of a program should be identified over the course of an outcome evaluation.

While generally not planned or intended, a program's existence always impacts other programs to a greater or lesser degree. An outcome evaluation examines the impact of the program on other programs, both within the agency and outside of it. For example, it might look at how the program is regarded within the agency and how its presence may have affected the morale of staff in other programs. Or, it might examine what programs outside the agency have been modified, cut back, or even eliminated in response to its presence.

Of course, there are many other potential unintended consequences of a program, many of them unique to the program itself. The effects of a program may be direct or indirect. They may be desirable or undesirable. They may be real or simply perceived to be real (it may not matter in terms of their consequences).

Sometimes a program successfully addresses one problem but creates or exacerbates another one. Or, a program can help to identify a new problem, perhaps one that may have a higher priority than the one the program addressed. A program can help to unite and mobilize the community, or it can divide and polarize it. It can cause us to re-examine ethical or legal issues, or the whole way we view a problem or those who experience it. The message to the evaluator is this: Invariably something happens because of a program's presence that no one anticipated. Ask questions and be on the lookout for unintended consequences. They just may be the most important findings of your outcome evaluation.

How Efficient Was the Program?

As I have already suggested, demonstrating that a program has achieved most of its outcome objectives is not, in itself, sufficient evidence that the program has been successful or is valuable. Admittedly, it suggests that the program was effective, at least to some degree. However, in a cost-conscious world, another question invariably must be asked—Yes, but at what cost? That is the question of the program's efficiency.

Some writers present **efficiency assessment** as a specialized type of program evaluation.[1] I have not done so because it seems to me that efficiency assessment in some form or other is just a part of any good outcome evaluation. Outcome evaluations must examine any successes that the program achieved in relation to the financial cost of producing them. How else can it be determined if a program was really "worth it"?

Depending on the nature of the program being evaluated and its objectives, the process of examining program efficiency can be a very structured, objective one, or it can be much more subjective and based more on impressions than on hard data. Two well-known, time-honored ways to approach the task of analyzing the efficiency of a program are cost-benefit analysis and cost-effectiveness analysis.

Cost-Benefit Analysis.   **Cost-benefit analysis** can be used when it is possible to measure both the costs and the benefits of a program in monetary terms (dollars and cents). This can be accomplished fairly easily in business and manufacturing. The benefits of programs with known costs (such as a publicity campaign or one involving sales representatives) can be compared with tangible benefits such as increased sales or earnings. In social programs, we can usually determine the cost of a program in monetary terms. However, putting a dollar value on its benefits can be a lot more difficult.

Cost-benefit analysis is most likely to be possible in evaluating programs where the following conditions are present:

1. A goal of the program is the prevention of a problem.
2. Social indicators make it possible to estimate only how many people may have been prevented from having the problem as a result of the program.
3. At least some of the costs of the problem can be estimated in monetary units.

When it can be used, cost-benefit analysis can be very helpful for measuring a program's efficiency. When it demonstrates that a program costs less money than it saves (it has a positive **cost-benefit ratio**), its findings can then be used for "selling" a program to a skeptical general public or to others who might be considering providing financial support for it. For example, a cost-benefit analysis might be used to evaluate a program designed to reduce the spread of HIV infection among high-risk clients, because we can both estimate how many people in the program (using normative data) would have contracted the virus if the program had not been offered, and the costs of their medical treatment. However, it would not be appropriate for comparing the cost of the program with other benefits of the program, the less tangible ones received by beneficiaries of the program who might otherwise have become infected—benefits that cannot be measured in dollars and cents. Nevertheless, just a demonstration of the overall savings in medical costs alone might be enough to convince some of the program's critics that the program is a "good investment."

Similarly, it might be possible to use cost-benefit analysis to evaluate the efficiency of a job-training program for people receiving cash assistance. If so, it could demonstrate to taxpayers how much money the program saved. The cost of the program could first be determined. Then an evaluator could (using available data) estimate the number of people who found work but who would have continued to receive assistance a certain length of time without benefit of the program. The monetary cost of their unemployment in either unemployment insurance benefits or public cash assistance benefits could also be estimated and the cost-benefit ratio established. However, cost-benefit analysis could not be used with other indirect benefits to program participants (for example, improved family relations, enhanced self-esteem, or a reduction in substance abuse) that they might have received because the program helped them to get work—they could not be measured in monetary terms.

Cost-Effectiveness Analysis.   If a cost-benefit analysis cannot be performed because a dollar value cannot be assigned to benefits (such as a safer community, a healthier workplace, or a less abusive living situation), it may still be possible to conduct a cost-effectiveness analysis. Cost-effectiveness analysis still requires that outcome objectives can be measured, but it is not necessary to assign a monetary value to them.

Cost-effectiveness analysis looks at "the relationship between project costs and outcomes, usually expressed as costs per unit of outcome achieved."[2] When it is possible to conduct a cost-effectiveness analysis (when costs can be monetarily quantified and benefits can be shown to have occurred), the goal is generally to assign a dollar value to each "success." For example, suppose the goal of an employee assistance program (EAP) is to help clients to stop missing work because of family problems. A program designed to accomplish this costs $50,000. Of the clients who complete the program, 25 meet the predetermined criterion for a "success"—perhaps they go one full month with perfect work attendance. That means that each success cost $2,000 ($50,000 ÷ 25 = $2,000). It would now be possible to compare the cost effectiveness of the program with others that share the same goal. If another program costs $4,000 per success, we could say that the first program is twice as cost effective as the other.

The previous example was a simple one; it was designed to present the general way that cost-effectiveness analysis works. (In fact, in the example a cost-benefit analysis might actually have been possible, because the company might be able to determine how many dollars an additional day of work would save the company.) The process of conducting a cost-effectiveness analysis can be made more difficult if accurate data have not been kept throughout the life cycle of the program. Usually the steps in completing a cost-effectiveness analysis are:

1. Specify the program's outcome objectives. (What will constitute a success?)
2. Compute the total cost of the program and subtract any client fees received.
3. Collect data on program outcomes, and identify the number of successes.
4. Divide the cost of the program by the number of successes it produced.

The first three steps are completed as part of any outcome evaluation. Completing a cost-effectiveness analysis (step 4) requires just a little extra mathematical work.

Often the costs and benefits in a cost-effectiveness analysis are really estimates; they cannot be assumed to be 100 percent accurate. Even a slight mistake in an estimate will affect either costs or benefits and can make what appears to be a cost-effective program not cost effective or vice versa. That is why, after completing the mathematics of a cost-effectiveness analysis, outcome evaluators often take on one additional task. They complete a **sensitivity analysis,** which is a listing of higher or lower estimates of costs and benefits and several recalculations of the cost-effectiveness ratio based on them. It reflects several "what if" scenarios. It is a relatively complicated process that involves the use of social indicators and some mathematical computations.[3]

In addition to helping to compare the cost effectiveness of a program with other programs with similar goals, a cost-effectiveness analysis can be very useful to administrators of organizations who may be considering implementing the same or a similar program. They can use it to decide if they can afford such a program or, given what they can afford, whether the anticipated benefits of such a program would justify implementing it. Of course, just because one program at a given time and place could produce a success at a cost of a certain number of dollars does not mean that the figure will be the same if the program is replicated at another time or place.

Even if the same program is continued within the same agency, its cost effectiveness is unlikely to remain constant. Many uncontrollable events or situations might affect the cost of a success in the future. For example, the cost of a success in an EAP program designed to reduce worker absenteeism might rise if the minimum wage requirement were adjusted upward, or if the cost of employee health insurance were to increase. Or, even if the cost of the program does not change, the number of successes might decline, perhaps because the program is able to recruit fewer clients, and thus the per capita cost of the remaining successes would increase. In fact, the most likely scenario is that changes will occur in both the cost of the program and the number of successes that it produces. The cost effectiveness of a program rarely remains stable.

Putting Efficiency in Perspective.   Both cost-benefit analysis and cost-effectiveness analysis make it a little easier for an evaluator to assess the efficiency of a program in an outcome evaluation. They provide additional yardsticks for comparing it with one or more other programs that may be addressing the same social problem. For example, a cost-benefit analysis can allow the evaluator to assess the program's **cost efficiency** (the amount that a program saved its stakeholders relative to some other program). A cost-effectiveness analysis may make it possible to talk in terms of the program's **cost effectiveness** (the cost of the program's successes relative to the cost of successes in other programs both within and outside the organization that share the same outcome objectives). However, decisions about the merit, worth, or value of programs are never simple. The efficiency of a program is just one indicator of a them.

In conducting an outcome evaluation, evaluators also need to remember that most programs in which social workers participate are not run like businesses. Program efficiency is not the only concern; sometimes it is not even the primary one. Many programs could be made more efficient, but for various reasons (often very good ones related to their concern for clients) their managers knowingly choose not to do so. Program managers have to balance efficiency with both equity (what is fair) and what they believe is best overall. Ethical concerns are often an issue too. While not a social program per se, a social work education program (a program with which readers are familiar), can illustrate this point. In a BSW or MSW program, it is probably not a cost-efficient use of faculty resources to teach an elective course in which there are only five students enrolled or to team-teach certain courses. However, the dean or department chair might set aside cost effeciency and decide to do them anyway if he or she believes that the course is needed and valuable or that team-teaching is the best way to present the content of the course. In short, it is the right thing to do.

To use another education example of how efficiency is only one factor in program decision making, suppose two applicants are competing for the last vacancy in a social work program. It could be argued that it is not a very efficient use of educational resources to admit the 50-year-old applicant to a social work program—the younger (20-year-old) applicant should be admitted in her place. The 20-year-old would have the potential to work many more years in the profession and thus have the potential to benefit more from her education or benefit more clients than the 50-year-old ever could. However, the program would not discriminate against the older applicant. That would be unfair and illegal. Besides, the number of years a social work graduate will work is only an estimate based in part on age; there is no guarantee that a younger graduate will work longer as a social worker or serve more clients than an older one.

To use another example, one involving a social program, a manager might know that continuing to treat clients with certain problems such as alcoholism would reduce the overall cost effectiveness of the program because offering such treatment is expensive and produces very few successes. Yet, there is no other program (such as Alcoholics Anonymous) available for alcoholism in the area. Thus, the program may continue to treat these clients—it is the ethical thing to do.

Even when making initial decisions about which program to offer, administrators cannot focus exclusively on efficiency. Sometimes they deliberately choose to offer a certain program even though they know it is probably less efficient than some other program. For example, suppose an administrator has to decide which of two related programs will be offered in his or her organization (or to decide which program will be continued and which will be dropped). If efficiency were the only consideration, the more cost-effective program would always be the logical choice. It would be the politically safe one; the organization's stakeholders would be unlikely to oppose it. However, because efficiency is just one issue to be considered, the administrator might choose the program that has proven to be *less* cost effective, and for one or more good reasons.

Suppose that the choice is between two job-training programs (program A and program B), both of which require the same resources. In the past, program A has produced more successes (defined as graduates of the program who found work) than program B, a program that costs the same. Thus, program A is clearly the more cost-effective program. So, why would an administrator ever choose program B over program A? There might be many reasons, including:

- Program A prepares all clients for the same jobs whether or not they show any interest in them; program B considers individual client preferences in determining which job-training services they will receive.
- Graduates of program A find work at only minimum-wage jobs, but those in program B find higher-paying employment.
- The long-term outcomes of program A (for example, job retention or the percent of its clients who are promoted to higher-level jobs) are not as good as those of program B. Thus, more clients in program A ultimately require additional training.
- While the number of successes in program A is higher, the percentage of successes is lower in program A than in program B (a program that serves fewer clients). Program A may be prohibitive because of its emotional impact on the large numbers of clients who complete it, but then are unable to find a job.

For any of the above reasons or others, choosing to offer a program that is not very cost effective might have been the correct decision—the fair, ethical, or even the politically wise one. While the efficiency of a program is one criterion that can be applied in an outcome evaluation of a program, it should not be allowed to assume too much weight. After all, social work itself is generally not a very efficient enterprise. Thus, it might be expected that some very valuable programs will sometimes not stand up too well to tests of their efficiency. Most importantly, social workers cannot allow efficiency to be more important than what is in the overall best interests of our clients.

USE OF THE LOGIC MODEL

Chapter 8 discussed the importance of a program having a fully conceptualized and articulated program model. Over the years, many methods have been used to accomplish this. The method currently most in vogue involves the use of something called the **logic model.** In fact, there is no single logic model. Logic model is a generic term. Different variations of it exist, adapted to the specific characteristics of programs. They provide a framework for describing the components of a program model, the program components first introduced in Chapter 6. Evaluators, and many funding organizations, expect and often require some variation of a logic model to be used for conceptualizing a program and what it hopes to accomplish.

All variations of a logic model contain inputs, activities, outputs, and outcomes. Some are more elaborate and more detailed. Table 9.1 is an example of one variation (a relatively simple one).

Logic models require program formulators to articulate both a program's components and the linkages among them. They require a distinction among a program's activities, outputs, and outcomes. In many programs, this distinction can be easily made and understood. For example, in developing a program model for a job-training program, it is fairly easy to see that the major activities are what

TABLE 9.1   The Components of a Logic Model

			OUTCOMES		
INPUTS	ACTIVITIES	OUTPUTS	*Short-term*	*Intermediate*	*Long-term*
Resources expended for the program	What was done within the program; how inputs were used to produce outcomes	Products of a program's activities; what was produced by the program	How the problem was reduced by the program; how its clients have benefited	Continued growth and application of change or learning from the program	Ultimate effects of the program on clients and others

the program and its staff members do to prepare its clients to seek employment. The major output is the number of people who complete the program. The outcome is the number or percentage of its graduates who find work that meets certain criteria. Longer-term objectives might be keeping a job over some length of time or job advancement. A logic model for such a program is straightforward. It lends itself to outcome evaluations that can use statistical analysis and other methods to arrive at definitive decisions about the success of the program.

Problems in Application

Managers in some programs have a more difficult time describing their programs using a logic model. Programs that struggle most with it seem to be those that do not simply work with clients around some problem to try to eliminate or reduce it, that is, to affect some change. Their clients may not have a problem at all. The program may be designed to prevent a problem, to maintain a certain level of functioning for as long as possible, or to take people who are functioning well and help them to function even better. Many of these programs are well-established, highly respected programs that receive widespread community support. However, when forced to fit their programs into a logic model they have a difficult time. For example, consider the plight of programs such as Boy Scouts, Big Brothers and Big Sisters, or 4-H. These programs are based largely on the premise that participating in certain activities (for example, camping, attending a ball game with an adult, or raising a calf, respectively) are beneficial in themselves, probably a correct assumption. They are believed to help to enhance self-esteem or build character, two program outcomes often specified. However, how does one prove the connection?

Applying a logic model in some programs can produce many difficult questions. For them, the difference between activities, outcomes, and outputs (and sometimes even indicators) is often unclear. Take the example of park bench building. Building a park bench or completing some similar community service is a common activity in the Boy Scouts, one that can earn merit badges and promotions. However, could it also be considered an outcome? It could be argued that the bench is a benefit for the community, which may be one desired outcome of the program. What about the number of park benches built within a scout troop? Is it a program output? Is it an outcome? What about the number of benches an individual boy builds? Is it an output or an outcome? It could be argued that it is an outcome because there is probably a correlation between number of benches a boy builds and benefits to him in the form of enhanced self-esteem or better character. Or, does that make it an indicator of the program's success? What if a boy quits school to be able to build more park benches? At what point does building ever more park benches stop benefiting a boy and become an unhealthy obsession, an indicator that the program is unsuccessful in achieving some other outcomes?

What about the number of boys who remain in the Boy Scouts a certain number of years? Is that an output or an outcome? Is it an indicator of program effectiveness? If we can accept the assertion that participation in Boy Scouts is beneficial in itself, staying in Scouts longer should continue to enhance self-esteem and build character. And, the fact that a large percentage of boys stay a long time may also suggest that the program is a good one. Or, it simply may be an indication that there is little else for boys to do in the community, or that they are neglecting other activities such as participating in school, religious activities, or dating. But, assuming high retention is indicative of a "good" program, does this necessarily mean that the program is a successful one? If a successful outcome is defined as building self-esteem or good character, it may be or it may not be. There are many "good" activity programs for youth that do not do this (or even claim to do it). The activities are often viewed as an end in themselves—they may, for example, keep young people from being involved in youth gangs or in selling drugs, but that would be hard to demonstrate. Or they may be only "feel good" programs, providing enjoyable wholesome activities for their clients.

If self-esteem and good character (both hard to define and measure) are two of a scouting program's outcome objectives, how do we operationalize them using indicators that are better than, say, park benches built or length of time that boys remain in scouting? It isn't easy. Perhaps, we could use long-term outcomes such as percent of former Boy Scouts who finish high school, avoid legal trouble, or find financial success in life. They are probably characteristic of young men with high self-esteem and good character. But that would require long-term follow-up of program participants, which would be logistically hard to accomplish. Besides, finishing high school, avoiding legal trouble, and financial success are also some of the characteristics of a successful sociopath!

Even if former Scouts can be shown to be more successful in life or are "better off" in some other way than boys who never got into scouting, does that prove that a scouting program was responsible? After all, it could be argued that boys who enter scouting are not typical or representative of all boys to begin with. Their parents are likely to have been scouts and to believe in scouting. They and their parents may be seeking wholesome activities for them, something that does not occur in many families. Perhaps scouting takes boys who are already functioning well and only helps them to function better. No wonder organizations like the Boy Scouts struggle with using a logic model!

Misuse of the Logic Model

In outcome evaluations, sometimes programs are evaluated on both (1) how well they describe their programs using a logic model, and (2) the degree to which they can demonstrate that their outcomes are achieved. When this occurs, the failure to describe a program well and to demonstrate that it has achieved its outcome objectives can be costly when funding decisions are made.

The use of these two evaluation criteria can put some programs in a disadvantageous position while competing with other, dissimilar programs for their share of a fixed or even shrinking pool of money. Is it unfair to judge a program like the Boy Scouts, Big Brothers and Big Sisters, or 4-H using the same criteria that are applied to, for example, a job-training program or an education program? Perhaps. In a job-training program or an education one, (1) a logic model is an easy fit, and (2) achievement of outcome objectives can be easily demonstrated. And, as previously discussed, programs such as scouting struggle both to make the model fit and to demonstrate their effectiveness.

There is an even more basic issue, however. Should how well a program is described using a logic model (the first criterion) be an evaluation criterion at all? After all, a logic model is primarily a management tool, and it works better for some programs than others. Besides, to give "points" or award money for how well a program is described using a logic model seems to be rewarding a program for how well it is able to perform a management task, not for what it actually accomplishes— its true value. Is this only another example of a means-end displacement? I believe so, because a good logic model is a means to an end (a well-conceptualized, well-integrated program). It is not a very good indicator of program effectiveness or value.

The process of trying to fit a program to a logic model causes leaders to re-examine their programs and outcome objectives in new ways, and to better conceptualize what they are hoping to accomplish, and that is good. It also requires them to identify or develop valid indicators of program success, another plus. Thus, attempting to use a logic model can be a valuable exercise, even when not done voluntarily or when the task is not entirely successful. However, how successfully a program is ultimately described using a logic model is often a function of (1) the nature of the program itself, and (2) the creative writing skills of its manager. It is not a good indicator of program success. In an outcome evaluation, program effectiveness should be evaluated only by the degree to which a program has demonstrated its value and any other indicators of program success (for example, achievement of outcome objectives or efficiency).

Of course, if a program is not yet to the point where it can be expected to demonstrate achievement of outcome objectives, a formative evaluation (Chapter 8) is more appropriate than an outcome one. Then there may be some rationale for taking how well a program is described using a logic model as an evaluation criterion. It is a fairly good indicator of how well a program "has it together" at an early stage of its life cycle. Achievement of program outcome objectives could still be used as a second evaluation criterion, but it would have to be modified. The program would be judged only on how well it has done to date, or whether it appears to be on course to achieve outcome objectives.

WHAT MAKES A GOOD OUTCOME EVALUATION?

No matter what specific design is implemented, an outcome evaluation should possess certain characteristics. They tend to overlap somewhat. However, taken as a group they provide a reasonably complete description of what constitutes a good outcome evaluation.

Feasibility

Every outcome evaluation (just like any other program evaluation) is limited by certain constraints. Time and money are two obvious ones. However, there are others, for example, access to data, the ability to accurately measure key variables, and ethical limitations on the use of control groups or other research methods that might place clients at risk. It makes no sense to design an evaluation that cannot be conducted within the constraints that are present. It is better to use a less-ambitious design for an outcome evaluation—one that can be implemented and completed within these constraints—than to try to implement a more sophisticated one that is just not feasible. Either alternative is likely to leave some questions unanswered or only partially answered. But the simpler, more feasible design, because it can be fully implemented, should provide at least tentative answers to all of the major research questions.

Objectivity

There is a reason why outcome evaluations are most often conducted by outside evaluators. They do not (or at least should not) have a vested interest in the future of a given program. Their position of neutrality allows them to be more objective in evaluating a program than, say, the person who designed the program or a person whose job may depend on the program's continued existence.

In a program outcome evaluation, objectivity means something very specific. It means that the evaluator collects and evaluates data with an open mind. He or she does not have a preconceived idea of what the data will ultimately suggest. In an objective outcome evaluation, the evaluation is designed to learn the truth about a program and its value, not to produce predetermined results. Whenever possible, data are allowed to "speak for themselves." However, this does not imply that only data whose validity can be unequivocally confirmed are used in an outcome evaluation. Some findings and recommendations are likely to be based on evaluator impressions or other "soft" data.

Accuracy

In an outcome evaluation, accuracy is the degree to which an evaluator "got it right." It relates most directly to the quality of data collected, whether others perceive them to be indicative of reality. Accuracy is best achieved by making sound research design decisions when, for example, selecting how key variables will be measured, drawing samples for data collection, or selecting which potential data sources will be used.

People employed in the program are often the best judges of whether an outcome evaluation seems to be drawing accurate conclusions. They can help the evaluator to know if he or she is getting a reasonably accurate perception of the program. A quizzical look or a comment from a staff member that seems to say, Where did *that* idea come from? is often an indication that the evaluation methods employed have created some misperception about the program. It suggests that the evaluator had better use additional data sources or do whatever else is necessary to correct any inaccuracies before the final report is written.

Fairness

Outcome evaluations invariably uncover different opinions and perceptions. The evaluator frequently learns that there are people within or outside a program who hold diametrically opposite views of some aspect of the program. One group, when asked to evaluate it, may describe it as strong; others may describe the same aspect as a program weakness. In fact, both assessments may be accurate from the perspectives of those who make them. For example, one staff member who prefers to function with considerable autonomy may evaluate a somewhat laid-back manager's support for service delivery as ideal; another who requires considerable assistance may evaluate it as inadequate.

In outcome evaluations, fairness entails presenting a balanced picture of the program in the report, including any disagreements about it that may exist. The evaluation will be perceived as unfair if the report does not reflect the different sides of some issue where there was clearly a lack of consensus.

Usefulness

An outcome evaluation is useful if it helps its stakeholders to make informed decisions about the program's future. That requires asking all the right questions, and learning the answers to them. The most important product of an outcome evaluation should be a clear picture of the program (its overall value and the degree to which it is effective). It should suggest to its stakeholders whether the program should be continued or discontinued and, if it is to continue, what changes should be made to improve it. Anything less would not be very useful.

ETHICAL PROBLEMS AND ISSUES

Many of the ethical issues encountered in outcome evaluation are the same ones encountered in all forms of evaluation research. Issues such as protection of the confidentiality of people who provide evaluation data and voluntary informed consent need to be addressed, often through correspondence with IRBs. However, some other ethical problems and issues occur sometimes in outcome evaluations. They relate primarily to the way that the findings of outcome evaluations are used.

Ethics and Design

If the individual or individuals conducting an outcome evaluation apply the criteria for a good evaluation described above, most ethical problems can be avoided. However, if they are less concerned with them or choose to deliberately ignore them, ethical problems are almost certain to result.

There is often a considerable amount at stake in the findings of an outcome evaluation: money, jobs, or the reputation of the organization in which a program is housed, for example. Because of this, an evaluator may feel pressured to produce favorable findings. As noted in Chapter 7, needs assessments are also sometimes conducted under pressure. Unethical researchers who bow to it can easily design them so that they will find what they want to find, to justify a program, or to keep it from being implemented. In many ways, the ethical temptations and issues that exist in outcome evaluations are similar to those in needs assessments. They are less prevalent in other types of program evaluations such as program monitoring or formative evaluations in which there is less at stake and the primary goal is to improve an existing program.

There are many different ways that unethical evaluators have been known to manipulate the findings of an outcome evaluation. If the evaluator is knowledgeable about research methods and statistical analysis, almost any desired findings can be produced. Consider a few examples related to the design employed:

1. *The design itself.* Research designs differ in important ways for a good reason—they are suited to specific situations or to answer certain questions. (This point will be illustrated in Chapters 10 and 11.) A research design for an outcome evaluation should be selected because it is the appropriate one, based on all of the factors that are present and what they suggest about the fairest way to evaluate the program. However, an unethical evaluator can select a research design that will virtually guarantee that a program will appear successful if that is the goal, or choose a design that will make the program appear to have failed.

2. *Selective focus.* It is not unusual for a program to have many objectives and subobjectives. Some are more achievable than others. When making overall judgments about a program and its worth and recommendations about its future, they should all be evaluated and given their appropriate weighting. However, an unethical evaluator can choose to focus on those outcome objectives that have been achieved while barely mentioning those that were not achieved, or vice versa.

3. *Selective sampling.* When forming focus groups or when selecting a sample of staff members or clients for confidential interviews, a random sampling method should be used to increase the likelihood of producing a representative sample. An unethical evaluator can deliberately select cases in such a way that the desired opinions about the program, or some aspect of it, will be obtained.

4. *Methods of data collection.* The methods of data collection selected should be those deemed most likely to acquire a candid, true picture of a program. Similarly, the decision as to the number of sources used should be based on how many different perspectives on the program are necessary to be able to arrive at "the truth." An unethical evaluator can select only a single data source, the one believed to have perceptions of the program that are consistent with the findings that are sought. Or, the unethical evaluator might collect data in a forum (such as a meeting with the program's manager present) where factors such as fear or intimidation will help to produce the desired results.

5. *Interpretation of data.* As noted previously, the data from an outcome evaluation should be allowed to "speak for themselves." They should be presented and displayed completely and in a way that facilitates their understanding by the reader of the report. Only appropriate statistical analysis should be used and the limitations and implications of its findings should be interpreted and presented honestly. An unethical researcher (especially one who is presenting findings to a less-sophisticated audience) can easily distort the findings. It is an exaggeration to say that anyone can "lie with statistics." However, it is certainly possible to convince other people who are less knowledgeable about them that they suggest conclusions that are really false. This can be done many ways, for example, by using distorted graphs that give the wrong impression, by treating association or correlation as if they are the same as causation, or by exaggerating the importance of the statistically significant relationships that is almost certain to be present if the number of clients in a program is large.

Other Ethical Issues

Unethical evaluators who yield to the pressure from others to present a program as effective or ineffective are most likely to use the design of the evaluation to produce the desired results. Evaluators who are both knowledgeable of research methods *and* want to do what is ethically right will design an evaluation so that it presents a reasonably accurate picture of the program. However, even if an outcome evaluation is designed to be fair and objective, other ethical problems can still arise.

Dissemination of Findings.   The questions of how to disseminate evaluation findings and to whom they should be made available would seem, on the surface, to be easy ones to answer. Often they are not. Many social programs are unpopular with some segments of society or with the general public. They may serve clients who have been stigmatized for some reason, such as people with mental illness or people who have been convicted of a crime. They may offer unpopular services such as refugee resettlement or abortion referrals, or (especially if they receive public financial support), they may simply be perceived as too costly or wasteful. All too frequently, some individuals or groups are eagerly waiting to confirm some strongly held stereotype about a program or its clients, to find some proof that their beliefs are correct.

Suppose the findings of an outcome evaluation are generally favorable, but illuminate some relatively minor problems in the program, for example, that clients frequently must be provided with small financial incentives to continue in the program, or that they will not participate unless provided with transportation. Ethically, the evaluator should describe the problem in the report of the evaluation. However, if the report becomes public knowledge, its critics will likely use it to attack the program in an attempt to discredit it as being too costly or for "coddling" its clients. There is no easy answer to a dilemma like this one. Sometimes a compromise can be reached—a general reference to the problem can be made in the report and the specifics of it shared only with program managers. Or, the report can be circulated to only those people who will use it constructively and can (hopefully) be trusted not to share it with others less positive toward the program.

Now let's consider a slightly different ethical dilemma. Suppose the outcome evaluation is again favorable, it shows that the program has been very effective in addressing some client problem, for example, in improving their child-rearing practices. However, as part of the evaluation, the evaluator did what a good outcome evaluator frequently does—construct a demographic profile of the clients served by the program. Unfortunately, as it is completed the evaluator notices that it tends to support a derogatory ethnic stereotype often held by the general public. For example, it may reveal that a disproportionate number of the clients have never been married, are unemployed, and are not actively seeking work. It is customary to include the client profile in the appendices of an outcome evaluation report. But if the evaluator includes them, they will almost certainly be used by some people as evidence that the stereotypes are accurate and to try to build resistance to the program among other people who previously had not been very critical of it. Again, there is no easy solution. Perhaps, some of the demographic characteristics of the clients of the program could simply be omitted if they are not essential to understanding the program and those it serves. However, if they are later revealed, the credibility of the whole outcome evaluation may be challenged.

Using Only One Evaluator. Another ethical dilemma is created by the common practice of hiring one program evaluator (or it could be a team of evaluators) to conduct all evaluations over the life cycle of a program. This seems like a logical practice on the surface, since the evaluator would have the opportunity to work closely with the program and to understand it thoroughly. The program evaluator might be involved in designing a needs assessment, conducting a formative evaluation at the appropriate time, and conducting the outcome evaluation for the program.

Here is the problem with this arrangement. As I have suggested, the role of the evaluator is supposed to be different when conducting these different forms of evaluation. An ethical dilemma can result because (1) it is not easy to shift roles, and (2) the different roles can place the evaluator in a difficult position. For example, if one has been the formative evaluator for a program (primarily a consultant), how does one objectively evaluate and judge the program as an outcome evaluator? Perhaps the program managers made all of the changes that the evaluator suggested in his or her formative evaluation, and the program still did not achieve its objectives. What then? To be critical of the program in the outcome evaluation would, in one sense, require the evaluator to be critical of his or her work as a consultant.

The unethical way to handle the dilemma might be to overlook the program's lack of success (using some unethical tactics related to design). However, a more ethical response, if the program is perceived to be unlikely to demonstrate success, would be to resign and let someone else conduct the outcome evaluation. Of course, the way to avoid this kind of ethical dilemma in the first place would be for a program to hire different evaluators to perform the different types of evaluation.

Role conflicts.   Not all ethical dilemmas are difficult to avoid—in some situations, the correct, ethical course of action is obvious. However, resolving the dilemmas can be difficult for other reasons. It often entails sacrificing what is desirable for the evaluator, or even risking what is best for clients by removing one's self from a "conflict of interest" situation. How can this occur? Here is an example. Often, a national organization (or a university) will apply for and receive a large grant from some federal agency. The organization will administer the grant and will be allowed to use a specified portion of the money for its administrative expenses (overhead). However, most of the money will be used to fund various "pilot programs" designed to address some social problem (for example, homelessness or family violence) in an innovative way. Various agencies respond to a Request for Proposals (RFP) disseminated by the grantee organization and submit a proposal for such a program. The proposals judged to be the best are selected and funded.

A steering committee is formed consisting of various individuals, some of whom are knowledgeable of the problem and its methods of intervention because they are administrators of related programs. Among other duties, the members are expected to conduct on-site formative and outcome evaluations of the pilot programs. Usually this causes no ethical dilemma. However, suppose that one committee member is assigned to conduct an outcome evaluation on a project that fared very poorly on its formative evaluation and apparently is still struggling. The evaluator knows that she is likely to be in the position of either recommending the continuation of the program for another three-year cycle, or recommending that its funding be terminated and the money given instead to another new pilot program. And, coincidentally, she has already developed a very good model for a program within her own agency and plans to seek funding for it.

What is the ethical course of action? The ethical solution is quite self-evident. It is to decline to perform the outcome evaluation, and request that someone else perform it. (She should also inform the other committee members of her plan to submit a proposal and offer to resign from the committee.) However, the ethical course of action could come at some cost to the evaluator. If she had acted less ethically, she could have helped to confirm that the program was unsuccessful, recommend that its funding be terminated, and she would have had a good chance of receiving its funding to support her own program.

This type of ethical dilemma is not all that uncommon in conducting outcome evaluations. Because some of the most likely people to conduct outcome evaluations of programs are those from programs with a similar focus (and who thus compete for funding with the organization being evaluated), the potential for conflicts of interest is frequently present.

OUTCOME EVALUATION REPORTS

The report of an outcome evaluation often is organized much like that of other program evaluations. However, because an outcome evaluation is conducted at a different point in the life cycle of a program, some areas will receive more emphasis;

others receive less. The report often is longer than that of, say, a formative or process evaluation and contains more data and "hard" evidence (of program effectiveness or ineffectiveness). Certain content areas are expected to be contained in a report of an outcome evaluation; others are optional, depending on its focus, how it is to be used, and by whom. The sequencing of topics also varies among reports, but it should flow logically. Box 9.1 suggests one way this can be done.

BOX 9.1

A FORMAT FOR AN OUTCOME EVALUATION REPORT

1. *Executive summary.* This is a brief synopsis of the evaluation design that was used, its major findings about the effectiveness of the program, and its major recommendations. It is an abstract or précis of the report. (It is the only part that some people will read.)
2. *Description of the program.* The program's goals and objectives are stated and elaborated on, if necessary. The organization in which the program is housed is described (along with its mission), and the relationship of the program to it is spelled out. The program's activities are generally included in the description.
3. *Statement of outcome objectives.* These generally are "borrowed" verbatim from program documents, frequently from the program's logic model if one has been used.
4. *Research design.* The specific methods used to evaluate the program are described. The research questions are stated. There is a narrative description of how answers were sought to each of them (data sources, instruments used, statistical analysis, etc.). References are made to the appendices where appropriate.
5. *Findings.* Data are presented, but not discussed. They are likely to include a summary description of clients served and of program outputs and factual summaries of analyses of program effectiveness. If conducted, the findings of cost-benefit or cost-effectiveness analyses are reported. There may be frequent references to tables, graphs, and results of statistical analyses in the appendices.
6. *Discussion of findings.* The research questions are addressed in sequence. There are conclusions regarding their answers along with the rationale for each.
7. *Recommendations.* Based on the findings, recommendations about the future of the program and what should be done with it are provided. They are in response to the major purpose of the evaluation (what decisions rest in part on the findings of the evaluation).
8. *Appendices.* The appendices contain material that is summarized or simply referred to elsewhere in the report (for example, demographic profiles of clients served, program budgets, data collection instruments, full results of surveys, narrative summaries from focus groups, results of statistical analysis conducted). If a brochure describing the program exists, it is often included. Materials are included here so that they can be referred to by the reader who may wish to verify that the conclusions and recommendations are justified or who simply wants to view the findings in greater detail.

Sometimes there is a tendency on the part of evaluators to try to impress the reader of their reports with their research knowledge, knowledge of statistical analysis, or command of the language. This is a mistake. A report is most valuable when it is read and understood. The readers of an outcome evaluation research report may be knowledgeable researchers and scholars themselves but, more likely, they will not be. And they will not want to reveal their ignorance or to have to go to a textbook or dictionary to find out what a term means or how a procedure is conducted.

It is best to avoid research jargon whenever possible. When it must be used for clarity, it never hurts to provide a definition or brief explanation. Readers of the report who are knowledgeable researchers will not be insulted; they will just skip over it. Many others will appreciate it. For example, rather than simply stating that "A disproportionate stratified random sampling method was used to form a focus group of treatment staff members," it would be helpful to include additional sentences such as, "This sampling method was used to ensure that there would be an equal number of males and females in the staff focus group. If a proportionate sampling method had been used, the focus group would have consisted of only one male, since only 20 percent of the treatment staff members are male. I did not believe any one individual could or should represent the 'male perspective' on the program."

CONCLUDING THOUGHTS

When many social work practitioners hear the term "program evaluation," they immediately think of outcome evaluations. Not only are they the best-known type of program evaluation, they are the one that most directly affects their lives and their careers. What we learn from outcome evaluations helps to shape the future of social work practice in many ways.

This chapter focused on those characteristics that outcome evaluations share in common. However, when it comes to research designs, outcome evaluations vary widely. They run the gamut—from exploratory, to descriptive, to explanatory. Sometimes, they even take the form of a true experiment, when ethical and logistical obstacles do not prevent it. In the next two chapters, we will look at some designs that are suited to different purposes and conditions and how they might be applied to measure the effectiveness and overall value of different programs.

KEY TERMS

efficiency assessment	sensitivity analysis	logic model
cost-benefit analysis	cost efficiency	
cost-benefit ratio	cost effectiveness	

STUDY QUESTIONS

1. What terms best describe the role of the evaluator in an outcome evaluation?

2. What are some ways that an outcome evaluation (even one of a failed program) can contribute to our professional body of knowledge?

3. What are two common methods for evaluating the efficiency of a program? How do they differ?

4. Explain how a cost-benefit analysis could be used as part of an outcome evaluation of a program that is designed to prevent juvenile delinquency.

5. What does a sensitivity analysis contribute to a cost-effectiveness analysis? Why is one often necessary?

6. When is the most cost-effective program not necessarily the best one, or the one that should be continued?

7. What is a logic model? How is it often used in an outcome evaluation?

8. What are the major characteristics of a "good" outcome evaluation? How can they be used to avoid ethical dilemmas?

9. What are some of the ways that an unethical evaluator might use research design to manipulate the findings of an outcome evaluation?

10. What are some policies about using research jargon in the report of an outcome evaluation?

REFERENCES

1. Nugent, W., Sieppert, J., & Hudson, W. (2001). *Practice evaluation for the 21st century.* Belmont, CA: Brooks/Cole, 34.

2. Rossi, P., & Freeman, H. (1982). *Evaluation: A systematic approach.* Beverly Hills, CA: Sage, 16.

3. Royse, D., et al. (2001). *Program evaluation: An introduction* (3rd Ed.). Belmont, CA: Brooks/Cole, 254–255.

CHAPTER TEN

PREEXPLANATORY OUTCOME EVALUATIONS

All research has a design—a plan for conducting it. Evaluation research is no exception. In evaluation research, a research design is the way that an evaluator goes about evaluating the effectiveness of a service or a program. Chapter 5 examined some research designs that practitioners frequently use to evaluate the effectiveness of their services in single system research. Chapters 7 and 8 looked at examples of how an evaluator might go about answering important research questions about potential programs or programs that were not yet ready for outcome evaluations. While not highly structured or (to use the research term) rigorous, they were research designs nevertheless. This chapter and the next examine some (of the many) time-proven designs, each with its own label, that can be used to help determine whether a program has been successful in achieving its outcome objectives.

The examples of research designs in this chapter are often described collectively as preexperimental.[1] However, a more accurate description is "preexplanatory," because they do not meet the conditions for even a quasi-experimental design, much less those of a true experiment. Thus, this is the term I have chosen to use.

Preexplanatory research designs, such as those discussed in this chapter and the explanatory ones in the next chapter, are suitable for use in many kinds of research. The reader is likely to have first encountered them in a basic course on research methods in social work or a related field such as psychology or sociology. Some of them (such as the longitudinal case study) are sometimes used to see how a program is progressing and to suggest needed changes to it as in, for example, program monitoring or formative evaluations (Chapter 8). However, I have chosen to wait until this chapter and the next one to discuss them in detail because they are most likely to be applied in their purest forms (or with minor modifications) in outcome evaluations.

RESEARCH DESIGNS IN OUTCOME EVALUATIONS

In time-limited programs, outcome evaluations are generally completed when programs are nearing their conclusion or when they have already finished their work. In more permanent, on-going programs, they can be conducted whenever the program has been operational long enough that it should have been successful in achieving its objectives. In programs that have been around many years, outcome evaluations may be conducted at regular intervals (for example, every five or ten years) to learn if the program is continuing to achieve its outcome objectives.

If outside funding is sought, an evaluation plan is usually required to be included as part of the request for funding (grant proposal). Even if it is not required, planning for an outcome evaluation should occur prior to a program's implementation. Once a program is underway, an evaluator's design options often become limited.

Designing an outcome evaluation entails making many decisions about what questions need to be asked and how they will be answered. While there are always some decisions that reflect the uniqueness of a given program, other decisions are common to all evaluations. A research design is likely to reflect decisions related to:

- Measurement of program outcomes
- When and how often outcomes will be measured
- Use and composition of control groups
- Methods for evaluating program efficiency
- Sources of data
- Sampling methods
- Data collection methods
- Control for threats to internal validity
- Statistical analysis of data

If the decisions are good ones, and the design that is constructed, selected, or adapted is effective, the evaluation process will produce good data. The data will in turn make it possible to evaluate a program's value, that is, to complete an outcome evaluation and to make good recommendations about the program's future.

DESIGN NOMENCLATURE

The same design labels that are used in basic research to describe the general characteristics of research designs are applied in outcome evaluations. For example, the terms exploratory, descriptive, and explanatory are sometimes used to describe the overall characteristic of an evaluation design. However, as we shall see, other common research terminology is applied a little differently and may have a specialized meaning in outcome evaluations. For example:

1. *Problem.* The social problem or human need that the program sought to address.
2. *Outcome objective(s).* What a program has stated that it hopes to accomplish, generally a decrease in or elimination of a problem, or the meeting of some need of its clients.

3. *Group.* Those clients who participated in the program. Sometimes it is defined more narrowly as "those clients who completed the program." In explanatory designs, the term "experimental group" is often used.
4. *Control group.* A generic term often used to describe a group of people who were not clients in the program. Less frequently in outcome evaluations, another program serves as a control group. A control group provides a source of comparison and is used to attempt to address the problem of threats to internal validity.
5. *True control group.* Those clients or potential clients who were randomly selected from some population *and* assigned to a control group through a process of randomization (or "random assignment"), as were clients in the program—the experimental group. Clients in a **true control group** do not participate in the program or interact with it in any way. True control groups are a characteristic of experimental research designs.
6. *Nonequivalent control group.* Those clients or potential clients who were selected to serve as a control group because of their similarity to clients in the program are known as a **nonequivalent control group.** Because they were not assigned to the control group through randomization, they are not a true control group, and thus cannot be assumed to be equivalent to program participants in all respects.
7. *Pretest.* A measurement of the severity of the problem (the dependent variable) taken only prior to the implementation of a program.
8. *Posttest.* A measurement of the severity of the problem (the dependent variable) taken following clients' participation in the program. When used with a pretest, it allows the evaluator to learn how much change occurred in the problem over the course of the program for its clients or, if a control group is used, how much change occurred for clients in both the program and in the control group.

Research designs (at least the general sequence of events in the design) can be described symbolically. When this is done in evaluation, the notations are the same as in basic research, but they have precise meanings:

- X = the program (either its beginning or in its entirety)
- O = the only measurement of the problem
- O_1 = the first measurement of the problem
- $O_2, O_3,$ and so forth = subsequent measurements of the problem
- R = random assignment of clients or prospective clients to one or more groups

GETTING NEEDED ANSWERS

When planning for an outcome evaluation, evaluators often first decide which general type of research design (exploratory, descriptive, or explanatory) is most likely to provide the needed answers to their research questions. In basic research, the primary criterion for making this decision is the current state of knowledge about a problem. For example, exploratory designs are most appropriate when some problem or phenomenon has only been recently identified or is not well understood. Descriptive designs seek to measure certain relevant variables to increase our understanding of a problem and its severity, who it affects, and so forth. Explanatory research, building on the findings of the other types, tests for relationships between variables, often for cause–effect relationships. There is a logical progression over time—exploratory studies come first and are followed by descriptive ones that, in turn, make it possible to conduct explanatory ones. In short, the question, How much do we already know about the problem? determines what type of research design is most appropriate and should be used.

In program evaluations, the current state of knowledge about a problem plays a lesser role in selecting a research design. The general type of design of a program evaluation is based primarily on the kind of questions that the research seeks to answer and the obstacles that may exist for answering them. For example, needs assessments (Chapter 7) seek to learn if a program is needed and, if so, what form it should take. That is why they tend to be exploratory and descriptive. Formative evaluations or process evaluations (Chapter 8) seek answers to questions about a program's functioning. That is why their designs tend to be primarily descriptive in nature. Outcome evaluations seek answers to still other questions— questions about a program's success. Designs can be primarily descriptive (like those described later in this chapter) or explanatory (like those described in the next chapter). Sometimes, for a variety of logistical reasons, they are even primarily exploratory.

As noted in Chapter 9, a central question in outcome evaluations is, Was the program effective? It is usually relatively easy to determine whether a program's outcome objectives were achieved. However, answering the question, How certain can I be that it was the program (and not something else) that produced the achievement of its objectives? can be much more difficult. If this cannot be done, the possibility remains that, even though a program's objectives were achieved, the program may not, in fact, have been valuable.

An experimental design can determine whether success at achieving program objectives is indeed attributable to a program and, thus, can provide a direct indication of a program's value. In the ideal world, all outcome evaluations would be conducted using experimental designs, preferably in their most rigorous forms. However, in the real world, that is not always possible. There are often one or more obstacles to the use of experimental designs and even to the somewhat less rigorous quasi-experimental ones.

Often, designing an outcome evaluation entails a conflict between what we would like to do and what we can do. Thus, evaluators frequently must rely on preexplanatory designs—descriptive or even exploratory ones. Preexplanatory designs offer some good alternatives. They can answer many questions about the overall effectiveness of a program and whether its outcome objectives were achieved. However, because they lack the design rigor of explanatory research, they generally do not allow us to determine with certainty that a program (and not something else) either produced the desired results or prevented them from occurring.

OBSTACLES TO USE OF EXPLANATORY DESIGNS

Even though evaluators know that they can provide the most definitive answers about program effectiveness, experimental and quasi-experimental research designs are not always used in outcome evaluations. Some of the reasons why evaluators resort to preexplanatory designs instead are the same as those in basic research. Others are related to the nature of evaluation research. The reasons are interrelated, that is, they all relate to the requirements of explanatory research.

Ethical Concerns

Two of the characteristics of true experiments—use of control groups and the random assignment to them and experimental groups—often present ethical issues. An experimental group (participants in a program) and its control group would have to be composed of clients, or at least prospective clients. Clients are people. They have rights, many of which are protected by our professional code of ethics. One of these rights is to receive timely, needed assistance.

In the best-known form of an experiment, the evaluator or program administrator would be required to draw two random samples of clients from a population of clients with a particular problem and randomly assign them either to the program or to a true control group. If, through randomization, they were assigned to the control group, they would not receive any services or interact with the experimental group members in any way. If the two groups were relatively large (say, thirty or more in each group), it could be assumed that random assignment would equalize them in relation to any potentially confounding variables. The most common threats to internal validity would also have been controlled, because there is no reason to believe that they would not affect both groups equally. Thus, if the findings of the research proved to be statistically significant, we could conclude that the program (and nothing else) caused differences in the severity of the problem between the two groups.

The research design would be "clean." We could arrive at definitive answers about a program's effectiveness, thus avoiding the problem of wasting future resources and wasting the time and other investment of clients on an ineffective program. But can we really do that to potential clients? Sometimes, in the interest of finding safe and effective intervention methods (as, for example, in some prescription drug trials), such a procedure is allowed. But often, the answer is no. Especially in situations when clients are in acute distress of some sort, to withhold services to them for purposes of research would be unethical and would never be permitted by an IRB.

The question of withholding assistance to control-group clients sometimes can be addressed much as it is addressed in single-system research. Control groups can receive "the usual treatment" instead (what they would receive if the program did not exist). We could still use random assignment to the program and its control group to make the two groups equivalent, but clients in the control group would at least receive services known to be effective in the past. However, even if control group members receive the usual services or participate in another program, ethical questions still exist. For example, we might ask:

- How can I justify using randomization to assign clients to different programs or to receive certain services when my professional judgment suggests which program or service might be most beneficial to a given client?
- How can I justify randomly assigning any client to another program or existing services if I really believe that the program to be evaluated is better?
- How can I justify not simply assigning those clients with the most severe problem to the program with the greater potential to help them?

These questions and other similar ones that suggest that an explanatory design might be detrimental to some clients are ethically troublesome. Sometimes they cannot be answered satisfactorily—concern over them simply precludes the use of an explanatory design of any kind. However, the underlying issues can sometimes be resolved. For example, if the program is a short one and the problem is not acute, there might be a solution to all three questions above. We could conduct the research as planned but ensure that, if the program does prove to be more effective, clients in a control group will be invited to participate in it after the conclusion of the outcome evaluation. Of course, this solution might not be feasible because of its extra cost or some other reason.

Logistical Problems

Even if all ethical obstacles to the use of an explanatory design can be overcome, there still may be logistical obstacles to its use. Usually the logistical obstacles to the use of an experimental design relate to an inability to create a true, equivalent control group(s). For example, it may not be possible to simply use randomization to assign clients to the program or to another (perhaps, an older) program because:

- There may be a limited number of clients who meet the criteria for inclusion in the program. They all need to be in the program in order for it to function as planned and be cost effective. Thus, there are no available clients to constitute a true control group.
- Clients may know about the differences between programs and have a distinct preference for the one being evaluated. If randomly assigned to the control group, they may refuse to participate. Even if they comply, their attitudes toward the program may be different from that of clients in the experimental group and may affect their performance in the program. Or, they

may temporarily leave the program, hoping that if they later reapply for services they will be assigned to the experimental group. That may produce a different level of experimental mortality within the two groups.

- The physical layout of the organization in which programs are housed may make it impossible to prevent interaction among the staff or clients of the programs. Staff members in the control group may learn of innovative methods used by staff in the experimental group and may decide to implement them, or clients might learn about them and demand that they be used in their program too. Clients in the control group may thus be exposed to some of the services of the program being evaluated (receiving an "overlap of treatments").
- The organization may not be able to assign staff members randomly to one program or another. Thus, for example, the control group may have more- or less-experienced staff than the program being evaluated or the staffs may differ in relation to some other potentially confounding variables.
- The organization may not be able to assign staff members exclusively to one program or another and thus, some of the interventions used in the program being evaluated may unintentionally be used in the control group and vice versa, resulting in an "overlap of treatments."
- Because of organizational constraints, facilities and resources for experimental and control-group programs may not be comparable.

Nature of the Program

The very nature of a program and its objectives can be an obstacle to the use of explanatory designs for outcome evaluations. Some programs are both unique and attract only certain individuals (for example, some recreational programs for older people). No comparable program exists, or its clients are so different because of a self-selection process that forming or identifying an equivalent control group would be difficult, if not impossible.

Other programs have no specific start-up date. Clients are not assigned to them, as they would be in an experimental design. They only evolve, serving just a client or two at first. Then they add more services and other activities, and more clients are served. Eventually, a program per se with its own identity and its own staff emerges. If it is reasonably effective in serving enough clients and delivering needed services, it may continue as a permanent part of the organization in which it exists.

In other programs, as discussed in Chapter 8, the problem is very large and, for all practical purposes, unsolvable (for example, there will always be victims of oppression, the homeless, unwanted children, and the working poor). Even a highly successful program can expect to have a relatively small impact on the scope of the problem itself; the problem will continue to exist. All the program can hope to accomplish is to help to meet some needs of a limited number of people who experience it, a very small percentage of people with the problem (and not even a very representative sample of them). An example of this type of program might be "Meals on Wheels" or the example from previous chapters, an international adoption program.

An international adoption program could not hope to achieve a significant decline in the major problems that it addresses (unwanted children and infertility). It would have much less ambitious goals, for example, to address the needs of a relatively small number of children and potential adoptive parents. Program participants (potential adoptive parents) would have to be recruited, not randomly selected. They would also not be representative of potential adoptive parents as a group in relation to key variables such as age, marital status, income, or education. Who could serve as their control group? People recruited but then denied international adoption services? That would be unethical. Parents who complete domestic adoptions? We could not force this alternative on clients. There is a self-selection process that determines the type of adoption services people seek. A true control could not be constructed and even a good equivalent one could not be identified. Such a program is not well suited to an outcome evaluation that uses an experimental design or even a quasi-experimental one.

When evaluating such programs, once again, the difficulty relates primarily to the problem of identifying or constructing an equivalent control group. To use another example, how could an evaluator use a true, explanatory design for performing an outcome evaluation of an after-school program designed to serve a limited number of children? Who would comprise a control group? It would be logistically (and ethically) impossible to randomly assign certain children to not participate in the program or any other program. A control group also could not simply consist of a group of children not in the program, because they would differ from children in the program in some important ways (for example, employment status of parents, number of parents in the home, or socioeconomic status). Such a program would not have a simple reference point. Thus, it would be hard to know if the program was really successful. Compared to what? A less rigorous design would most likely have to be used, one that would employ more qualitative research methods and that would be regarded as more descriptive than explanatory. If it can be determined that the program is fully utilized and it seems to be meeting the needs of targeted families (two likely indicators of outcome achievement), it would probably be deemed a success.

Inadequate Planning

The use of explanatory designs requires adequate planning. Often this entails being involved with a program before its onset, first selecting potential clients and then controlling their random assignment to the program and to control groups and, if required, conducting measurements of the problem's severity (the dependent variable) before the program is implemented. An evaluator cannot come on the scene after a program is underway and implement an explanatory design correctly. Sometimes the evaluator simply is hired too late or is brought in to replace an evaluator who has resigned and has not done the necessary work (random selection, random assignment, pretest measurement, and so forth) that should have been done. Or, if necessary data were collected, they may have been lost or there may be questions about their validity. Sometimes even evaluators who were involved with a program from its beginning simply fail to understand the importance of performing all tasks in a timely manner and thus their behaviors preclude the use of explanatory designs in outcome evaluations.

CHARACTERISTICS OF PREEXPLANATORY OUTCOME EVALUATIONS

In one sense, the term preexplanatory outcome evaluation sounds like a bit of an oxymoron. How can exploratory and descriptive designs be used to determine whether a program has achieved its outcome objectives when they are regarded as among the least rigorous forms of research? Nevertheless, preexplanatory designs can be and are used successfully in outcome evaluations. They can provide very useful information about a program's effectiveness and its overall value. They just produce more tentative answers than explanatory designs.

Hypotheses

In preexplanatory designs, the general research hypothesis is the same as when more rigorous designs are used. Most frequently it is the directional hypothesis, The program was effective. However, in preexplanatory designs, hypotheses are tested more indirectly than in explanatory ones. Statistical tests of significance may not be used or, when they are, they yield only tentative answers to central research questions.

Specific hypotheses (those related to the program and its outcome objectives) are usually stated. If there is a nonequivalent control group, the independent variable is the group in which clients or potential clients were located (program or control). Or, if the control group is another related program, the independent variable is the program in which a client participated. Its value categories are "control" or "program" (the one being evaluated). If a before-and-after (pretest/posttest) design is used, the independent variable is "time of measurement" (before or after the program). Most often, the dependent variable is "amount of change in the problem." However, depending on the program and its goals, it could be something else such as "prevention of a problem among its clients," maintaining the status quo, or some other indicator of program success.

Data Collection and Analysis

Preexplanatory designs tend to rely fairly heavily on qualitative research methods for hypothesis testing. They may still entail collecting quantitative data (for example, the percent of clients who have benefited from a program). However, because they sometimes lack a reference point (such as an equivalent control group), numbers and measurements of variables may not be very meaningful. For example, it may be impossible to know if the percent of clients who appear to have benefited from a program really suggests that the program was a valuable one unless normative data from other similar programs are available with which to compare it.

There are two reasons why evaluators use statistical tests of significance less frequently in preexplanatory designs than in experimental designs. First, some qualitative data do not lend themselves very well to this kind of analysis. Second, even when quantitative data are available for data analysis, statistical testing does not always serve a useful purpose. What value is there in learning that sampling error or chance was unlikely to have produced the apparent success or failure of a program if other factors—threats to internal validity—were not controlled and could easily have produced it?

There are a few occasions when tests of statistical inference can be valuable in a preexplanatory outcome evaluation, however. When normative data are available, they can be used to examine to what degree a program varies from the "norm." For example, if there are demographic data available on all clients who have a particular problem, statistical analysis can be used to determine whether the sample of clients in a program is representative of them in relation to certain potentially confounding variables. If so, at least the apparent success of a program cannot be attributed to sampling bias. Or, if the "usual" success rates of programs that address the program is known, statistical analysis can be used to determine whether a higher than usual success rate of a program is statistically significant. Tests to perform these analyses would be those used to compare samples with populations, for example, the one sample t-test or chi square "goodness of fit."[2]

Like all forms of evaluation research, preexplanatory designs try to go beyond simple numbers in attempting to understand some phenomenon (for example, to learn how staff members perceive the program or how they experienced it). This often entails the use of data sources such as focus groups, key informants, and confidential personal interviews. Large amounts of these more qualitative types of data may be collected and then, inductively, the evaluator tries to conceptualize what they seem to mean about the value of a program. When presented in a report as findings, they often take the form of narrative summaries or conclusions, supported by direct quotations.

Sometimes, evaluators or program staff members solicit **testimonials** from clients as indicators of a program's value. They consist of written accounts of how the program benefited individual clients, written in their own words. When included, testimonials may have an emotional impact on some readers of the report and may help to convince them that a program is valuable. However, for many people they are not very credible evidence of a program's effectiveness. They do not describe the experiences of a random sample of the program's clients. When readers of evaluation reports see them, they also may speculate as to how much coercion was used to acquire them, who actually wrote them, or if their authors might be the *only* clients who were helped by the program. When conducting a preexplanatory outcome evaluation, it is always possible to find evidence of a program's success that has more credibility than testimonials. The most appropriate use of testimonials is for fund-raising (where they can often be quite effective), not as data in an outcome evaluation.

Some Design Possibilities

We will now look at five common preexplanatory designs and some of the ways that they could be used in an outcome evaluation. Each could provide a reasonably good measurement of the degree to which a program's activities and the achievement of its outcome objectives are related. While these designs have been rigorously applied in many outcome evaluations, there have also been numerous other occasions when some of their features (but not all) have been used in an outcome evaluation design. On still other occasions, elements of one have been combined with elements of another (or some other design altogether) to produce a design for an outcome evaluation. In constructing a unique design or in deciding to rely on an established one such as those that follow (perhaps with modifications), the issue is always the same—what methods will provide the best possible picture of the program and its value?

To help in understanding the examples of preexplanatory design options that follow, I will suggest briefly how each could be used in an outcome evaluation of a job-training program, and (in more detail) in the less-typical program example used in previous chapters, an international adoption program in a private family service agency. To review, the three outcome objectives of the adoption program as stated in Chapter 8 are:

1. To provide a viable option for those prospective adoptive parents who may not qualify for domestic adoption services because of one or more demographic characteristics.
2. To provide a viable option for those prospective adoptive parents who, for various reasons, might prefer to adopt a child from a foreign country over a domestic adoption.
3. To have successfully placed forty children from foreign orphanages in loving homes by the end of the second year of the program's operation.

One-Group Posttest Only.   This design simply requires the evaluator to measure the problem or needs of clients who participated in the program at the time of completion or soon after they completed the program. Collateral evidence of program effectiveness is also acquired, if possible, for example, personal observations, anecdotes, or case histories of clients. Then some judgment is made about the program's effectiveness. If clients seem to have less of the problem than before they entered the program or otherwise have benefited from the program, the program may be regarded as effective.

The **one-group posttest only** design is used mostly in those situations where, for some reason, no plans were made for an outcome evaluation until the program was well underway or another more rigorous design could not be implemented as planned. Its findings tend to be viewed as little more than an informed guess about the value of a program. It is also recognized that the design can provide tentative answers to only a limited number of questions. For example, if used to evaluate the effectiveness of a job-training program, it could determine whether some outcome objective was achieved, such as 60 percent of clients were candidates for employment within one week of the program's completion. However, unless normative data from similar programs are available, it could not be determined if a 60 percent rate of success was high, average, or low. And, of course, it could not determine what else might have produced the achieved level of success.

The design also is referred to as the "one shot case study," although it does not generally entail a case study in the usual research sense. Whichever label is used, it is diagrammed as:

$$X \qquad O$$

Application. In evaluating the success of an international adoptions program, the research hypotheses (specific to the three outcome objectives) for this design might be stated as follows:

1. Prospective adoptive parents who might not qualify for domestic adoption services will both value and utilize the program.
2. Prospective adoptive parents who do not choose to pursue domestic adoption will both value and utilize the program.
3. By the end of its second year, the program will have successfully placed at least forty children from foreign orphanages into North American homes.

The evaluation would be undertaken as the program completed its third year. The evaluator would have considerable freedom in implementing this design in order to determine whether there was support for any or all of the hypotheses. He or she could use any potential data sources (choosing those believed to be most appropriate). They would be helpful for describing the program, who it served, and how clients and staff members perceived it. To address the first two objectives (whether the program had, in fact, provided options for those who either chose not to or would not have qualified for a domestic adoption placement), the evaluator probably would rely on a number of data sources. Personal observations might be important. So would findings from focus groups and confidential interviews with staff and potential adoptive parents who either were or are active clients of the program. Demographic profiles of clients gleaned from program records might also be useful. Any former clients who had already completed adoptions could be surveyed or, preferably, they could be interviewed in order to learn their opinions of the program. A completed adoption would (or would not) be considered a "success" based on the evaluator's personal observations and the conclusions of the adoption workers who worked most closely with the clients. The ultimate decision about whether there was support for the first two hypotheses would be a judgment of the evaluator, based on a synthesis of the perspectives of many individuals and groups.

The task of evaluating whether the third outcome objective was achieved would be simpler and more straightforward. Records data would reveal whether there had been at least forty successful adoptive placements by the end of the second year of the program's evaluation. (Similarly, a review of the budget and an interview with the program director could help to determine whether the program had reached its goal of becoming self-supporting through client fees by the end of its third year.) Finding these answers would be the same no matter which outcome evaluation design was used.

In the process of making personal observations and collecting data in other ways that involve very few constraints (unlike the way evaluation is conducted using more structured designs), the evaluator would invariably form a variety of perceptions and impressions of the program and its quality. However, they might not relate directly to its outcome objectives. Nevertheless, they would be helpful, if shared, and would likely be included in the outcome evaluation report. For example, it might be learned that the program turned out to be far less controversial in the community than the professional literature[3] suggested it might be. However, the evaluation process may have revealed other problems, such as morale issues or interpersonal conflict. For example, he or she might observe tension between staff members who work in the program and those in other agency programs because of what are perceived as workload inequities or the opportunities for foreign travel that program staff have, but that other staff members lack. There might be some other causes for resentment of the program within the agency, for example, it might be perceived as having a higher priority than other programs, have better relations with the general public, or be more elitist, because it serves more affluent clients who can afford the high costs of international adoptions.

Of course, the serendipitous observations and impressions that an unstructured design like the one group posttest only affords could also detect some desirable features of the program that were not previously identified. For example, staff in other programs may express pride in having the program as part of their agency, or may appreciate being able to provide options to applicants who are not good candidates for domestic adoptions. Or it may be learned that the program's staff has experienced little or no staff turnover since it was implemented, an indication that morale within the program is high.

Two Static Group Comparison.   An important difference between a **two static group comparison** design (also known as "posttest only, nonequivalent groups") and the previous one is the presence of a reference point: a nonequivalent control group. Its presence makes it possible to compare clients who have just completed the program with those who were comparable in some way, but did not participate in the program. If the clients in the program appear to have been served better than those in the control group, the program may have been effective. However, because the members of the control group (and those in the program) were not randomly selected or assigned to the two groups, it cannot be assumed that the groups were equivalent before the program began.

This design is most often used when there is available a "ready-made" group of people who seem to be a kind of natural control group. For example, a pilot program to reduce school dropout among adolescents might be evaluated by comparing the percent of adolescents still enrolled in school at the end of the program with that of an identified group of other at-risk adolescents. They did not enroll in the program or (better yet), perhaps even attempted to participate in the program but had to be denied entry because of some impartial reason such as space limitations.

The two static group comparison design is also sometimes used to compare the effectiveness of two similar programs that share the same outcome objectives. Ideally, they might also have similar costs, number of clients served, and duration. For example, we might compare a new job-training program with another, established program. The established program's clients could serve as a nonequivalent control group and the rate of success in achievement of program objectives of the two programs could be compared to produce a tentative conclusion as to which may be the more effective program. Of course, when this is done, we cannot assume that the two groups of clients were identical in all respects in the first place, because they were not randomly selected and assigned to one program or the other. Various confounding variables may be present more or in different form in one program than in the other. Thus, the established program is not an equivalent control group. The design is diagrammed as:

$$
\begin{array}{cc}
X & O_1 \\
\hline
& O_2
\end{array}
$$

Application.   In using this design to conduct an outcome evaluation of our international adoption program, there would be at least two options. Either would employ a nonequivalent control group. It would serve as a reference point, a standard by which the program (and the achievement of its first two objectives) could be evaluated. (Achievement of the third objective would be evaluated in this design and all others in this chapter using records data as described in the previous discussion.)

The nonequivalent control group could be comprised of active clients in the domestic adoptions program. They and clients and staff from the international adoptions program could both be interviewed, surveyed, and be observed in focus groups using similar methods to try to determine whether the addition of the new program truly provided service alternatives and helped to better address the needs of all prospective adoptive parents. If the two static group comparison design were used with domestic adoption clients serving as a nonequivalent control group, research hypotheses (specific to the first two outcome objectives) would be tested. For example, they might be:

1. Clients in the international adoption program will be older and will be more likely to come from nontraditional families than clients in the domestic adoptions program.

2. A sizeable percentage of clients in the international adoption program would qualify as adoptive parents in the domestic adoption program.

How could the evaluator find support for the research hypotheses using this design? The demographic differences between clients in the two programs could be analyzed to learn if, for example, the program served very many clients who would not have qualified for domestic adoptions. If so, that would suggest that the first outcome objective may have been achieved to some extent. Support for the second hypothesis would have to come in even more indirect ways. Most of the requirements of the domestic adoptions program could be ascertained from its program policies and rules. Any informal policies that may exist (such as those relating to age, marital status, or sexual orientation) might have to be revealed through confidential interviews with program staff members. Once all requirements for qualifying as adoptive parents in the domestic adoptions program have been identified, they could be compared with the characteristics of clients of the international adoptions program to determine what percentage of clients would meet them. If the percentage is fairly large (say 30 percent or more), that would tend to suggest that the program may have achieved its second outcome objective. Of course, it might also suggest that the program may have drawn some potential adoptive parents away from the domestic adoptions program, a possible negative effect of the program.

The general question of whether the new program provided a "viable option" (the term used in the first two outcome objective statements) for potential adoptive parents might be answered in other ways too. For example, in the process of interviewing clients of the international adoptions program it might be revealed that many of them would have failed to complete the adoption process if the program had not been in place along with the features that it provides. Interviews with clients in the domestic adoptions program might reveal that many of them considered all adoption possibilities (including international adoption) and appreciated the opportunity to at least have additional options to consider. However, interviews might also reveal that, in considering international adoption, some domestic adoption clients learned that they simply could not afford it, or that they were not able to meet the international travel requirements. Thus, international adoption was never a "viable option," for them.

A second alternative for a nonequivalent control group might be another, relatively new international adoption program (perhaps in another state) that shared the same or similar outcome objectives. Surveys and, if the cost would not be too prohibitive, face-to-face methods of data collection could be used to compare perceptions of clients and staff members of the two programs in relation to the first two objectives. If a comparable program served as a control group, it would allow the evaluator to determine whether, overall, the program seemed to do a better job of meeting outcome objectives than the other, comparable program. This would also afford an opportunity to provide a different perspective on the third outcome objective, specifically whether the other program produced more or fewer completed placements in its first two years than its "control group." (It could also reveal whether it took more than three years to become financially self-supporting, a program goal.) For this reason alone, this might be a better alternative (budget permitting) than using clients in the domestic adoptions program in the agency as a control group. Generally, the more similar the control group is to the program, the more useful the comparison between it and the program being evaluated becomes. If another international adoption program were used as a control group, two research hypotheses (designed to provide a start toward assessing the achievement of the first two outcome objectives) might be:

1. The program will have served a greater number of older clients and more clients from nontraditional families than the other international adoption program.
2. The program will have served more clients who meet the requirements for domestic adoption than the other international adoption program.

On first glance, it might appear that the hypotheses are in conflict with each other—if one can be supported, how can the other also gain support? If the program attracted a larger number of older clients and more clients from nontraditional families than the other program, how could it also have served more clients who meet more traditional, domestic adoption requirements? It is possible to do both. For example, if the program simply served considerably more clients than the other program, it could have served a larger number of older clients, more clients from nontraditional families, *and* more clients who met the requirements for domestic adoption.

If the other program were used as a control group, records data on client characteristics from the two programs also could be used to see if there is support for the two hypotheses. However, even if "the numbers" seemed to offer support for them, that in itself would fall short of demonstrating that the program's outcome objectives were achieved. Why? The numbers (and the research hypotheses) relate only indirectly to the program's first two outcome objectives. They may be one possible indicator of program success, or they may be little more than an output. Achievement of the program's outcome objectives could only be assessed using another international adoption program as a control group by collecting additional data, those more directly related to the "viable option" question. The two programs might be compared in this regard using a sample of all clients in both programs and conducting confidential interviews and focus groups. This would suggest whether the program really achieved its first two outcome objectives better than the other program.

Even though either control group option would be of some help in evaluating the outcome objectives of the program, the two static group comparison research design is not an especially good fit for our hypothetical program overall because of the nature of the program and what it seeks to accomplish. The addition of a control group may add an additional perspective on program effectiveness, but a control group may be unnecessary for evaluating the outcome achievements of the program. It is of limited help in answering the main question that an evaluator would seek to answer, Did the program successfully meet a need of some potential adoptive parents not previously served by its agency? To answer that question, it might only be necessary to evaluate the program itself by observing and collecting data from its clients and staff members in several different ways and then trying to make sense of it all. One or more of the other, simpler designs described in this chapter could accomplish that.

Longitudinal Case Study.   The **longitudinal case study** design requires multiple, regular measurements of the problem (the dependent variable) in the program. There is no control group. The first measurement is made prior to or when clients first enter the program.

If applied to a job-training program, the design could be used to measure some variable such as "employability" at regular intervals over the course of the program. It would reveal, for example, at what point clients first produced an acceptable job résumé, when they learned to dress appropriately for a job interview, or when they first presented themselves well in a role play exercise with a prospective employer.

The design documents the presence of change over the course of the program. What's more, it can help to suggest when change occurs most rapidly (perhaps, coinciding with some program service or component), when it slows down, or even reverses itself. It can even reveal when (and if) the program may reach a "point of diminishing returns" and could perhaps produce the same benefits in less time.

The design cannot rule out the possibility that other factors (besides the program) may have produced the changes. However, it may actually suggest what they might be if certain types of data are collected. For example, in an in-patient program designed to treat some emotional illness, data about changes in house rules or changes in the use of certain medications might be identified as alternative explanations (to the program) for changes in the problem. Similarly, a longitudinal case study design may document that physical abuse of partners of clients in a program did not decline much in the first four weeks of a program, but then continued to decline steadily after that. However, the evaluation may also record that, at the beginning of the fourth week a new physical fitness center opened up in town and a large percentage of the clients in the program became members of it. A conclusion could be that the program is effective but takes a while to generate change. Or, it could suggest that the activities of the fitness center may be the real reason why the program's outcome objectives were achieved—the program may have had nothing to do with it!

This design bears some similarities to program monitoring (Chapter 8). However, it is more structured and more focused (on achievement of outcome objectives) than monitoring. Of course, when used in an outcome evaluation the design also should be implemented by an outside evaluator, a person not associated with the program. As noted earlier, monitoring is generally conducted by program managers or quality control specialists. The design is diagrammed as:

$$X \quad O_1 \quad O_2 \quad O_3 \quad \ldots$$

Application.   If this design were to be used in an outcome evaluation of the international adoption program, research hypotheses related to the first two outcome objectives might be:

1. During its first three years, the program will attract an ever-growing number of clients who do not qualify for domestic adoption services because of one or more demographic characteristics.
2. During its first three years, the program will attract an ever-growing number of clients who qualify for domestic adoption services, but prefer not to use them for a variety of reasons.

Note that, as different designs are used, they suggest the use of different research hypotheses to attempt to evaluate the achievement of a program's outcome objectives. Thus, they also change the focus of the evaluation somewhat. The two hypotheses above (like the other ones used in this chapter) seek to take advantage of the special features of the design being used, in this case, the multiple measurements of the same variables that are required.

As in the previous example, the hypotheses focus on what might be regarded as program outputs, not outcomes per se. However, examining whether there is support for them could certainly help in determining whether outcome objectives (increasing "viable options") were achieved. If there is found to be support for them and if many of the program's clients were drawn from one of the agency's usual sources (general inquiries), that may suggest support for the outcome objectives. In addition, unlike the previous two designs, this design could document *when* increases in certain types of clients occurred and can thus at least allow for speculation as to what else (besides the program or its reputation) may have produced them.

The design would entail collecting data and asking the same questions (those related to outcome objectives and progress toward achieving them) at regular intervals over the course of the first three years of the program, perhaps at 6 months intervals. While doing this would provide indications as to whether the objectives were achieved over the course of the program, it could provide some other valuable program insights as well. Thus, like some of the evaluation methods in Chapter 8, the evaluation could also have the potential to provide feed-forward, at least informally. For example, it might tell the evaluator that some objectives were achieved ahead of schedule. In relation to the third outcome objective, it might reveal that the program had already completed forty successful adoption placements after only eighteen months. It might also reveal that the program had a large number of other prospective adoptive parents awaiting approval for adoption. At the same time, it might show that the program as currently staffed was a long way from its goal of being self-supporting at thirty-six months. Impressions from the data collected at eighteen months could be shared informally with the program's administrator who could then respond to them. He or she could decide to assign more staff to conduct home studies or adjust client fees upward to increase the likelihood that the goal of a self-supporting program after three years might be achieved.

Cross-Sectional Survey. As in all cross-sectional research, this design hopes to measure certain variables at a single point in time, at some key juncture. Theoretically, a **cross-sectional survey** can be conducted at any time. However, in an outcome evaluation, it is generally used to evaluate the achievement of intermediate and long-term outcomes following completion of a time-limited program. To conduct a cross-sectional survey while the program is just underway would make no sense—it would be premature to expect a program to demonstrate achievement of its outcome objectives. That is when formative evaluations sometimes are conducted. To conduct a cross-sectional survey near a program's completion would still be premature; a more appropriate evaluation at that stage might be a process evaluation. To conduct one at the program's conclusion might be appropriate, but we have already discussed a design that does essentially the same thing—the one group posttest only design.

The design is best suited to time-limited programs in which (1) its clients are a cohort, that is, they all begin and complete the program at the same time, and (2) it is desirable to complete all aspects of the evaluation at the same time. Why is it sometimes important to conduct all measurements of program success at the same time? The major advantage to conducting an evaluation this way is that it prevents the time when the measurement is taken from becoming a confounding variable. Suppose, for example, that client perceptions of a program were measured for some clients just after completing the program, for some six months after it, and for still others a year or two after completing it. The length of time between program completion and measurement could produce different measurements of indicators of program success, for example, faulty memories and intervening events might influence clients' perceptions of the program.

The design is sometimes used as an "add-on" to some other design, such as the longitudinal case study, to help determine whether intermediate or long-term objectives (as well as short-term ones) were been achieved. For example, for evaluating the intermediate or long-term success of a job-training program, former clients might be surveyed five or ten years after the program's completion. They might be asked if they are satisfied with their current job, are using the skills that they were taught, have been regularly employed, have continued in their career advancement, if they have received regular merit raises since leaving the program, and so forth.

This design is usually not diagrammed, since there is no sequence of measurements to display. The diagram would be simply:

$$O$$

Application. On the surface, it would appear that this design would not be well-suited for use in an outcome evaluation of our hypothetical international adoptions program because such a program would not be time-limited and clients would not participate in it as a cohort. However, as we shall see, with a little creativity it might actually work quite well. If this design were used, the research hypotheses might be:

1. Clients of the program will perceive that the program's existence has provided a viable option for them in seeking to become adoptive parents.
2. Staff members of the agency will perceive that the program's existence has provided a viable option for the agency's clients in seeking to become adoptive parents.

Once again, notice how different research designs are used to answer somewhat different research questions and thus, to test somewhat different research hypotheses. The hypotheses for this design seem to address the program's first two outcome objectives more directly than the hypotheses that would be appropriate for the other designs that we have examined. This may suggest that, of those designs discussed so far, this one, despite its simplicity, may actually be the best suited for conducting an outcome evaluation of our hypothetical program.

Primarily qualitative research methods would be appropriate because what is measured is perceptions (of adoption options), rather than a measurement of, for example, certain behaviors or facts. The evaluation should take place after there have been a fairly large number of clients served by it. Determining if there is support for the hypotheses would require a heavy reliance on interviews with past and present program staff and with past and present clients of the program. Perhaps even client-satisfaction surveys might be used. If so, collaborative evidence would be sought, because clients (especially those who are about to become or are already proud parents thanks to the program) are very likely to be highly complimentary of the program and its services. It might come from others associated with the program or even from potential adoptive parents who are not clients of the program, if they can be identified.

The design might be implemented exactly as the program completes, say, its fifth year. Data collection would be completed in the shortest time possible by using multiple trained evaluators and carefully coordinated data collection designed to produce a "snapshot in time" of the program and its merit to date.

The design, while it could be made to work for use in an outcome evaluation of the program overall, has its shortcomings. In a program of this nature (one that is not time-limited and in which a cohort of clients do not complete the program at a single point in time), conducting all measurements of client perceptions of the program at one time can produce certain problems and make interpretation of findings difficult. It can actually introduce the potentially confounding variable "time of measurement" (in a slightly different sense) rather than controlling for it. For example, suppose we used it after the program's fifth year as suggested. When measurements are taken, some staff members might have been part of the program from its onset; others may be relatively new to it. Some may still be employed within it; others would not be. These factors could easily influence perceptions of the program. Should all staff perceptions receive equal weighting?

Similarly, if all measurements were conducted after five years of the program's operation, clients would be at various stages of the adoptive and post-adoptive process, and that might affect their perceptions of the program. This variable (how far along clients are in the adoption process) could easily be measured and recorded for each client or former client. It could then be treated as an independent variable and statistical analysis could be used to see if it really is related to client perceptions of the program, as we might hypothesize. Whether it is found that it is or it is not might be a valuable collateral finding (not central to the assessment of program effectiveness) for the program's stakeholders as they seek ways to improve the program. Nevertheless, it might be concluded that it would be better to avoid the potentially confounding variable "time of measurement" altogether by not using this design. It might be preferable to, for example, conduct a follow-up survey for all clients as they reach the same stage of the adoption process (perhaps, six months following adoption of a child), even though that would require that data collection might be spread out over several years.

One-Group Pretest-Posttest.   In the **one-group pretest-posttest** design, the presence of a pretest of the sample (clients in the program) allows the evaluator to learn how much change in the problem occurred among clients who completed the program. For example, if the design were used to evaluate a job-training program, we might measure "employability" prior to the program and again after it to measure the amount of change that occurred among people who completed the program. Of course, employability and actually getting and keeping a good job are not the same. Used this way, the design would not provide a very direct indication of the success of the program. In addition, there are several other major shortcomings of the design that always exist when it is used in outcome evaluations. They include:

- Because the design lacks any kind of control group, we have no way of knowing how much change would have occurred if clients had not been in the program.
- The design does not tell us *when* any changes occurred and thus is less informative than the longitudinal case study. For example, it does not do as good a job of suggesting what else (besides the program) might have produced changes.
- The presence of a pretest opens up the possibility that the pretest itself may have been responsible for at least some of the changes that occurred. For example, clients may have learned from it or it may have affected their attitudes about the program in some way.
- The design can produce misleading conclusions about program effectiveness because of the problem of client attrition. Usually, the pretest measurements are of clients who completed the program as they began the program; the posttest measurements are of those same clients as they completed it. Absent from the data are any measurements of those who dropped out, people who may have felt that the program was not helping them or was otherwise not worth their time. Thus, the posttest may be positively biased, and the changes between the pretest and the posttest may be greater than they would have been if data from all of the program's clients could have been included in the analysis.

Despite these limitations, the design can be used effectively for some outcome evaluations. Sometimes they are just not that important. Where client attrition is not an issue (such as in some institutional settings like prisons) or when program goals are to change larger systems like communities or organizations, the design can provide a fairly accurate assessment of whether outcome objectives were achieved. For example, it can be used to determine whether, following a program designed to increase political participation in a community, voter turnout increased by some targeted percentage. Of course, the design cannot tell whether an especially attractive candidate (or a despised one), the weather, or the absence of a home football game on election day may have caused the increase rather than the program.

This design is a popular one for evaluating the effectiveness of educational programs such as one-day workshops. The design virtually guarantees that the program will appear successful. Why? Even if clients in the program were only minimally attentive and slept only part of the time during the program, they will almost certainly leave the program with more knowledge than when they entered it. There is just not enough time to forget!

When the design is used (inappropriately, in my opinion) to evaluate a short program with educational objectives, statistical analysis is often used to provide even more "proof" of the program's effectiveness. The two-sample matched t-test is frequently used or one of its nonparametric alternatives, such as the Mann-Whitney U test.[4] A reader of the outcome evaluation report who is not knowledgeable about statistical analysis is likely to be impressed to learn that the amount of increase in knowledge among clients was statistically significant. However, a statistically significant change need not be a substantive one; if clients retained any knowledge at all (which is highly likely), statistical significance is almost invariably achieved, especially if the program contained a relatively large number of people.

In short, the design is simple to implement, and often ends up providing support for program success. However, it may not provide a true assessment of the effectiveness of certain types of programs such as brief educational programs or workshops. It would be more useful to measure such variables as long-term retention or application of learning than the short-term retention that this design measures. That could be accomplished using a cross sectional survey at some time after the program's completion.

The one group pretest-posttest design is diagrammed as:

$$O_1 \quad X \quad O_2$$

Application. The one group pretest-posttest design in its purest form would not be very useful for evaluating the first two outcome achievements of our international adoption program because the outcomes are not specific changes in the clients who complete the program. Of course, we might expect certain changes to occur—some clients would become new parents while some would not. However, as noted previously, the number of completed adoptions alone would probably be considered an output, and thus not directly related to the first two objectives. It is more relevant as an indicator of program success in relation to the third outcome, the number of children successfully placed during the first two years.

To use the design (or at least a reasonable facsimile) we would have to "cheat" a little. The groups of clients in the pretest and posttests would not be the same clients but two groups of clients (applicants for services) who could be regarded as very similar. If we did this, the design could provide at least some indication of whether the first two outcome objectives were achieved.

How would the evaluation work? Prior to the program's implementation, all applicants over a certain period of time (say, three months) could be apprised of what adoptive services the agency currently offered (O_1). Then they could be surveyed or interviewed about their perception of the agency's services. They could be asked the degree to which it provided the adoption options that they deemed most appropriate for themselves and their families. Then, after the program was operational for a while, perhaps after three years, the same procedure could be completed with all new applicants for agency services during a similar time interval (O_2), and the results of the pretest and posttest compared. Interviews with or surveys of current clients of the program and its previous clients could also be undertaken and compared with the results of the posttest as a kind of reliability check on the posttest data. The research hypotheses might be stated as:

1. Prior to the program's implementation, fewer applicants who do not meet the requirements for a domestic adoption will perceive that the agency will meet their needs as prospective adoptive parents than similar applicants seeking services after the program is fully operational.
2. Prior to the program's implementation, fewer applicants who meet the requirements for a domestic adoption will perceive that the agency will meet their needs as prospective adoptive parents than similar applicants seeking services after the program is fully operational.

In evaluating the findings of the pretest-posttest comparison, some statistical analysis could be used. For example, whether the measurements were taken before (pretest) or after (posttest) the program was implemented would be the independent variable. Whether or not applicants perceived that the agency's programs met their needs could be regarded as the dependent variable. Another easily measured indicator of the success of the program might be whether applicants ultimately completed their applications for services. Then cross-tabulation of the independent and dependent variables could be completed and the chi-square test of independence could be used. The cross-tabulation and results of statistical analysis might look like Table 10.1.

The statistical analysis, even if it produced statistical significance as in Table 10.1, would fall far short of conclusive evidence that the first and second outcome objectives were achieved, or that the program overall was successful. If the pretest and posttest samples are fairly large (as in Table 10.1), statistical significance is a virtual certainty. Thus, it would still be necessary to make some impor-

TABLE 10.1   Cross-Tabulation and Chi-square Analysis:
A One-Group Pretest-Posttest Design

	COMPLETION OF APPLICATION		
Time of Measurement	*Yes*	*No*	*Totals*
Before the Program	61	45	106
After the Program	91	14	105
Totals	152	59	211

$$X^2 = 20.83, df = 1, p < .0001$$

tant, relatively subjective judgments based on other data sources (interviews, focus groups, and so forth) before any conclusions regarding support for the research hypotheses could be drawn. For example:

1. Is the *amount* of change in the attitudes and perceptions of applicants about agency programs since the program was implemented large enough to conclude that the first two objectives have been sufficiently achieved?
2. What other factors (threats to internal validity) may have produced the changes in attitudes and perceptions?
3. Do demographic profiles of the program's clients suggest that it is serving the clients it was intended to serve?
4. Does the program appear to have drawn away potential adoptive parents from the agency's domestic adoption programs?
5. Why do a sizeable number (fourteen) of applicants still believe that the agency is not capable of meeting their needs as potential adoptive parents despite the presence of the international adoptions program?

Design Selection

Some preexplanatory designs are clearly more appropriate for use in some programs and less appropriate in others. Each is designed to address some questions more than others. Selecting a research design or constructing one entails asking questions such as, What is the main thing I want to learn about the program in order to draw conclusions about its effectiveness? or, What would best convince me that the program was valuable? Box 10.1 describes the central question addressed by each of the five designs that were just discussed.

As should be clear by now, there is one question that, by their very nature, no preexplanatory design can ever answer definitively. It is, How certain can I be that it was the program that caused the outcome objectives to be achieved (or not achieved)?

■ ■ ■ ■ ■

BOX 10.1

**QUESTIONS OFTEN ADDRESSED BY PREEXPLANATORY
DESIGNS IN OUTCOME EVALUATIONS**

One-group posttest only—What is the severity of the problem following the program?

Two static group comparison—Comparatively speaking, how effective was the program?

Longitudinal case study—When and under what circumstances did changes occur?

Cross-sectional survey—At some point in time, how effective was the program?

One-group pretest-posttest—How much change occurred over the course of the program?

CONCLUDING THOUGHTS

Explanatory research designs cannot be used in outcome evaluations of many social programs because of problems relating to the selection and use of experimental and control groups. The examples of research designs presented in this chapter as a group represent some very serviceable alternatives to consider and, perhaps build on, for outcome evaluations.

The hypothetical example of an international adoption program may be getting a little old (and tortured) at this point. Rest assured, it will not be used in the next chapter, since it would be even more inappropriate for illustrating explanatory designs than preexplanatory ones. However, the example has served us well. It was ideally suited to our discussion of needs assessments and evaluations designed to improve ongoing programs. By using it to suggest how the five designs in this chapter might actually work, it has illustrated other important points. First, any of the designs *could* be used (at least with some modification) to attempt to assess the program's outcome achievement. This is often the case. Secondly, as was observed, *none* of the designs in themselves would provide a complete, and probably not a very accurate, picture of the success of the program. That is also often the case. What would have to be done (and often has to be done) is this. The evaluator would consider the strengths and weaknesses of many existing designs for providing the necessary data to make decisions and recommendations about the program. Then he or she would create a unique design (perhaps a hybrid of two or more of the designs in this chapter or in other texts containing some elements of one and some elements of others) that would promise to do a better job than any one of them. It would address the program's outcome objectives as directly as possible, but would also seek to provide any other useful feedback sought by its stakeholders about the overall value of the program. It would thus provide a fair and balanced evaluation of the program's achievements, and would be helpful for making decisions about the program's future.

KEY TERMS

true control group
nonequivalent control group
testimonials

one-group posttest only
two static group comparison
longitudinal case study

cross-sectional survey
one-group pretest-posttest

STUDY QUESTIONS

1. What is the difference between a true control group and other control groups?

2. What type of research design is considered "ideal" for conducting outcome evaluations? What are some of the reasons why it often cannot be used to evaluate the effectiveness of social programs?

3. What question can an experimental design answer that a preexplanatory design or even a quasi-experimental one cannot definitively answer?

4. In what type of programs are preexplanatory designs most likely to be used in conducting outcome evaluations?

5. What does it mean when we say that preexplanatory designs rely heavily on qualitative research methods for determining if a program has been successful?

6. How does the lack of a pretest in a one-group posttest only design limit its findings? Why would an evaluator sometimes use the design anyway?

7. What might be an example of a nonequivalent control group for an outcome evaluation of a child-abuse prevention program that works with families judged to be "at risk" for child abuse?

8. What can a longitudinal case study design tell the evaluator about changes in the problem or needs of clients that other preexplanatory designs cannot?

9. What is an important criterion for determining whether a research design might be well-suited to conducting an outcome evaluation of a program?

10. What are some of the limitations of the one-group pretest-posttest design? Why is it not appropriate for an outcome evaluation of a short-term educational program?

REFERENCES

1. See, e.g., Royse, D., et al. (2001). *Program evaluation: An introduction.* Belmont, CA: Brooks/Cole, 219–226; or Ginsberg, L. (2001). *Social work evaluation: Principles and methods.* Needham Heights, MA: Allyn & Bacon, 169–172.

2. See, e.g., Weinbach, R., & Grinnell, R., Jr. (2004). *Statistics for social workers* (6th ed.). Boston: Allyn & Bacon, 219–226.

3. Hollingsworth, L. (2003). International adoption among families in the United States: Considerations of social justice. *Social Work, 48*(2), 209–217.

4. Weinbach & Grinnell, Jr., op. cit., 238–240.

CHAPTER ELEVEN

■ ■ ■ ■ ■

EXPLANATORY OUTCOME EVALUATIONS

The designs discussed in Chapter 10 sometimes can be used effectively to demonstrate that the outcome objectives of a program have been achieved. But they cannot demonstrate a cause/effect relationship between the program and the achievement of its objectives. They leave open the real possibility that something else (not the program) produced it. The designs examined in this chapter address this possibility. Stated another way, they attempt to control for the various threats to internal validity that can mislead us into false conclusions about the effectiveness of a program.

When using explanatory research designs to conduct outcome evaluations we hope to demonstrate causation—that a program (and nothing else) produced a desirable change in a problem for its clients or some other desirable outcome. To accomplish this, certain conditions must be present:

1. The intervention must coincide with or precede (in time) the desirable outcome.
2. There must be co-variance (association or correlation) between the presence or absence of the program (the independent variable) and the desirable outcome.
3. All other explanations for the desirable outcome must be ruled out.

INTERNAL VALIDITY AND OUTCOME EVALUATIONS

To discuss research designs that control threats to internal validity, it would be useful to list the most commonly cited ones again and examine the forms they might take in an outcome evaluation. One of the "usual suspects," direction of causation, is not a threat in an outcome evaluation. It addresses the issue of whether the independent variable produced changes in the dependent variable or if it might have been the other way around. Of course, it would make little sense to speculate that maybe the dependent variable (change in the problem addressed) produced change in the independent variable (absence or presence of the program or the group—experimental or control—that clients were in). That would be impossible. However, unless controlled, it is necessary to consider other threats to internal validity. Here are the forms that some of the more common ones take in an outcome evaluation:

1. *History.* Over the course of a program, many events can occur that can affect the program's achievement of its outcomes. Some may endanger it; others may contribute to or even explain it. For example, consider the plight of a hypothetical program designed to lower anxiety level among clients that ran from 9/1/01 through 9/20/01. About halfway through the program, the terrorist acts of 9/11/01 occurred, events that probably made most everyone more anxious. If, after an outcome evaluation, the program appeared to be unsuccessful in achieving its outcome objective of reducing client anxiety, the events of 9/11 may help to explain its apparent lack of success. Conversely, in a different example, the apparent success of a program to get older clients more active outside of the home may be explained totally or in part by the fact that a new attractive senior center began operation in the community during the course of the program.

2. *Maturation or passage of time.* Some behaviors and other phenomena just naturally change on their own. This may explain why a program appeared to be successful or unsuccessful in achieving its outcome objectives. For example, a year-long after-school program may not be able to claim full credit for improvement in the cooperative play of its participants. The children may have simply "grown out of" some uncooperative behaviors as they matured. Or, another program working with teenage clients and hoping to increase respect toward authority figures may not be able to demonstrate any improvement. However, it may have prevented the increase in disrespectful behaviors that usually goes along with progressing into the teen years (maturation?).

3. *Statistical regression to the mean.* If only the most extreme cases are placed in a program (those clients with the highest or lowest measurements of the dependent variable), they are likely to appear to improve, but it may be because of this threat to internal validity. This is often the case in situations where clients are referred to a program because of the extreme severity of their problem or they are selected because they appear to be most in need of the services offered by a program. If there is no control group with clients who reflect the same severity of the problem, it is difficult to know if any improvement took place because of the program. Suppose there is a pretest given to all clients diagnosed as clinically depressed. Those with the lowest scores that day are placed into a program to treat depression. Then they are measured again for clinical depression at the end of the program and they show a statistically significant improvement (they have scores revealing less depression as a group than when tested before the program). The program may have helped them with their depression, or they may simply have "regressed to the mean," that is, they may now reflect more typical measurements of a variable that tends to

fluctuate, clinical depression. Since they were the clients who tested as most depressed on the first day of testing, they were more likely to reflect improvement than get worse, even if the program was totally ineffective. In a sense, they "had nowhere to go but up."

4. *Testing.* When a before-and-after design is used, it might seem logical to use the same test as both the pretest and posttest. When this is done, several things can happen that might make a program appear to be effective when it was not. For example, the program may be an educational one designed to increase knowledge of sexually transmittable diseases (STDs). Clients in the program would be tested on their knowledge before the program. Then, after testing and during the course of the program, questions from the exam might be discussed with other clients. ("What did you put for question 12?") Then at the end of the program, they take the same test again, remembering most of their correct answers (which were confirmed by the program) and remember not to repeat the incorrect ones that were proved wrong by their conversations with others and their test grades. Thus, it may have been the testing and its aftermath (rather than the program) that produced all or most of the improvement in test scores.

5. *Instrumentation.* Sometimes, in order to try to control for the testing threat to internal validity, different pretests and posttests of the dependent variable are used in a before-and-after research design. But that can produce another threat, instrumentation, if the tests are not exactly comparable. Suppose (using the previous example) that the posttest measurement of STDs is a little easier than the pretest one. Then it will appear that the program was successful, but the "improvement" was really caused by instrumentation. Of course, if a more difficult posttest was used than the pretest one, clients might show little or no improvement in their knowledge of STDs. Then instrumentation might obscure the fact of the program's effectiveness.

6. *Selection bias.* If a control group is used but it is a nonequivalent one (rather than a true control group), any difference between the control group and clients who participated in the program in relation to the dependent variable may have been caused by one or more important differences between the two groups. For example, the clients in the STDs education program may be clients who are at risk of contracting STDs who voluntarily enroll for the program. The nonequivalent control group may also be people who are considered "high risk," but did not enroll for the program. If the program participants show a greater improvement in their knowledge than those in the control group, it may be because the program was effective. But it may also be because they were more highly motivated (fearful?) to learn about STDs, as suggested by the fact that they volunteered to learn more about it, while the people in the control group did not.

7. *Overlap of "treatments."* This threat to internal validity can exist for different reasons. If a control group is used, it might be "contaminated" in some way, for example, it may actually receive some of the same services as clients in the program. (This would not be unusual—very few if any programs are totally

new or fail to borrow something from existing programs.) Or, clients in the program may interact with those in the control group and describe what they have learned to do for themselves from the program that helps with the problem. For example, they may describe and provide instruction in relaxation techniques or biofeedback as a means of reducing stress. Or, clients in a program may also be receiving other services not part of the program that may affect the problem that the program is designed to address. For example, a program to treat perpetrators of child abuse may demonstrate a statistically significant decline in abuse among those who complete the program. However, the decline in abuse among its participants may be more attributable to the employment counseling or budgeting services they received from another agency or program than to the program itself.

8. *Experimental mortality.* Experimental mortality refers to the phenomenon of clients dropping out of a program and how it can bias a research sample. When clients leave a program before its completion, they may do so somewhat randomly, but frequently they do not. If a fairly large number of clients leave a program before completing it, an outcome evaluation involving only clients completing the program may suggest that the program was highly successful. However, experimental mortality may have created a sampling bias—clients most pleased with the help they were receiving completed the program; those who believed it was no help are those most likely to have dropped out prior to the program's completion. Rarely, the opposite phenomenon can occur. A program may appear unsuccessful if clients have their problem solved quickly and leave the program because they believe they need no more help. Then, those who complete the program may give the erroneous impression that it was not very successful. Consider the example of a "marital enrichment" program. Which couples will likely complete the program? Will their assessment of the program or the quality of their marriages be truly representative of all the program's participants? Probably those who drop out of the program will be those most likely to have concluded it is of little or no benefit. Possibly a few would be those whose marriage was already so much improved by the program that they believed they no longer needed the program. Either way, a measurement of only clients who completed the program could lead to erroneous conclusions about the program's effectiveness. The threat of experimental mortality can be minimized (but not eliminated) by including data from clients who did not complete the program, if that is feasible.

STATISTICAL ANALYSIS AND OUTCOME EVALUATIONS

Up to this point in our discussion of evaluation research, perhaps to the delight of the reader, there has been little mention of statistical analysis. Even in Chapter 10 where preexplanatory research designs for outcome evaluations were presented, statistical testing was only briefly mentioned. That is because when using preexplanatory designs, any conclusions about program effectiveness are necessarily inconclusive. Statistical analysis is of limited value, because there are so many other explanations for why a program may appear to have been effective (threats to internal validity) that are left uncontrolled and thus cast doubt on any conclusions about program effectiveness. However, when it is possible to use explanatory (quasi-experimental and experimental) designs, much greater emphasis is placed on statistical tests of inference for making determinations about program effectiveness. (In short, if you dislike statistical analysis, your luck just ran out.) How important is statistical analysis in explanatory research designs? As we shall see, depending on its findings and whether they are put into meaningful perspective, statistical analysis can be very valuable or of virtually no importance at all!

Of course, if the wrong statistical test is used or it is used inappropriately, the findings can actually be misleading. The selection of a statistical test often can be a complicated decision—well beyond the focus of this book. It involves an understanding of both the assumptions for a test's use and enough understanding of the conditions that are present to be able to determine whether those assumptions have been adequately met. Thus, the tests that are mentioned later in this chapter should be regarded as no more than "possibilities"—they might be appropriate or they might not, depending on the exact nature of the data collected, the way that sampling occurred, the size of samples, and so forth.

Inference

As the reader may recall from studying statistics, statistical inference relies on mathematics and the concept known as a sampling distribution. Using formulae developed by mathematicians, it allows us to determine the mathematical probability (p-value) that a relationship between variables found within our data could have been produced by sampling error, the natural tendency of samples to differ from their populations and from each other. Stated another way, it tells us how safe it would be to *infer* that the relationship is a real one that exists beyond our sample.

Now what does that all mean in the context of a program evaluation? Even when potential clients are randomly selected for a program and for one or more control groups, the groups can be assumed to be comparable, but not perfectly identical. That is because of sampling error, which is invariably present. In an explanatory outcome evaluation, statistical inference can tell us the probability that any difference between the experimental group (clients in a program) and its control group(s) was caused by sampling error (rather than by the program itself). For example, in an outcome evaluation of a job-training program, it could suggest whether (1) a new program may really work better than an older one for unemployed clients, or (2) it only appeared more effective than the older one because the clients in it differed from those in the older program in some important way. Perhaps (as a group) they were better motivated, had a higher educational level, or entered the program with more job skills.

In statistical analysis, a finding of a low *p*-value (usually $p < .05$) provides evidence that sampling error probably did not produce the relationship between the independent variable (which sample clients were in) and the dependent variable (changes in the problem or other benefits). In short, if it did, such an event would be so rare as to **"defy the laws of probability"**—it would happen only rarely (less than 5 percent of the time) because of sampling error.

If you have studied statistics, you might also remember that statistical significance is often misunderstood and thus overrated. Suppose that we learn that the 500 clients who completed a new job-training program have a statistically significant higher rate of success than those 500 clients who completed the old program. Should we be impressed with the success of the program? Does that mean that the new program is much more effective than the old one? Not necessarily. The very large sample sizes of the two groups (500) made the statistical analysis very powerful, that is, highly likely to provide statistical support for even very weak relationships between the independent and dependent variables. The rate of success in the two programs may actually have differed by very little, less than 3 percent to be precise. If the two groups had 1,000 clients each, statistical significance could result if the actual difference in the success rate of the two programs was even smaller. This underlines an important point—when samples are large (as in programs with large numbers of clients), even minimal program success is likely to be statistically significant. That is, the effect of the program may be real, but minimal. And, that can be a very important observation when drawing conclusions about the value of a program.

Statistical Testing and Program Impact

What is the role of statistical testing in outcome evaluations? People reading reports and making decisions about the future of programs expect to see the results of it. Thus, it is almost always necessary. However, unless the results are put into perspective, they may be of little value in assessing the value of a program (especially a larger one), and can actually be misleading. Almost any program will have some effect on a problem or some other benefit, sometimes a very small one. And, as previously noted, if the number of clients in a program is relatively large, even a slight change in its clients or other benefit to them will be statistically significant. In fact, a finding of a statistically significant relationship between the presence of a program and desirable changes in some problem it addressed is so common among larger programs that a *failure* to find one is more worthy of note. Conversely, if a program has only a small number of clients who participate in it, a finding of a statistically significant improvement in their problem may be virtually a mathematical impossibility, even though the program may be quite effective. In short, statistical significance can be virtually meaningless in itself.

What matters more than a finding of statistical significance (or a failure to find it) in making sense of the findings of an outcome evaluation? It often helps to learn how *much* the clients in a program may have benefited or how *much* more clients in it may have benefited than people in a true control group or in some other program. Stated another way, we want to know how *strong* the relationship between the independent variable (the presence or absence of the program) and the dependent variable (change in the problem or other benefits) really was. Knowing that can put a finding of statistical significance into a little better perspective and help to determine whether a program really is worthwhile. It requires that the evaluator do more than report whether a program produced a statistically significant outcome; he or she should help the reader of a report to understand how much difference a program may have really made.

In the previous example (the job-training program with 500 clients in the new program and another 500 in its control group), both variables were nominal level (new program/old program and success/failure) and chi-square analysis would most likely have been used. Reporting the percentages of success for the two groups (say 62.1 and 59.2 respectively) along with the finding of statistical significance ($p < .05$) would help to put the success of the program in perspective. Percentages can easily be derived through hand calculation or as an option when using any of the most popular computer software packages. When percentages are reported, the people who read the report can then decide for themselves whether a slightly less than 3 percent better success rate of the new program justifies either continuing it along with the old program or replacing the old program with it. Factors such as the respective costs of the two programs, staff attitudes about them, and so forth can be factored in to assist in making this determination.

When other statistical tests are used, another method for putting a finding of statistical significance into perspective can be used, reporting effect size, a topic introduced in Chapter 5. Effect size reflects how much of the variation in the dependent variable is associated with the independent variable (the program or its absence in the current discussion). Effect size is another way of reporting the strength of a relationship between variables using a variety of statistical procedures. Which procedure is the right one to use? It depends on the statistical test that is appropriate and the research design employed. The reader may need to consult an advanced statistics book to explore the various methods for computing effect size. I will mention just two of the more commonly used ones.

r^2. If statistical analysis produces a correlation coefficient (r-value), such as when Pearson's product moment correlation coefficient (Pearson's r) or one of its nonparametric alternatives is used, effect size is easily computed. We can simply square the correlation coefficient thus produced to find out (roughly) what percent of the variation in the dependent variable is associated with the variation in the independent variable. The resulting number (r^2) is called the **coefficient of determination.**

Suppose that part of the outcome evaluation for a program entails examining the correlation between the age of clients and the number of services that they used. Through statistical analysis we might learn that the correlation is positive and somewhat strong, say, $r = .52$. We could square this number ($.52^2 = .2704$). We could now conclude that about 27 percent of the variation in number of services used in the program was associated with age. Or, that about 73 percent (100 percent – 27% = 73%) of the variation in use of services is related to something other than age.

To use another example, in a program designed to increase anger-management skills among clients, we might learn using a before-and-after (pretest-posttest) design that younger clients in the program reflected a statistically significant higher increase in anger-management skills over the course of the program than older clients. The correlation between age and change in anger-management might be, say, –.55. We could square the correlation coefficient ($-.55^2 = .3025$) to get the coefficient of determination and thus learn that about 30 percent of the difference in increase in anger-management skills was associated with age, but 70 percent was related to something else (other factors).

ES.   If a control group (true or nonequivalent) is part of the research design (as is the case in all of the designs in this chapter), a simple formula can be used to compute effect size (referred to simply as **ES** in this case). It gives us a slightly different perspective on findings and involves computing two descriptive statistics, the mean and the standard deviation. The formula for ES is:

$$ES = \frac{\text{Experimental group mean} - \text{control group mean}}{\text{control group standard deviation}}$$

Let's use the previous example to illustrate how ES would be computed and what it would tell us. Suppose that all clients who completed the anger-management program had a mean (average) anger-management score of 81 on some standardized anger-management scale. Clients in the control group had a mean score of 75 with a standard deviation of three. Now we can compute ES as follows:

$$ES = \frac{81 - 75}{3}$$

$$= \frac{6}{3}$$

$$= 2.0$$

Now what does this mean? The average difference in anger-management (6 points) between the experimental and control groups would almost certainly be statistically significant unless the two samples were quite small. OK, now how would reporting ES put this finding into perspective? ES (2.0 in our example) refers to units of standard deviation in the anger management scores of the control group. It is the number of standard deviations from the mean score of the control group that an average (typical) client in the control group fell. Because ES was a positive number, it means that on completion of the program a typical client who completed it had an anger-management score that would have fallen two standard deviations above the mean score in the control group. If we were to use a table of the normal distribution found in any statistics book, we would learn that the average client in the program would have fallen at about the 98th percentile in the control group—he or she would have an anger-management score that was higher than about 98 percent of clients in the control group.

In this example, ES provides a strong endorsement of the program. However, if this were a real outcome evaluation we would not be through yet. It would be premature to declare the program a resounding success and make major changes such as doubling the size of the new anger-management program or sending all clients with anger-management problems through it. Why? As noted earlier, there are many reasons why a 6-point difference in anger management (even if it were to occur every time the research was replicated) may not justify these changes. For one thing, the 6-point difference in anger management between the old and new programs may not be that substantive. Perhaps scores on the measurement instrument range from 0–200. A difference of 6 points would be a difference of only 3 percent. An average score of 81 on it may also still leave clients with major anger-management problems that interfere with their holding a job, relating positively to family members or having other problems with social functioning. In other words, neither program may have been very effective in solving its clients' problem. Even if we were satisfied with the higher success level of the new program, the more successful program may be longer or much more costly than the older one. Or, it may be politically unpopular among certain stakeholders, staff members may not like working in it because it entails evening work hours, and so forth. Despite a "statistical endorsement" of the program, the best decision might still be to discontinue it.

Of course, sometimes even programs that seem to have a relatively small effect are still valuable or worthwhile. They may simply be the best programs around. For example, even the most successful programs for the treatment of pedophilia probably cannot produce impressive statistical evidence to document their effectiveness. There are many other factors to consider besides the results of statistical analysis in conducting an outcome evaluation. That is why outcome evaluations, just like other program evaluations, gather data from a variety of sources and generally rely on both quantitative and qualitative methods to arrive at conclusions about the merit, worth, or value of a program. They also focus on economic and political factors as well as ethical and practice issues and rely on a good dose of common sense.

QUASI-EXPERIMENTAL DESIGNS

As was already suggested, the best way to control for threats to internal validity is by the use of random selection and random assignment of clients to experimental and control groups. Later, this chapter looks at several specific designs that rely on these methods. But first, we will look at some examples of designs that are superior to those in Chapter 10, but still fall short of this ideal. They usually are referred to as quasi-experimental designs. These designs, although they lack a true control group, can still provide a tentative answer to the question, How do I know that it was the program and not something else that produced any changes in the problem? They do this in a way that is similar to the way that statistical inference works—with references to the laws of probability.

The Role of Probability

The concept of "defying the laws of probability" that is central to an understanding of statistical significance is also important for interpreting the findings from outcome evaluations that use quasi-experimental designs. The findings can be used to determine whether the presence of a program and achievement of its outcome objectives are more than just a coincidence. They can help us to decide whether it was the program and not something else that produced the desired outcomes.

How does this work? Many designs use a control group, one that is very similar or even "matched" in relation to possibly confounding variables. If clients in the program benefit more than people in the control group (in relation to the problem), perhaps much more, that may still be because the two groups were unequal to begin with. However, if the control group was chosen because its clients were similar to clients in the program, that is unlikely. A more likely explanation is that the program was effective.

Other designs lack a control group but measure the problem many times over an extended time period. If desirable change or other benefits to clients occur over the course of the program and, perhaps, continue after it (but did not occur before it), that too would seem to defy the laws of probability. It might be the result of a coincidence (such as some event that occurred at exactly the same time as the program), but it is unlikely to be. Still other designs use both an equivalent control group and multiple measurements of the problem over time. Then, suppose there is improvement in the problem for clients in the program only during the course of the program and it never occurs in the control group at all. Is that only a coincidence? It could be, but it is highly unlikely—that would defy the laws of probability.

A New Example

We are now ready to look at some quasi-experimental designs in a little more detail. In providing application examples for them and the experimental designs that follow, the familiar example of an international adoption program would not be appropriate here. The fictitious example that will be used instead is a new multifaceted outpatient treatment program for adolescent girls identified as suffering from extreme debilitating shyness. The program's primary outcome objective is to reduce shyness for those who complete the program, as measured by the (fictitious) standardized Smith and Jones (S&J) shyness scale. The scores on the scale range from 20 to 70. Higher scores reflect more shyness and lower scores reflect less shyness.

Of course, the program would have a number of other goals and objectives, those relating to, for example, the demographic characteristics of the clients served by the program, the unintended effects of the program, or to program efficiency (cost issues). Part of the outcome evaluation would entail evaluating the degree to which they have been achieved. However, we will focus here on the central outcome objective, reduction of shyness among its clients, and how we might design an outcome evaluation to determine whether it had been achieved.

More Design Possibilities

There are many possible research designs that could be used to learn whether the central outcome objective was achieved in our hypothetical shyness-reduction program. Some would be more desirable or more feasible than others. Nevertheless, for illustrative purposes, we will consider some of the designs that occur most frequently in outcome evaluations.

Nonequivalent Control Group.   There is no true control group in the **nonequivalent control group** design. However, the nonequivalent control group should be as similar to the clients in the program as possible. They may be clients in a similar program or those in "the usual" program. To the extent feasible, the control group should be matched in relation to potentially confounding variables. For example, if age is believed to be related to shyness, we would want to select a control group that, as a group, is similar in age to clients in the program. This design is diagrammed as:

$$\begin{array}{ccc} O_1 & X & O_2 \\ \hline O_3 & & O_4 \end{array}$$

First the problem is measured in both clients who will be in the program (O_1) and in the nonequivalent control group (O_3). Then the program (X) is offered but, of course, not to the control group. Then the problem is measured again in both groups (O_2 and O_4) at the conclusion of the program. The first two measurements (O_1 and O_3) are conducted to ascertain whether the experimental and control groups really are comparable in relation to the problem prior to the introduction of the program. If they are the same or nearly the same, any differences in the second pair of measurements is assumed to be attributable to the program, since both the experimental and control groups can be assumed to have been exposed to most of the same influences (threats to internal validity) over the course of the research. For example, if maturation or passage of time contributes to a reduction in the problem, both the experimental (program) and control group clients should be affected to the same degree by it. Thus, we can answer the question, Did the clients in the program show a higher rate of success than those in the control group? Because the design includes both a pretest (O_1) and posttest (O_2) of the clients in the program, we can also answer the question, How much improvement did clients in the program make?

Application.   To use this design in our shyness treatment program, we might identify or form a control group in one of several ways. For example, they might be clients in another existing program for treating shyness. Or they might be those adolescents identified as meeting the criteria for inclusion in the program but who, for logistical reasons (such as work schedules), were unable to participate in it. A far less-desirable alternative would be to form a control group from among clients who were referred to the program, but who chose not to participate in it. Their nonparticipation may reflect lower motivation or more extreme shyness than those adolescents in the program or some other factor that may be considered a confounding variable—the control group might not be comparable to the experimental group in one or more important ways.

Both groups would be administered the S&J scale immediately prior to, and immediately following, the completion of the program and average scores computed for each of the four measurements. Assuming that average scores in O_1 and O_3 were comparable, any differences in average group shyness levels at the time of the posttests (a comparison of O_2 and O_4) might be attributable to the program. The amount of change in shyness over the course of the program (O_2 minus O_1) would also be calculated. Along with a comparison of both posttests (O_2 and O_4), it would help to assess whether the program was "worth it," that is, whether the amount of change in shyness that occurred among its participants was substantive enough to justify the cost of the program.

Statistical Analysis.   If the samples had been carefully matched, there might be some justification for using the parametric two-sample dependent *t*-test. In fact, it is frequently done, although there might be some question as to whether its assumptions would have been adequately met in this example.[1] The test would be used to compare the mean (average) shyness score of the two posttest measurements (O_2 and O_4) to see if the difference is statistically significant. If it is, that would lend support for the research hypothesis that the program is more effective than whatever intervention, if any, was offered to the control group.

If the measurement of the dependent variable is a little better than ordinal level but cannot be considered interval/ratio level (as is often the case with measurements using scales) or if the dependent variable is not considered to be normally distributed, a nonparametric test such as the Wilcoxon sign test[2] should be considered. Since, in either case, clients were not randomly assigned to experimental and control groups, it might be safer (more justifiable) to use the nonparametric test.

Time Series.   There is no control group, not even an equivalent one, in a time-series design. In a sense, clients in the program "serve as their own controls," much as they do in single-system design. In fact, the design is very much like the ABA design discussed in Chapter 5. The design is longitudinal—the dependent variable is measured several times before the onset of the program, during it, and, in some variations, after it. Like all longitudinal designs, the **time series** allows the evaluator to learn both if changes occurred in the dependent variable and when they occurred. While it cannot control for all threats to internal validity, it can at least give some indication of the degree to which one of them, maturation or passage of time, may have produced change in the dependent variable.

Usually, maturity or passage of time tend to produce changes gradually. If a program is not effective, change should continue at about the same rate both prior to and during a program. It would "defy the laws of probability" if maturation or passage of time were to create dramatic change in the dependent variable at exactly the time that the program took place and less dramatically at other times. It could have been maturation or the passage of time that caused the dramatic change, but that would be highly unlikely.

If a program is effective, desirable changes should occur during it. (After its completion, they should continue or at least previous changes should be maintained—a desirable program impact). If this pattern does not occur, the program almost certainly was ineffective. In fact, this design is probably better at identifying ineffective programs than it is at providing support for program effectiveness. Lacking any kind of control group, many of the other threats to the internal validity are not well controlled. One variation of the design (in which measurement ends shortly after the program) is diagrammed below.

$$O_1 \quad O_2 \quad O_3 \quad O_4 \quad X \quad O_5$$

There is a variation of the design. In it, measurement of the dependent variable continues after the program for an extended time (similar to an ABA single-system design). Its diagram is as follows:

$$O_1 \quad O_2 \quad O_3 \quad O_4 \quad X \quad O_5 \quad O_6 \quad O_7 \quad O_8$$

Variations on the design can be adapted to the situation to help in assessing whether a specific outcome objective of a program has been achieved. For example, in the first variation, we could attempt to determine whether dramatic changes (in the dependent variable) were observed shortly after a program's completion. In the second variation, we could attempt to learn whether the program had a lasting impact, or whether its effects on the problem declined over time once clients were no longer in the program.

Application.   If some variation of the design were to be used to evaluate the shyness program, we would measure the shyness of clients using the S&J scale at regular intervals prior to the onset of the program. We would do this to either observe a pattern of changes in shyness (such as a decline related to maturation or passage of time) or, if change was not occurring, to construct a baseline (see Chapter 4). In the latter instance, the baseline might consist of the average score of all clients during the measurements prior to the program being implemented. Then the program would be offered. At its conclusion, clients would be measured again either once (the first diagram) or several more times (the second diagram) to attempt to see if the program produced desirable changes in the problem or, in the latter case, had a long-term impact on the problem.

Statistical Analysis. Because the only group in the design would be clients who completed the program (a before-and-after situation), the dependent *t*-test could be used, assuming interval/ratio measurement of shyness and that scores on the S&J scale overall tend to be quite normally distributed (are not too badly skewed). The test would compare the mean scores of all clients following their completion of the program with their mean scores for all measurements prior to completing the program. If a comparison of the mean scores reflects a reduction in the problem and the difference is statistically significant, it would be reasonably safe to conclude that the difference was not a function of chance or sampling error. If the assumptions for dependent *t* are not met, the Wilcoxon sign test or another similar nonparametric test could be substituted. Of course, because the design lacks a control group, several threats to the internal validity remain uncontrolled, and any conclusions about program effectiveness would have to be considered very tentative, no matter which test is used.

While not directly related to the central research hypothesis, it might also be useful to use correlation analysis (Pearson's *r* or a nonparametric alternative[3]) to compare, for each client, his or her average score on the measurements before the program with his or her score after the program. We might expect, logically, that those scoring highest prior to the program would score highest after it and vice versa (a strong positive linear correlation). If that were found to be the case, we might conclude that clients tended to benefit equally from the program. However, if that were not the case (either a low linear correlation or even a negative one), that would be an interesting finding. It would suggest that some clients benefited more than others from the program. Perhaps, the data would reveal who they were, or confidential interviews with clients and staff members or some other more qualitative research methods might reveal it. The finding could then be used to improve the program, perhaps by assigning to it only those clients whom the evaluation revealed would be most likely to benefit from it. Or, perhaps the program could be modified in some way so that clients might benefit more equally from it.

Multiple-Time Series. The ability of the previous design to lead to even tentative conclusions about a program's effectiveness is limited by its lack of a control group. However, if a nonequivalent control group can be found, a variation, the **multiple-time series** design is preferable. Like the previous design, it is longitudinal and consists of the same multiple measurements both before and after the program. However, each measurement is also conducted simultaneously with clients in the control group. It is diagrammed as follows (two variations):

$$O_1 \quad O_2 \quad O_3 \quad O_4 \quad X \quad O_5$$
$$O_6 \quad O_7 \quad O_8 \quad O_9 \quad\quad O_{10}$$

or,

$$O_1 \quad O_2 \quad O_3 \quad O_4 \quad X \quad O_5 \quad O_6 \quad O_7$$
$$O_8 \quad O_9 \quad O_{10} \quad O_{11} \quad\quad O_{12} \quad O_{13} \quad O_{14}$$

With this design, there is a reference point with which to compare the clients of a program—the control group. We have a kind of "effect size"—how much *more* clients improved in the program than those receiving some other form of intervention or no intervention. Evaluators often use the design for comparing two programs, a new one with another established one, to see if the new program is really superior to the older one. It does a good job of controlling most of the threats to internal validity. However, they are controlled only to the degree that the clients in the control group and those in the experimental group were comparable to begin with in relation to certain relevant variables, and had comparable experiences over the duration of the program. Any differences in the groups and their experiences just might explain any differences in the relative success of the two programs.

EXPERIMENTAL DESIGNS

Quasi-experimental designs are a big improvement over preexplanatory ones for addressing threats to internal validity. While they can lead to the conclusion that they are an unlikely explanation for the apparent success of a program, that is not the same as ruling them out altogether. However, if a true experimental design can be used, it is possible to conclude with reasonable certainty whether a program actually caused some desirable benefit for its clients because the ususal threats to internal validity (except experimental morbidity) are controlled.

Common Characteristics

Experimental designs are highly desirable. They also are the most rigorous of research designs. The general characteristics of a true experiment are widely known; they are taught in high school and even in elementary school. Briefly, they are:

- The presence of one or more control groups
- Random selection of cases, with random assignment to experimental and control groups
- Introduction of or manipulation of the independent variable within the experimental group(s)
- Control of potentially confounding variables, either physically, statistically, or (most often) by randomization

More Design Possibilities

As in the discussion of quasi-experimental designs earlier in this chapter, let's examine the three experimental designs most frequently used in outcome evaluations. We will continue using the example of the shyness-reduction program for adolescents to illustrate how the designs can be applied. One notable difference in experimental designs is the presence of the notation "R." It is a reminder that in experimental designs, control and experimental groups are created using random assignment.

Classical Experiment. The best-known experimental design, the **classical experiment,** is the one that high school science teachers have extolled for many decades. It consists of random selection and assignment of cases to an experimental group and a control group. Pretest measurements of the dependent variable (the problem in program evaluations) are made in both groups. Then the intervention (the program) is introduced to the experimental group only. Then the dependent variable is measured a second time. A diagram of the design is as follows:

$$R \quad O_1 \quad X \quad O_2$$
$$R \quad O_3 \qquad\quad O_4$$

Or, sometimes (to indicate that both pretests are conducted at the same time, as are both posttests) it is diagrammed as:

$$R \quad O_1 \quad X \quad O_2$$
$$R \quad O_1 \qquad\quad O_2$$

An underlying assumption of experimental designs is that random selection and randomization in assignment of cases to one or more experimental groups and to one or more control groups has the effect of making all of the groups equivalent. That means they are virtually identical in relation to the dependent variable (the severity of the problem) and any potentially confounding variables. That is what happens if the samples (groups) are reasonably large. Then any differences in posttest measurements (O_2 and O_4 in the first diagram) can only be attributable to the presence of the intervention (X) in the experimental group(s) and its absence in the control group(s). However, what if the samples are reasonably small? Knowing what we do about sampling error (that it is greater in smaller samples than in larger ones), we cannot assume that the samples are totally equivalent. Sampling error may have produced one or more important differences in the groups. The presence of a pretest of both groups in the classical experiment can verify whether they exist or whether the groups are truly equivalent, at least in relation to the dependent variable (the extent of the problem).

Because the design includes both a pretest and a posttest of the experimental group, it is also possible to determine how much change in the dependent variable the program may have produced. This can be helpful for assessing whether the amount of change produced by a program justifies its expense, that is, was it substantive enough to conclude that the program was successful.

Application. To use this design (as it is illustrated in the first diagram above) to evaluate the hypothetical shyness-reduction program, we would first need to develop a pool of clients who meet certain criteria, for example, they all received above a certain score on the S&J shyness scale. Then we would select the desired number at random from this pool, say, fifty clients in all, alternating between assigning them to the program and to a control group. Their S&J scores would serve as pretest measurements (O_1 and O_3). Then the program (X) would take place. At its conclusion, we would again test clients in both groups using the S&J scale (O_2 and O_4).

Given the chronic nature of the problem (shyness) and the fact that clients with the problem would not be in any acute distress, the twenty-five control group members might be offered no assistance; they might be put on a waiting list for the program or another one. This would probably not be unethical if the program was short and the wait would not be very long. In addition, because the waiting time would be short, control group clients would be unlikely to seek help elsewhere for their problem and would thus remain true control group members. Assuming that the groups were equivalent to begin with, the difference between scores in the posttests (O_2 and O_4) would reflect the amount of shyness reduction that the program produced.

If the program was longer, or if for any other reason it was concluded that it might be unethical to offer no assistance to clients in the control group, control group members might receive the usual counseling or other services that the organization offers. Then the difference between scores in the posttests (O_2 and O_4) would reflect how much better (or worse) the program worked for reducing shyness than the usual services offered for the problem. A comparison of the pretest (O_1) and posttest (O_2) scores of clients in the program would provide an indication of how much shyness reduction occurred among clients in the program.

Whichever control group option is used, if the shyness posttest scores in the experimental group are better among clients who were in the program than among clients in the control group, the difference may be attributable to the program. Statistical analysis could tell us the mathematical probability that the difference was attributable to sampling error.

Statistical Analysis.   The members of the two groups can be considered to be independent, that is, not related or linked in any way. If the dependent variable is interval or ratio level and normally distributed (as is the case with scales that have been "standardized") the two sample, independent *t*-test can be used.[4] It would compare the mean (average) posttest scores of the experimental and control groups and would tell us if the difference between them is statistically significant, that is, it has a low probability of being attributable to sampling error ($p < .05$).

If the dependent variable had been badly skewed (was not randomly distributed) within the population, a nonparametric alternative such as Mann-Whitney U or Kolmogorov-Smirnov[5] might be substituted. In a program where measurements of the dependent variable are only nominal level (for example, Stayed in school/Left school or Improved/No improvement/Got worse), a test like chi-square would be appropriate.

While it would be possible to use the two-sample dependent *t*-test or one of its nonparametric alternatives to compare the pretest (O_1) and posttest (O_2) scores of clients in the program, little would be gained by such analysis. Unless the program was completely ineffective, a finding of statistical significance would be highly likely. Such a finding would suggest only that clients in the program improved. That would be much less valuable than what could be learned by simply subtracting pretest scores (O_1) of clients in the program from their posttest scores (O_2) to learn how much improvement occurred or by a statistical comparison of experimental group and control group posttest scores (O_2 and O_4).

Posttest Only Control Group.   The **posttest only control group design** is just like the classical experiment design, except it has no pretest of the dependent variable. Sometimes a pretest is regarded as either unnecessary or undesirable prior to introducing the independent variable. An evaluator might consider it unnecessary if a program and its control group are both very large. Then, because of their size and the equalizing effects of randomization, sampling error would most likely be quite small. The groups could be assumed to be equivalent in all respects. Thus, unless the evaluator was interested in how much change occurred over the course of the program for its clients, it would be a waste of time to conduct a pretest of the dependent variable.

It also might be undesirable to conduct a pretest of the dependent variable for other reasons. Pretesting could produce change in the dependent variable. While this might not consitute a threat to internal validity (because it would affect both groups equally), it might make it more difficult to determine exactly how much impact the program had on it. Pretesting also might be too costly or might be logistically impossible. Perhaps, staff working with clients in the control group might resist conducting a pretest of control group members because they would have little investment in the evaluation. Or it may be feared that pretesting might interfere with the program's effectiveness in some way, perhaps by revealing some of the hidden objectives of the program.

The posttest only design requires a faith in randomization to create equivalent and experimental and control groups. The diagram of the design is:

$$R \quad X \quad O_1$$
$$R \qquad\quad O_2$$

Application.   This design might be another possibility for evaluating whether the central outcome objective of the shyness-reduction program was met. It would be appropriate if either (1) the number of clients in the program and in its control group was relatively large, or (2) it is believed that a pretest using the S&J scale would not be feasible for some reason, for example, it might in itself produce change in shyness.

A pool of clients believed to suffer from extreme shyness might be compiled by referrals from staff members conducting intake interviews over some time. Clients from this pool would be randomly selected and then randomly assigned to experimental groups and control groups (as in the classical experiment). However, the dependent variable (shyness) would not be measured for either group prior to completion of the program. Control group members would only be identified; their shyness would not be measured using the S&J scale until their posttest (O_2), which would be conducted at the same time as the posttest (O_1) for participants in the program.

If control group members received no assistance, but were placed on a waiting list for the program, the difference between scores in the posttests (O_1 and O_2) should reflect the amount of shyness reduction that the program produced. If control group members receive the usual counseling or other services that the organization offers, then the difference between scores in the posttests (O_1 and O_2) would reflect how much better (or worse) the program worked for reducing shyness than the usual services offered for the problem. However, because there was no pretest of clients in the program, it would be impossible to know how much they improved over the course of either program.

Statistical Analysis.   Since the focus of analysis would be on a comparison of the posttests of the clients in the program (O_1) and people in the control group (O_2), the same tests that were suggested for use in the classical experiment could be used. The two-sample independent *t*-test would be appropriate in many situations if its requirements can be met. If not, one of the nonparametric options noted in the previous section could be used.

Because the design does not include a pretest of the clients in the program, statistical analysis could not be used to directly determine if the amount of improvement in its clients is statistically significant. However, as noted earlier, such a determination is usually of little value anyway, less valuable than a comparison of the program's clients with the people in a true control group.

Solomon Four Group.   Among the best-known experimental designs, the **Solomon four group** is the most complex. Not surprisingly, it is not used too frequently, but reports of its use occur from time to time.[6] If ethical and logistical obstacles to its use can be overcome and sufficient planning occurs, the design is highly desirable. It has many of the same advantages of the classical experiment. However, it does a better job of controlling for one threat to internal validity, testing, than any design we have examined thus far.

As the title suggests, the Solomon four group design uses randomization to assign cases (clients) to four groups, two experimental groups and two control groups. One experimental group and one control group receive a pretest; the other two groups do not. A diagram of the design would look like this:

$$
\begin{array}{cccc}
R & O_1 & X & O_2 \\
R & O_3 & & O_4 \\
R & & X & O_5 \\
R & & & O_6
\end{array}
$$

In the diagram, the first line depicts an experimental group (clients in the program) that receives the pretest; the second line depicts a control group that also receives it (but does not receive the intervention). The third line depicts an experimental group that does not receive a pretest; line four depicts a control group that receives neither a pretest nor the intervention.

How does the design control for the effect of testing better than the true experiment or at least to better determine if it was at work? In a true experiment (lines one and two above) both groups are pretested, but clients in the experimental group enter the program where the pretest can be discussed among participants and what was learned from it can be reinforced. In contrast, clients in the control group are less likely to interact; in some control groups they may never meet. Thus, any differences between the experimental and control groups following the program may be attributable, at least in part, to testing and its aftermath. However, in the Solomon four group design it is possible to determine whether testing may have produced some change in the dependent variable in the experimental group. Here are two ways to tell:

1. Compare posttest scores of the two experimental groups (O_2 and O_5) with those of the two control groups (O_4 and O_6). If both groups who received the pretests (O_2 and O_4) have better scores than their counterparts who were not pretested, that may suggest the presence of a testing effect.
2. Compare the posttest scores of all four groups. First compare the scores of the experimental and control groups who were given a pretest (as in the classical experiment). Suppose the scores (O_2 and O_4) reflect a difference, one that might have been caused by testing and its aftermath in the experimental group. Now compare the posttest scores of the other two groups (O_5 and O_6), those from the two groups who received no pretest (lines three and four in the diagram above). If the difference is similar to the one in the first comparison (O_2 and O_4), that would suggest that it was not testing that produced all or part of the difference. If the difference disappears in the second analysis, testing may have produced it in the first comparison.

When the Solomon four group design is used in a laboratory setting or to evaluate some aspects of social work practice, it is possible to create and maintain two identical experimental groups. However, in a program outcome evaluation this is usually not realistic. It would entail either (1) setting up two absolutely identical programs with identical staff, offered at the same time and place, and so forth, or (2) putting both experimental groups into a single program but preventing those who had been pretested (line one above) from discussing their pretest with those who had not received one (line three above). Of the two, the second alternative is more feasible, but still not ideal.

Application.   If the Solomon four group design were used to evaluate our hypothetical shyness-reduction program, potential clients of the program would first be identified using some source such as case records, referrals, or intake histories. Then from among this pool, four groups (preferably of equal size) would be compiled using random selection and assignment. One of the control groups and one experimental group (future program participants) would then be pretested using the S&J scale. The clients in both of these groups would be instructed not to discuss the test or its content with anyone. The other two groups would not receive the pretest. Clients in both experimental groups would enter the program; clients in the two control groups either would receive no treatment and be placed on a waiting list or would receive the usual services offered by the organization. At the end of the program, all four groups would complete the S&J scale (a posttest). Comparisons of posttest scores from all four groups would help to determine whether (1) clients in the program did better as a group than those people in the control groups, and (2) the likelihood that any difference between the experimental groups and the control groups might have been produced by the pretest and its aftermath in the experimental group. There would be an attempt to confirm or refute any impressions thus formed through confidential interviews with clients, focus groups, and other, more qualitative approaches to data collection.

Statistical Analysis. In order to compare the posttest results of all four groups simultaneously, it would be necessary to use a test designed for situations in which the independent variable has more than two value categories. A possibility would be one-way analysis of variance (ANOVA) or a nonparametric alternative such as the Kruskal-Wallis test.[7] Either test would answer the basic question, Is there any difference among the groups in relation to the dependent variable? Then, if the results of analysis suggest that there is ($p < .05$), additional insight can be gained by comparing pairs of posttest scores. This analysis (for example, a comparison of the two groups who received the pretest or a comparison of the two groups who did not receive it) could be conducted using the two-sample independent t-test or, if conditions for its use cannot be met, one of its nonparametric alternatives.

COMPLETING THE PICTURE

The designs presented in this chapter (especially the experimental ones) can be used to inject a considerable amount of objectivity into an outcome evaluation. When implemented, they can produce findings that lend credibility to an evaluation report and its recommendations. However, as should be obvious by now, quantitative measurement, control of threats to internal validity, and findings of statistical significance in themselves are insufficient proof of a program's effectiveness or its overall merit, worth, or value.

The central questions that an outcome evaluation seeks to answer are generally the same, Was the program effective? and, How valuable was the program? They are designed to learn a program's impact on some problem. However, there are many different ways that the evaluator can attempt to learn the answer to these questions, some more direct than others. The explanatory designs presented in this chapter reflect methods to learn the answers to various questions related to program effectiveness. Boxes 11.1 and 11.2 contain examples of the type of question that each addresses when used in an outcome evaluation of a program that seeks to produce some desirable change among its clients, a frequent goal of social programs. Of course, if the goal of a program is problem prevention, basic need provi-

---

BOX 11.1

QUESTIONS OFTEN ADDRESSED BY QUASI-EXPERIMENTAL DESIGNS IN OUTCOME EVALUATIONS

Nonequivalent control group—Was the amount of change greater among the program's clients than within its control group?

Time series—Among clients of the program, what changes occurred after the program was introduced?

Multiple time series—Were the changes that occurred among clients in the program different from those within its control group?

BOX 11.2

QUESTIONS OFTEN ADDRESSED BY EXPERIMENTAL DESIGNS IN OUTCOME EVALUATIONS

Classical experiment—How much success did the program produce?

Posttest only control group—Did the program produce more success than its control group?

Solomon four group—How much did the pretest measurement of the problem contribute to the program's success?

---

sion, maintenance of health, broader system change, or something else other than change among individuals, the questions that each design could answer would be similar but somewhat different.

Often, programs have multiple outcome objectives that relate to the problem it seeks to address. For example, a real shyness-reduction program might have several related outcome objectives. These might include more frequent initiation of conversations, increased eye contact, and increased social interaction. (It could be argued that each is only an indicator of achievement of the central outcome objective—reduction of shyness.) Any of the designs described in this chapter could be used to evaluate the degree to which each was achieved, thus providing a more complete picture of whether the shyness-reduction program had been successful. There are even statistical tests available that would be able to examine the relationship between the achievement of all of these objectives (or indicators) and the program's presence in a single statistical operation.[8]

Of course, there is much more to an outcome evaluation than simply determining whether there is support for the hypothesis that one or more of a program's outcome objectives have been achieved. Many other aspects of a program and its worth are evaluated, some of which are only tangentially related to the achievements of its outcome objectives. They may relate to, for example, the quality of management within the program, its reputation in the community, staff morale, or cost effectiveness. The precise questions to be answered in a given outcome evaluation always depend on the program's stakeholders and what they need to know to make an informed decision about the future of the program. Thus, it is impossible to create a "one size fits all" model of a complete outcome evaluation.

In this chapter and the previous two, the focus has been on what makes outcome evaluations different from other types of program evaluations the questions they seek to answer. It should be remembered that when an outcome evaluation relies in part on one of the designs described or one not mentioned here, it constitutes only the skeleton, the bare frame on which a comprehensive outcome evaluation is constructed. These designs (and others not mentioned) merely describe how many case samples will be used, how they will be selected, what will happen to each, and when and how many measurements of the dependent variable will occur. That is all. A complete plan for a program evaluation contains much more. It includes many different ways of acquiring and synthesizing information. Both quantitative and qualitative methods are used, primarily to provide the checks and balances that are needed to arrive at a fair evaluation of the program.

Chapter 6 introduced the concept of convergent analysis in program evaluations, a variation of triangulation. It suggests the importance of using multiple sources of data. Thus, a complete outcome evaluation design is likely to include the use of "softer" data sources—some combination of evaluator observations, confidential interviews, key informants, focus groups, community forums and, yes, client-satisfaction surveys. It would have been redundant to describe their use in this chapter because they are used much the same as in needs assessments or formative evaluations. However, it is important to remember that they form an important part of outcome evaluations—they "flesh out" the skeleton that is the basic design and help to complete our understanding of a program. Sometimes, they even cast doubt on the findings derived by the quantitative analysis of data.

CONCLUDING THOUGHTS

When most social workers think of evaluation research they think of outcome evaluations. There is a reason for that, and for why I have devoted three chapters to the topic. Outcome evaluations have more impact on our programs and services than any other form of evaluation research. Social programs, social work jobs and, most important, services to our clients often are dependent on their findings.

The importance of outcome evaluations is unlikely to diminish during the twenty-first century. More likely, it will increase. We have already reached the point where an outcome evaluation design is a requirement of just about any grant proposal that seeks funding from sources outside of our organizations. (Requirements for needs assessments and formative evaluations also are now quite common). As outcome evaluations come to be normal and expected in outside-funded programs and we learn to appreciate their value, will they eventually be required for all programs, even those permanent ones with internal funding? I would not be surprised to see that happen. It would be a good thing.

The earlier chapters of this book were designed to expand the reader's thinking about evaluation research—to present its breadth and depth—to move beyond thinking of it as only outcome evaluations. In some ways, as we conclude our overview of the topic of evaluation research, we have come full circle. We are back to the topic of outcome evaluations. I believe that is appropriate. The need for good outcome evaluations is what started it all. They remain central to the entire enterprise of evaluation research.

KEY TERMS

"defy the laws of probability"
coefficient of determination
ES

time series
multiple-time series
classical experiment

posttest only control group
Solomon four group

STUDY QUESTIONS

1. Why is maturation often a threat to internal validity in programs that seek to change children's behaviors?

2. Why is statistical regression to the mean often a threat to internal validity in outcome evaluation designs of social programs that lack a control group?

3. If only 50 percent of clients fail to complete a program, would experimental mortality still constitute a threat to the internal validity of the findings of an outcome evaluation? Why, or why not?

4. Why is the conclusion that a program made a statistically significant change in a problem not necessarily an indication that the program was successful?

5. Explain how the "laws of probability" play an important role in the interpretation of findings from a quasi-experimental outcome evaluation.

6. What is the function of a control group in explanatory research? Describe what might happen to people selected to be in a control group.

7. How do experimental and quasi-experimental designs differ from each other?

8. What are some reasons why experimental designs are used infrequently in outcome evaluations of social programs?

9. Why do some experimental designs not contain a pretest of the dependent variable? When would this be acceptable in an outcome evaluation?

10. What threat to internal validity does a Solomon four group design control that other designs do not? In your opinion, how much of a threat is it in most program evaluations? Does the threat justify use of the design? Why, or why not?

REFERENCES

1. See, e.g., Evans, J. (1996). *Straightforward statistics for the behavioral sciences.* Pacific Grove, CA: Brooks/Cole, 326–327; or Shavelson, R. (1988). *Statistical reasoning for the behavioral sciences* (2nd ed.). Needham Heights, MA: Allyn & Bacon, 469–485.

2. See, e.g., Siegel, S. (1956). *Non-parametric statistics.* New York: McGraw-Hill, 75–83.

3. See, e.g., Weinbach, R., & Grinnell, R., Jr. (2004). *Statistics for social workers* (6th ed.). Boston: Allyn & Bacon, 136–164.

4. Ibid., 229–238.

5. Ibid., 238–242.

6. See, e.g., Fanney, V. (2003). Urban interdisciplinary program helps families prevent child neglect. *Social Work Education Reporter, 51*(3), 17–18.

7. Weinbach, & Grinnell, Jr., op. cit., 242–244.

8. Kachigan, S. (1986). *Statistical analysis.* New York: Radius Press, 329.

POSTSCRIPT

Books on basic research methodology and statistics tend to vary primarily in their presentation. In writing in these areas, my coauthors and I have always presented essentially the same material as many other authors have before us, only using different examples and a different organizational framework. There is a consistency in these areas. We all mean the same thing when we talk about reliability or validity, nominal-level or interval-level measurement, purposive sampling or systematic sampling, mean or median, chi-square or Pearson's r, and so forth. There is no debating these terms and their meaning—there is only what, by convention, is right or wrong.

In doing the research for the present book, I observed a very different situation. There is almost as much lack of consensus about evaluation research as there is consensus. Even many key terms are defined very differently from one book or article to another. I mentioned some of these discrepancies in the text; there are many others. Perhaps it is the relative newness of the whole enterprise—we may be still finding our way. For whatever reason, I frequently found myself asking, With which other writer should I agree this time? or sometimes, Should I risk taking a position that no other author has taken on some issue only because it just seems logical to me? Writing this book was much more like writing a management book than writing a research text—I often found myself ultimately suggesting "what works for me," rather than what is, by established tradition, correct.

Using class notes, existing literature, and my own experiences with evaluation research entailed a process not unlike the convergent analysis that is characteristic of good program evaluations. I drew from many sources and observations (some conflicting) and tried to make sense of it all. The product, the previous eleven chapters, present a mixture of ideas, some of which are "standard fare" and some of which are clearly my own opinions. Like a good social worker, I have risked a little. Some ideas and conceptualizations and even definitions are definitely in contradiction with what some writers have said, but in agreement with others.

In an effort to demystify evaluation research, I have sought the logical thread that I knew had to be there. Sometimes the logic was obvious; other times I may have had to stretch a little to find it. On a few occasions, to preserve the logical flow of it all, I even had to "invent," to describe what (in my opinion) should be or will be someday rather than what is.

In evaluation research, for every generalization it seems there are exceptions; for every principle there are still other exceptions. The previous eleven chapters described in narrative form how I think it all fits, a logical way to conceptualize the various types of evaluation research. As this book was nearly ready to go to press, a student shared a matrix that she had constructed to help her to study for an examination on the topic. It struck me that something like it might be a good way to summarize how evaluation research fits together or, more accurately, how in the ideal world that I have alluded to several times, it ought to fit together. Table P.1 reflects the logical thread that I sought (and sometimes had to create). It lays it all out, open to the reader's examination and criticism. I am, of course, open to changing it, if convinced that it is flawed. That is what makes the scientific method so great!

TABLE P.1   Contemporary Evaluation Research: Types and Characteristics

TYPE OF EVALUATION	PRIMARY PURPOSE	PRIMARY QUESTION	PERFORMED BY	PRIMARY ROLE	WHEN PERFORMED
Single System	Evaluate individual effectiveness	Did the intervention make a difference?	Practitioners	Social worker	Any time
Needs assessment	Determine program need	Is the program needed?	Manager, outside evaluator	Researcher	Before, or after changes have occurred
Program monitoring	Program improvement	How are *we* doing?	Manager, quality control expert	Manager	Throughout
Formative	Program improvement	How are *they* doing?	Outside evaluator	Consultant Fact finder	Early–middle
Process	Program understanding	What happened?	Outside evaluator	Detective/ systems analyst	Middle–late
Outcome	Decision making about program future	Was the program successful? How valuable is it?	Outside evaluator	Judge/ evaluator	Late–post